This
Mt. N
Couns

D0327288

Integrative Life Planning

Integrative Life Planning

Critical Tasks for Career Development and Changing Life Patterns

L. Sunny Hansen

Jossey-Bass Publishers • San Francisco

Copyright © 1997 by Jossey-Bass Inc., Publishers, 350 Sansome Street, San Francisco, California 94104. All rights reserved. No part of this publication may be reproduced, stored in a retrieval system, or transmitted, in any form or by any means, electronic, mechanical, photocopying, recording, or otherwise, without the prior written permission of the publisher.

Substantial discounts on bulk quantities of Jossey-Bass books are available to corporations, professional associations, and other organizations. For details and discount information, contact the special sales department at Jossey-Bass Inc., Publishers (415) 433–1740; Fax (800) 605–2665.

For sales outside the United States, please contact your local Simon & Schuster International office.

TCF Manufactured in the United States of America on Lyons Falls Turin Book. This paper is acid-free and 100 percent totally chlorine-free.

www.josseybass.com

Credit are on page 359.

Library of Congress Cataloging-in-Publication Data

Hansen, Lorraine Sundal.
    Integrative life planning : critical tasks for career development
and changing life patterns / L. Sunny Hansen.—1st ed
        p.   cm.
    Includes bibliographical references and index.
    ISBN 0–7879–0200–4 (cloth : acid-free paper)
    1. Career development.   2. Career changes.   I. Title.
HF5549.5.C35H363   1996
650.1—dc20
                                                            96–10134
                                                            CIP

FIRST EDITION
HB Printing   10 9 8 7 6 5 4 3 2

Contents

To Henry Borow

*Mentor, friend, colleague, from whom I have
learned a lot about work and other life roles*

and

To Tor, Sonja, and Tor

*My family, whose love, support, and example
were critical to the task of writing this book*

Preface

"Workers Need a New Source of Job Security"
"Corporate Killers: Wall Street Loves Layoffs, but the Public
    Scared as Hell. Is There a Better Way?"
"As Work Is Redefined, Millions Become Casualties"
"Thousands of Résumés Later, Manager Still Seeks Job"
"Precise Work, Painful Cuts: Layoffs Stun Blue-Collar Force"

This dramatic sampler of headlines that appeared in newspapers and news magazines the week before this manuscript was finalized illustrates one of the themes of this book—the changing American work environment. That subject dominated the headlines during much of the time I worked on this project. I am writing from the viewpoint of career professionals—those of us who are trying to help people not only survive but also prepare for life and work in the twenty-first century. I argue that we need a new philosophy of career planning; new attitudes about work, family, and other life roles; new ways of relating to others; and a new sense of the purpose of work in community.

For some time career development professionals have realized that the traditional approaches to career planning are not quite adequate for these times. Many have criticized theories of career and vocational behavior as not being congruent with what is happening in people's lives. Dramatic changes in education, work, and family, in business, industry, and technology, in human development, and in global boundaries have made the world a far more uncertain place. Old paradigms of matching people to jobs have given way to new paradigms of career and life planning, but we do not know exactly what form the new approaches should take.

The Need for This Book

This book is the result of a decade-long attempt to provide career professionals with a new conceptual framework to assist their clients in preparing for life and work in the twenty-first century. Preparing the book has been a large and exhausting undertaking. The book is designed to stimulate those who work with students, clients, and employees in a variety of settings to develop a new mindset and a new worldview, to think in new ways about how they can best help others make life choices and decisions in a constantly changing world. It is congruent with trends away from the mechanistic, fragmented, reductionist view of the world and toward the new connected, holistic, integrated view of people and community.

The new model is called *Integrative Life Planning (ILP)*. ILP represents a movement away from the traditional "trait and factor" approach to career planning—studying self, studying jobs, and then matching them—and toward a holistic approach to planning one's life course. It draws heavily on career development theory and particularly that of the late Donald Super, who defined career—much more broadly than most—as the development and implementation of a self-concept with satisfaction to self and benefit to society and as a sequence of roles a person holds in a lifetime, of which occupation is only one.

Although the expanded concept of career has been around for some time, the old meaning of career still dominates. Most people still think of career as job or occupation. After teaching career development courses for about twenty-five years at the University of Minnesota, I decided I needed to develop a new term and a new concept. I introduced the Integrative Life Planning concept in 1987 at the first national conference of the National Career Development Association in Orlando, Florida, where it met with considerable enthusiasm from career professionals. Since that time the model has been changed and refined after exposure to several hundred practitioners in workshops and classes and during its emergence in book form over the last four years.

A number of professionals in career development and organizational development are beginning to look at career in new ways. A national conference in Ohio in 1992 brought together theorists and practitioners seeking convergence in vocational and career development theories. A second conference in 1994 began to develop a theory of career counseling practice or career intervention. In reporting these, Mark Savickas suggested that Frank Parsons's logical rational model was a solution for vocational guidance at the beginning of the twentieth century and that Donald Super's career development theory was a solution for the second half of this century but that new solutions are now needed that are appropriate to the context of people's lives and to career counseling practice as we end this century and move into the new one.

The Integrative Life Planning Model offers a comprehensive framework as part of the solution. It helps people make life choices and decisions in a context of changing families, work, learning, and leisure—and of the world becoming a global community. The early model focused heavily on helping individuals find an occupation from a dwindling occupational pie, but the second encouraged exploration of life roles; the latter has proved difficult to implement.

The 1990s find us with a whole new range of issues that need consideration as we plan for the future. Many global and local problems need our attention. In addition, there are issues relating to the changing nature of work and work patterns, the career development of women and men, the link between work and family, interpersonal effectiveness in increasingly diverse workplaces, the place of spirituality, meaning, and purpose in life, and personal transitions and organizational change.

Organizational career development specialists and management consultants are also writing about other dramatic changes occurring in workplaces that will dictate very different patterns of career development in organizations in the future. Douglas T. ("Tim") Hall first wrote about the "protean career" in 1976. Now, in 1996, it is becoming a reality. The protean career, which takes it name from the Greek myth of Proteus, can take many forms. It refers to individuals who change and adapt quickly, experience relational growth, and are self-directed continuous learners. William Bridges (1993, 1994a, 1994b) similarly predicts that career planning in the twenty-first century will call for individuals who can adapt to change in a "dejobbed" society and sell themselves as entrepreneurs or "vendors." Jeremy Rifkin (1995) goes further, predicting the end of work. The two fields of individual career development and organizational career development are coming together in ways described in this book—with emphasis on the interaction of the individual and the organizational career in a changing society.

I believe that ILP fills a gap in providing an interdisciplinary framework for examining both the context of and the choices in people's lives. The process of delineating the concept put me in touch with literature from a variety of disciplines, including psychology, career development, family social science, multiculturalism, organizational development, adult development, economics, sociology, futurism, and even theology. In this sense the book is nontraditional, going beyond the boundaries of my counseling and career development field to tap the thinking of other fields. I reviewed literature that was both subjective and objective, academic and popular, personal and professional. In a sense the book represents an attempt to get out of a box. It helps us look at changing needs of women and men locally and globally, and it puts a strong emphasis on career not only for personal gain but also for community well-being.

Intended Audience

Because of its scope, I believe that this book will be of interest to a wide range of readers. It is designed specifically for any who consider themselves career specialists in educational institutions, business organizations, government, or agencies. In my intended audience I include career counselors, career coaches, career center directors, counselor educators, college student development personnel, academic advisers, human resource development managers, organizational development specialists, labor market information specialists, futurists, management consultants, employee assistance specialists, school counselors, career therapists, outplacement counselors or consultants, and, of course, students. Faculty who teach career development, organizational development, adult education, and human resource development may also find it helpful as a primary or supplementary text. It may also be of interest to family counselors and to career planners and changers themselves. In the text, when not referring to people in specific settings, I use the terms *career professionals, career counselors,* and *career practitioners* interchangeably.

My hope is that the concepts, issues, trends, and strategies I describe will serve as a useful resource for both theorists and practitioners. More than anything, this book invites career professionals to read, reflect, and act on the ideas expressed and determine relevance for their work. It is not a book of answers. Rather, it raises many questions and offers an approach to career and life planning that people increasingly are seeking. It is not a "how to" book that defines exactly how the concept can be implemented. However, it does offer ideas for ways in which ILP can be applied through workshops, classes, and other career interventions. A book on practice will have to come next; doubtless it will include creative ideas of practitioners who have developed their own ILP models and strategies.

Organization and Concept of the Book

The Integrative Life Planning concept provides a framework for putting career professionals in touch with aspects of career development that have often been neglected or ignored. It identifies six critical tasks or life themes that people will need to attend to as they plan for the future in the twenty-first century. The concept goes far beyond selecting an occupation. It seeks to show connections between the various tasks and the needs of individuals, families, and communities. Thus, this is a book about connectedness and wholeness to help reconcile dreams and hopes with the local and global needs society faces in the 1990s.

Each of the six critical tasks of ILP is presented in one chapter, starting with Chapter Three. Each chapter discusses related background and issues, trends, and the thinking of researchers and practitioners from different disciplines. I also include personal and family experiences and examples to illustrate or accentuate certain points. I hope that these discussions will be of value to career professionals as they work with various clients.

Chapter One, "Integrative Life Planning: A New Way of Thinking About Career Development," sets the stage by discussing some of the limitations of traditional approaches to career development and the rationale and need for new ones. I introduce the concept of Integrative Life Planning, the principles on which it is based, and the six critical tasks or life themes that comprise its dimensions. Although trait and factor approaches will probably always be with us, ILP offers an alternative framework for those seeking to live more holistic and perhaps altruistic lives.

Chapter Two, "Tracing the Interdisciplinary Origins of ILP," presents the ILP knowledge base. It includes a brief summary of such areas of literature as life-span and adult development theories, career-development theory, gender-role theory, and multicultural theory and concepts. Because of the scope of this book, the literature cited is necessarily selective rather than comprehensive. As is evident throughout, I draw on both qualitative studies and quantitative research findings relating to the critical tasks.

The six critical tasks of ILP are explained, beginning with Chapter Three, "Critical Task 1: Finding Work That Needs Doing in Changing Global Contexts." Out of 10,233 global challenges, I identify and discuss ten that seem especially important to me in relating to ILP and our need to "think globally and act locally," as the saying goes. Chapter Four, "Critical Task 2: Weaving Our Lives into a Meaningful Whole," discusses the Four Ls of ILP, *Labor, Love, Learning,* and *Leisure*. This discussion is followed by an examination of major influences on the career development of both women and men. I introduce a model of self-sufficiency and connectedness as a means to help men and women move away from traditional gender roles and function as partners.

Chapter Five, "Critical Task 3: Connecting Family and Work," reviews the many types of families that exist in the United States and identifies a number of issues causing role conflicts, especially in two-earner families and in organizations. I also suggest some interventions that can facilitate work-family roles and relationships and I explain the need for new mindsets if new family patterns are to succeed. The fourth critical task, understanding our own uniqueness while valuing the diversity of others, is presented in Chapter Six, "Critical Task 4: Valuing Pluralism and Inclusivity." With the changing demographics of our population and an increasingly diverse workforce, it is essential that workers develop interpersonal attitudes and skills to help them understand the world of "the other." The terms *pluralism* and *multiculturalism* are discussed, as are issues of race and gender in multicultural career counseling. The point is made that there are traditions such as domestic battering, sexual mutilation, and bride burning that violate human beings (often women) and that these traditions should not be tolerated. Empowerment is emphasized as an important concept for women and men of all backgrounds.

In Chapter Seven, "Critical Task 5: Exploring Spirituality and Life Purpose," brings into consciousness the need for most human beings to explore spirituality—the core of the person, for integration and wholeness, regardless of religious belief. The chapter also discusses the relationship of spirituality to values, money, and materialism. Different sources and meanings of spirituality are cited along with popular approaches to addressing these issues in career planning.

Chapter Eight, "Critical Task 6: Managing Personal Transitions and Organizational Change," is one of the most important chapters in the book because it describes transition models, links personal transitions and decisions, explains the concept of Positive Uncertainty, and discusses organizational changes that affect personal careers. The chapter also raises questions about discrepancies between popular philosophies of organizational leadership and actual corporate practices that are devastating men and women today. The case study of a job loss presented is my own personal example of how job loss affects families.

The final chapter, "Integrating Lives, Shaping Society: Implications for Career Professionals," summarizes the ILP concept and the six critical tasks, showing their relationships within ILP and the community. Implications for the life planning process are presented, along with suggestions for ways in which career professionals can become change agents. Examples are given of programs and interventions that past ILP workshop participants have created. The chapter ends with the Circle of Life activity that is an integral part of Integrative Life Planning. The Resource section, "Applying ILP— Strategies for Practice," presents possible strategies that practitioners may use to implement different parts of ILP.

Quilt as Metaphor

Integrative Life Planning uses the quilt and quilters as metaphors. In pioneer days, quilts were made largely by women. Today they are made by others as well, as illustrated by the AIDS Quilt made in memory of the people who have died of AIDS. Quilts often are works of art and represent milestones in people's lives. The pieces of quilts are put together to make a whole although each piece may tell its own story.

ILP is like a quilt for many reasons. On one level, the ILP quilt represents the global world or context in which dramatic changes are affecting persons, families, communities, nations, and the planet. On another level, it represents the career world—career development and planning and ways in which professional knowledge and practice are changing. It also represents the ILP model, its six critical tasks that are so much a part of contemporary life but often have been neglected or overlooked in traditional career planning. The tasks form the core of the Integrative Life Planning quilt and are the patches or pieces that together create its basic design. On a fourth level, the quilt represents a few pieces of my own life, pieces of my experience that are directly relevant to ILP, for they have shaped me and my thinking about career and life planning, and my own options, barriers, and decisions.

It has been a risk to write this book, but then I have taken lots of risks in my life, most of the time with positive consequences. I went off to college without much money (even more difficult for people with financial constraints today); applied to study in England and had to give up scholarships and take out loans to finish college but gained a life-changing experience finding my roots in Norway; traveled through the southern United States with a friend from India and had eye-opening experiences with racism; worked in an academic environment at a time when racism, sexism, and other *isms* were not considered important so that I often felt like a voice in the wilderness (this has changed now, fortunately); made a conscious change from a traditional to a more democratic and liberal Congregational religion; married a Norwegian in my early thirties and had a son and daughter in my late thirties; worked at several kinds of jobs and lived and lectured in several countries; worked for social justice and social change from junior high school on; created a program called BORN FREE; and served and led professional associations and other organizations.

These were many risks for a young woman from a small town in southern Minnesota. But as a nontraditional woman, I have been blessed with opportunities never dreamed of. My quilt indeed has been a large one, with a few pieces yet to complete. Trying to put together the pieces of career development—in some new ways that will inform and inspire professionals to act for change—

represents a synthesis of my life work, values, and hopes for constructive change in the profession, in work and family, in community, and in society.

Acknowledgments

I am indebted to many people whose support I have had for the several years this book has been in preparation as well as earlier in my professional career. I would like to acknowledge each of them:

My professional colleagues and friends who have mentored me, including Henry Borow—who hired me as his secretary while I was an undergraduate and introduced me to the field of vocational guidance and career development—and his wife, Marion, who also became a lifelong friend. Their dual-career marriage provided an early role model for me.

Tom Skovholt, coordinator of the Counseling and Student Personnel Psychology Program (CSPP)—longtime colleague, friend, supporter, and kindred spirit on many of the issues of counseling and career development, gender roles, and multiculturalism.

All those colleagues and career professionals too numerous to name whose ideas appear in these pages and have informed and influenced my own, and who permitted me to use their work.

The many professional organizations that have helped me grow: the American Counseling Association and its divisions and especially the National Career Development Association.

The College of Education and Human Development (where I spent most of my professional career), particularly Dean Robert Bruininks and Educational Psychology Department Chair Mark Davison, who facilitated my sabbatical year (1993–94) to work on the book.

The critical but constructive manuscript reviewers whose careful reading and valuable suggestions made this immeasurably better than the first draft: Nancy Schlossberg, professor at the University of Maryland; Lee Richmond, professor at Loyola University in Baltimore; and Douglas T. ("Tim") Hall, professor at Boston University.

The many career development and counseling theorists and practitioners who have inspired me over the years and influenced my work, most notably the late Donald E. Super.

The staff at Jossey-Bass, who have been a pleasure to work with, including Gale Erlandson, my senior editor, whose insightful comments and suggestions on the manuscript and support and encouragement kept me going; Rachel Livsey, editorial assistant, who monitored my progress and provided many resources; Joanne Clapp Fullagar, senior production editor, and her staff, whose editorial skills helped bring this to closure; and Susan Cho, marketing.

David Rivers, lawyer-turned-graduate student in the CSPP program, whose eye for detail was helpful in preparing the bibliography.

Students in my counseling and career development courses who stimulated my thinking with their Integrated Career Development papers, the creation of which was a meaningful class assignment for many years; and workshop participants who provided helpful and constructive feedback on ILP and were enormously creative in their innovative projects to implement the concept.

Master's and doctoral advisees who often risked choosing nontraditional topics and methods in their research and with whom I shared a process of mutual learning, care, and respect.

Carla Hill—CSPP office supervisor, secretary, and friend—who formatted the manuscript and has been dedicated, competent, and loyal for many years, for her diligence in handling the word processing, communication, and numerous other details associated with an ambitious project like this.

My lifelong friend Phyllis Kragseth, who read the manuscript with an English teacher's eye, a friend's heart, and a cheerleader's enthusiasm.

And my family: our daughter, Sonja, whose many talents, from mathematics to art and sports, never cease to amaze me, and our son, Tor, who has so far followed in his father's engineering footsteps, and both of whom, through the various stages of growing up, provided living examples of what I was reading and writing about in counseling and career development; and, finally, my husband, Tor, a truly "together" person who is also friend, partner, and storyteller and the most egalitarian man I know.

White Bear Lake, Minnesota   L. SUNNY HANSEN
July 1996

The Author

L. Sunny Hansen (Lorraine Sundal Hansen) is professor of counseling and student personnel psychology in the Department of Educational Psychology at the University of Minnesota. She received her B.S. degree in English and Journalism (1951), her M.A. in Education-English and Curriculum and Instruction (1957), and her Ph.D. in Education-Counseling and Guidance (1962), all from the University of Minnesota. She was founder and director of BORN FREE and is now director of the BORN FREE Center, which is focused on applied research and educational interventions for culture, gender, and career. She has been an English teacher, counselor, and counselor educator for more than three decades.

Hansen's research and development interests are in the areas of career development and career planning, gender roles, multicultural counseling, and international counseling and guidance. She has authored or coauthored several books, monographs, and articles, including "BORN FREE: A Collaborative Approach to Reducing Sex-Role Stereotyping in Educational Institutions," "Integrated Career Development," "Career Development Trends and Issues in the United States," "Interrelationship of Gender and Career," "Gender Issues in Multicultural Counseling," *Growing Smart: What's Working for Girls in Schools, Career Patterns of Selected Women Leaders, Career Development and Counseling of Women,* and *Eliminating Sex-Role Stereotyping in Schools.* The creation of innovative programs, courses, and media around the theme of career development also has been a focus for her.

Hansen has been honored by her profession with the National ACA Professional Development Award (1995) from the American Counseling Association (of which she served as president); NCDA Eminent Career Award (1990) from the National Career Development Association (of which she also was president); the National

Distinguished Mentor Award (1985) from the Association for Counselor Education and Supervision; the Distinguished Achievement Award (1990) from the Minnesota Association for Counseling and Development; the Jules Kerlan Outstanding Achievement Award from the Minnesota Career Development Association; and the Outstanding Career Development Award from the Minnesota Chapter of the American Society for Training and Development. She also is a fellow of the American Psychological Association and a national certified counselor and a national certified career counselor.

Hansen's impact has been felt in more than fifteen countries where she has been an invited lecturer, workshop presenter, and Fulbright scholar. She was a vice president and board member of the International Round Table for the Advancement of Counseling (IRTAC) and is an editorial board member of its journal, *IJAC*.

Integrative Life Planning

Chapter One

Integrative Life Planning: A New Way of Thinking About Career Development

ILP adds complexity by examining so many issues when guiding an individual toward a career. In the old "trait and factor" approach, if you knew the subject had a father who was in the business of delivering milk door to door, and the young man liked the out-of-doors, admired his father, and had a strong back, your work was done! The depth of investigation was considerably less intense, and once that determination was made, the client was pretty well set on that path for life. ILP moves to a view of making life and career decisions right up to the last breath.
—A woman in midlife who attended an ILP
    workshop

Several versions of a Snoopy cartoon speak indirectly to the theme of this book. Snoopy is out running (a relatively new popular pastime in American society), and the various parts of his body are speaking to each other, some in accusatory language. One of the legs asks the other the purpose in all the running. The heart reminds the other parts that if it goes, so will the rest of the body. The brain concurs that it probably is important to take care of the heart. The final word of advice is to be quiet and keep moving.

1

The message, of course, is that one part of the body is dependent on other parts, and all are connected and must work together to maintain the whole. *Interconnectedness, relatedness, wholeness* are frequently repeated words in this book, but they are words that are not common to traditional career development texts or career planning practice.

In this book we build on the new paradigm that evolved in the early 1980s. By *paradigm* we mean new ways of solving old problems (Ferguson, 1980; Capra, 1982; Kuhn, 1962). Ferguson in particular cited the new paradigms in various fields—for example, medicine, religion, education—to support her thesis that people were beginning to "conspire" (that is, to breathe together) to bring about change in society. She believed that out of personal change would come social change and particularly a change toward connectedness. Capra had a similar message when he described how the old reductionist, mechanistic way of ordering the universe—the logical, rational, competitive, fragmented, objective Newtonian interpretation—was changing, being replaced by a new physics worldview that was subjective, nurturing, cooperative, and connected. Capra credited the women's movement of the 1960s and 1970s with some responsibility for this shift.

Since the 1980s new paradigms are being "discovered" in a number of disciplines. Traditional Western medicine is moving away from strictly scientific principles to approaches that include holistic health, attention to mind, body, and spirit, and spiritual healing (Siegel, 1989). Economics is being challenged to move away from considering only the gross national product (GNP) as a means of measuring the progress of nations to include more human indicators, such as Hazel Henderson's Country Futures Indicators, which focus on social as well as economic progress. Henderson says that GNP and gross domestic product (GDP) are not inclusive enough indices of a nation's growth and describes new alternatives—"paradigms in progress" and "life beyond economics"—including "sustainable, equitable, people-centered development" (1995, p. 116). From her futurist outlook, she also notes how love relationships between women and men are being redefined, a topic of continuing importance in the 1990s and in Integrative Life Planning.

Futurist Joel Barker (1993) defines paradigms as "the business of discovering the future." He suggests that successful organizations will be those that anticipate paradigms and paradigm shifts and have leaders and managers who understand and act on them. Organizational management specialists also offer new paradigms for work, career, and organizations. They suggest that work in the future may be very different, requiring new structures, leadership, and approaches to career development (Hall, 1996; Mirvis and Hall, 1994). Mirvis and Hall describe a boundaryless career and boundaryless organizations that require a great deal of flexibility, adaptability, and self-direction. Hall advocates a new form of career that he calls the *protean career.* The protean career implies an ability to shift and change in career cycles over a lifetime—very different from the one-job-for-life mindset. Others call for new definitions of work. For example, Matthew Fox (1994) calls for the reinvention of work as a process of finding work that needs doing. Mary Sue Richardson (1993) calls for a new location of work that includes both home and the occupational workplace and for a broad definition of work that includes paid and unpaid work, family work, volunteer work, and community work. She believes that the twenty-first century will require a focus not on work as occupation but as all the forms of work in which men and women engage.

I believe we need a paradigm shift in career and life planning. Although the traditional, logical, rational matching of people and jobs—often called "the trait and factor" approach—will probably always be with us (unless there are no jobs to match people to), the dramatic changes in society—both global and national—in work, family, education, demographics, and roles and relationships of women and men of all backgrounds, require career professionals to find new ways to help their clients make complex life choices and decisions. I believe too that the issues faced by all nations, such as environmental degradation, human rights, multiculturalism, and violence, dictate a new philosophy of career planning in which the focus is not so much on individual occupational choice for personal satisfaction and livelihood as on multiple choices over a lifetime not only for individual wholeness but for life with meaning, that is, for work that benefits self and community.

Career Needs: Past and Present

It is easy to find people who claim that present approaches to career decision making do not always work. When students in my career development classes introduce themselves to one another with a few words about their own career development, some say, "I just fell into a career" (usually meaning a job) or "I happened to be at the right place at the right time" or "I still don't know what I want to be when I grow up" or "My counselor (or teacher) said I probably couldn't get into college, so I went to college to prove them wrong—and here I am!" Some report that they were fired or "downsized" and are in transition. Others recount leaving a job to find a new life path and realizing that it was the best thing they ever did. Few indicate that they know what career development is, have gotten help from a career counselor, or have learned how to go about career planning. Indeed, unless they are taught, people do not have an understanding of the multiple dimensions and complexities of career development and planning.

Although information is considered important in the Information Age, both anecdotal sources and formal surveys reveal that the public still views "career" primarily as "job" and that the outcome of vocational planning is often choosing a job. Many career services delivered through labor market offices, federal career information projects, recent legislative thrusts such as "Tech Prep," "School-to-Work Transitions," and work-based learning focus on preparing youth and adults for jobs that presumably will be waiting for them when they become "work-ready."

The many computer-assisted career information systems also encourage this narrowing down to a particular job. Such approaches tend to reflect an assumption that career planning is a linear process of preparing people for and fitting them into one right job, an assumption that does not fit with the multiple career transitions people are making in the United States or today's larger global society. Although everyone acknowledges that information is important, most would agree that information is not enough in the complex process of career decision making. Many years ago Martin Katz (1963), creator of the System of Interactive Guidance and Information (SIGI) computer-assisted decision-making system, astutely observed that career decisions are choices among values and values systems. He translated words into action by making values the core of his SIGI system.

Many people are beginning to recognize that career development is a lifelong process that occurs over an entire life span and consists of more than choosing an occupation. Many career professionals, however, have been trained in a linear model in which occupational information is paramount to preparing for the worker role. Most career services, whether delivered by labor market information centers, employment action centers, career planning centers, career development centers, outplacement centers, or the new legislatively mandated "one-stop" community career centers, have as their primary goal to help the individual make an occupational choice or a transition—to fit into a particular occupation or job after going through self-assessment, testing, educational or occupational exploration, and the job search. This model still dominates most career counseling practice.

It is true that some agencies, such as women's centers, and some private practitioners help clients look at career planning more holistically. Still, the great majority of career services still focus on occupational choice, job search, and job placement. Because many women's agencies recognize the economic needs of women as well as their desire for more holistic lives, which include relationships as well as achievements, they have approached career planning from broader life-roles or work-family perspectives.

Single parents, many of them women living at the poverty level, often focus on getting a job or getting off welfare. They are in a double bind if they want to get a job while doing long-term career planning because if they get a job that pays too much, they may lose health care benefits and if they lose health care benefits, they may be forced back on welfare to protect their families. They also face problems in getting adequate and affordable child care and transportation. In times of a tight economy and high unemployment, many find themselves with few options.

Unfortunately, political efforts in 1996 to "change welfare as we know it" and get rid of the welfare system seem to have come from a blame-the-victim mentality. While moving out of welfare dependency and getting training and jobs are desirable objectives, there is no assurance that jobs will be available when training is completed. In addition, it is unclear if the legislators who want to change the laws have any idea of the complexity of the problem that they have magnified but that actually accounts for only 4 percent of the national budget. The career planning process for single people, male and female, with and without children, and especially those with low incomes, will present special challenges in the twenty-first century.

The Expanded Concept of Career

The old matching model that marked the beginning of vocational guidance at the turn of the last century, while still used by some job placement and career professionals, does not seem sufficient or expansive enough for the kind of postindustrial society in which we live. Donald Super (1951) was one of the first important theorists to introduce the expanded concept of career. He defined career as a sequence of positions one holds during a lifetime of which occupation is only one. Super (1980) introduced the analogy of roles and theaters in a person's life, using what he called the *Life Career Rainbow* to illustrate. The rainbow includes nine major life roles: child, student, leisurite, citizen, worker, parent, spouse, pensioner, and homemaker. The theaters are those of work, home, family, leisure, and community. Super also posited that individuals move through developmental stages of growth: exploration, establishment, maintenance, and decline—the latter stage, now renamed "disengagement," includes the stages of decelerating, retirement planning, and retirement living.

In the business sector, a less psychological approach to career planning has been used in organizational career development. While education-based models generally have focused on the individual, organizational models have emphasized the institution and a blending of the individual's goals with those of the institution, with the latter being primary. Increasingly, human resource programs define career development as the problem of the individual, not the organization. While managers formerly aimed to be "coaches" for the career development of their employees, the new trend is for individuals to be more self-directed and proactive in their own promotions and advancements, to make their needs known, to empower themselves. Although strategies to find the "best fit" between employee and job still dominate many businesses, they are likely to change with the dramatic changes in the workplace and organizations that are already occurring.

The Case for New Approaches

Thus, while trait and factor approaches to career planning are still widely practiced, I argue that more broadly based approaches are needed. They are needed primarily because the old models were designed for a different period in time and society and have neglected or excluded (perhaps unconsciously) some of the critical personal issues influencing career development today. The following section presents seven reasons that career development must change as we move toward the new millennium.

Changing Societies

Leaders in many fields agree that the major characteristic of the twenty-first century will be change. Change is already occurring so fast and in so many areas that it is difficult to keep up with it. Change is now a constant in work, family, education, leisure, demographics, technology, politics, and so on. Increasingly, the *changing contexts* of people's lives are being recognized as major influences in their career opportunities and decisions, rather than only their internal influences, such as interests, abilities, and aptitudes. These changing contexts require new paradigms—new strategies for solving the old, lifelong problems of making career decisions and career transitions at different stages in our lives, perhaps with new orientations and motivations, which include not just self but also society. Paying attention to these contexts is a major development in counseling, psychology, and career planning.

Changing Career Definitions

The narrow definitions of career as job and of career planning as fitting into a job—the old linear model—are often still used. It is hard to change the mindset. In this scenario, people scan the environment for information and compete for their piece of a limited pie rather than see multiple possibilities in themselves and in society, in work and in all of life's roles. As already discussed, Super

(1951) provided the earliest and most lasting expanded definition of career and career development: "a continuous, lifelong process of developing and implementing a self-concept, testing that self-concept against reality, with satisfaction to self and *benefit to society*" (p. 88, emphasis added). We will return to his broad definition of career throughout the book.

One of Super's main points is that people have multiple *potentialities*. When they make career decisions, they are choosing to develop one talent over another. In contrast, traditional career planning and vocational guidance assumes that there is one perfect fit for a person's talents. It is a reductionist approach.

The organizational management literature also speaks to changing career patterns. The old assumptions of job security and stability are being challenged, and with blue-collar, white-collar, and older workers being "downsized," there is considerable uncertainty and anger while new rules are being developed for worker-employee relationships. Instead of the old "relational" career patterns, where workers provided skills or services and received salaries, benefits, and lifetime work in return, the new "transactional" careers are those in which contingent workers sell skills through time-limited contracts that offer few or no benefits. These new organizational policies and structures require greater adaptability on the part of workers along with self-development and self-management of careers (Mirvis and Hall, 1994). For the core workers (those who survive downsizing or are hired on a long-term basis), the new patterns also require greater emphasis on psychological success through deeper relationships with co-workers, especially in increasingly diverse work settings (Hall, 1996).

Changing Demographics

The demographic changes projected for the United States are well known (Johnston and Packer, 1987). An increasingly diverse and multicultural society will require career professionals to be more skillful in dealing with differences—whether the differences are of race, religion, ethnicity, class, age, gender, disability, sexual orientation, or country of origin—and in helping students and workers successfully do the same. Interpersonal relationships always have been important both on and off the job, but in the future career professionals will have to pay even greater attention to helping individuals build mutual respect, trust, and self-esteem and value differences. In the past, career assistance has focused mostly on white middle-class populations; in the future, career professionals will need new theories, knowledge, and strategies to interact effectively with more diverse populations in both their work settings and their personal lives (Brown and Minor, 1989, 1992).

Changing Lives

Although women's and men's lives are changing around the world—as was suggested by the 1995 United Nations International Women's Conference in Beijing and by increasing evidence of a men's movement—the rate and nature of change vary depending on economics, politics, religion, history, and social and cultural traditions. Roles and relationships between men and women have changed dramatically in the twentieth century, particularly in the Western nations, as women increasingly participate in the labor force. Men's roles have changed, too. Many men participate more in family, especially as their work is restructured and they are allowed to spend more time with their families. An extensive body of literature has emerged both on conflicts and convergence in work and family. Career professionals need training to understand the reciprocal effects of family and work and to help partners develop mutual respect, manage conflict, and promote work-family balance. They will also need to help reduce the stereotypes and biases that exist in a society that still encourages dominant-subordinate relationships.

Changing Organizations and Workplaces

Organizational structures and workplaces are changing in ways that may make traditional approaches to career planning and counseling obsolete or inadequate. Restructuring of work, downsizing, mergers, and takeovers all have powerful impacts on work and workers. In addition to the dramatic increase in layoffs among blue-collar and white-collar workers in both the United States and Europe, the old one-job-for-life pattern is being replaced. Today there are part-time workers, variously called contingent workers, portfolio persons, contract workers, even "throwaway" workers. Organizations are moving toward work teams, bottom-up decision making, new types of managers, and fewer hierarchies.

A widespread fear, described countless times in the media, is that the traditional workplace is changing in negative ways and that job security is a thing of the past. People talk of the loss of "the loyalty factor" and the development of a new psychological contract between employer and employee. David Noer describes this condition, especially among surviving employees, in *Healing the Wounds* (1993). William Bridges, in *JobShift* (1994b), asks "Where have all the jobs gone?" as he envisions the "dejobbing" of society, that is, a trend in which each worker becomes an entrepreneur, performs tasks rather than a job, and learns to live with rapid change and "temporariness."

Obviously, the old models of fitting people into jobs will become useless if there are no jobs to fit into. That new concepts of career and life planning will be needed if such changes take place seems self-evident.

Personal Transitions and Changing Work Patterns

Traditional approaches to career planning assume that society is static, that individuals do not change, and that work choices are made for a lifetime. But we need only look at the burgeoning literature on career transitions (for example, Bridges, 1980; Schlossberg, 1991; Brammer, 1991) to realize that those assumptions are no longer correct. The most frequent estimate is that the average adult will make five to seven major career changes in a lifetime. William Charland in *Career Shifting* (1993) stresses the importance of "starting over in a changing economy" and emphasizes, as have many other career authors, the importance of retraining and lifelong learning. In analyzing emerging work and learning opportunities, he cites labor market estimates that in the United States each year, a third of all job roles are in transition, a third of all technical schools become obsolete, and a third of all workers leave their jobs. Indeed, transitions have become commonplace and transition counseling has become central in the career development and human resource professions. Part of the career professional's task is to help individuals rethink the relationship between personal transitions, their own values, and organizational and social change.

Individualism, Spirituality, and Community

Another important change is the glimmering recognition that the exaggerated emphasis on individualism—so true especially in the United States—leads to fragmented individuals and a fragmented society in which egotistical decisions dominate and holistic development is ignored. Considerable literature exists on development and wellness of the whole person and the connection between body, mind, and spirit. Since the 1970s, the literature has placed a growing emphasis on work and spirituality and the search for meaning and purpose. There is also some recognition that life choices and decisions need to relate to societal issues and the common good. The best indication of this trend is the growing call for attention to "community" in such books as *The Spirit of Community* (Etzioni, 1993) and to spirituality and "connectedness" in such books as *The Reinvention of Work* (Fox, 1994). Professionals can contribute to this movement by helping career planners put less emphasis on work as satisfaction to self and more on work as benefit to society. They can also help people see the connectedness of the various parts of their lives—that is, the relationships between women and men, family and work, the rational and the emotional, the intellectual, physical, and spiritual, the personal life and the career, the local, national, and global—and the integration of the parts into a whole.

Integrative Life Planning (ILP): An Alternative Concept

In this book I introduce the concept of Integrative Life Planning (ILP), a comprehensive model that brings together many aspects of people's lives in ways that I hope will help them and their career guides see the "big picture" of their lives, their communities, and the larger society. ILP presents an alternative way of thinking about career and life planning with both a philosophical framework and practical strategies that career professionals can use or adapt to implement the concept. This work is in harmony with many other works of postmodern thought that call for connectedness, pluralism, spirituality, subjectivity, wholeness, and community. Among them are two already mentioned in this chapter—Hazel Henderson's *Paradigms in Progress* and Matthew Fox's *Reinvention of Work*—and Thomas Moore's *Care of the Soul* (1992), along with much of the multicultural literature that emphasizes these themes. Rather than giving a lot of answers, ILP provides career professionals with a comprehensive framework to consider using in their own settings with their unique populations.

The Quilt and Quilters as Metaphor

When I began to delineate a model of ILP in 1987, I chose a quilt and quilters as metaphors for what I wanted to say and what the ILP approach to career planning represents. Quilting is an important tradition in many cultures, usually performed by women. The quilt itself is constructed from pieces that fit together to make a whole. The pieces are fastened together with care to create a product—actually, a work of art—that provides warmth and symbolizes nurturing. The art of quilting can be learned by anyone interested in taking pieces and putting them together, connecting them in ways that hold meaning both for the maker and the user. Quilters are people who engage in this process in order to help others make quilts of their lives. Thus, the quilt metaphor can be used to convey many messages and to offer an idea of how to weave together the personal, the professional, and the practical.

The quilt can also be understood on many levels. On one level, it represents the global world or context in which dramatic changes are occurring, affecting persons, families, communities, nations, and the planet. On a second level, it represents the career world, the field of career development and planning and the ways in which professional knowledge and practice are changing, with new frontiers of knowledge and new ways of knowing driving the way we think about ourselves, our society, and the planet. On a third level, it represents the ILP model itself, with its critical tasks—which will be presented in the following chapters—that are so much a part of our lives today but are pieces that often are neglected or omitted in traditional career planning. The critical tasks form the core of Integrative Life Planning.

On yet another level, the quilt represents a few of the pieces of my own life, pieces of my experience that are directly relevant to the ILP themes, for they have shaped me and my thinking about career and life planning and my own options, barriers, and decisions. The pieces represent a synthesis of my thought and my voice, with conscious linking of the personal and professional. This quilt weaves some of my personal story together with the local, national, and international scene in which it was played out. In my life quilt, the personal is part of the professional because the combination of these experiences influenced the development of the Integrative Life Planning Model. The model evolved as I read a lot, experienced a lot, and reflected a lot, all against the backdrop of a university work environment, a Norwegian American home environment, and a two-career family environment that included two special children.

This book is a departure from the objective, empirical norms of academia that dominate vocational, career, and educational psychology in most research universities. It acknowledges the new knowledge produced in the last fifteen years as a valid representation of new voices, especially women and ethnic minorities. It represents the tensions I felt as the only full-time female professor in my program over that time. It also includes the frayed-at-the-edges feeling I got trying to bring about change in a system that sometimes seemed like a block of concrete more than connected pieces of a quilt. Yet I was able to survive, grow, and work for change in that system, largely because of support and affirmation from the outside, both national and international.

Indeed, this metaphorical quilt has so many meanings that I could not possibly discuss them all in one book; instead, I focus on several of them. These are the global-local context and its implications for change in people's life options and decisions; the professional context and the movement from traditional vocational guidance to contemporary career development and, transcending that, to Integrative Life Planning; and the personal context, the kinds of personal and professional experiences I have had that are relevant to this model and out of which ILP has evolved. The quilt symbolizes all this as well as all those I have met and all that I have had the opportunity to do and be with the help of my family, students, colleagues, and friends.

ILP: The Conceptual Framework

I will now provide an introduction to the ILP concept—I will explain what the ILP quilt looks like. First, it is important to understand that ILP is a concept *in process.* Its form differs in several ways from that first presented in 1987 although it also retains many of the same basic elements. Ultimately, I hope that ILP will provide career professionals with a different worldview about career development, introduce them to integrative ways of helping their clients, students, and organizations, and stimulate them to create new tools and instruments for doing so.

Planning Versus *Patterns*

While developing the ILP concept, I have vacillated between the descriptive terms Integrative Life *Planning* and Integrative Life *Patterns. Planning* implies a linear rational process or detailed method for achieving or making something, in this case a career, usually with a known outcome. And indeed, ILP resembles traditional career planning, but it is different in that it is integrative, that is, it focuses not only on job or work but on wholeness, bringing together the parts of a life. In contrast, the term *pattern,* often associated with sewing, means a guide to use in making things although the user does not always know how they will turn out even if the model is good. The term *pattern* thus seems to me to be more fluid, perhaps more "right brain," embracing both predictability and uncertainty. Yet patterns are also integrative; they bring parts together to make a whole. In fact, I believe the word *pattern* more aptly characterizes the ILP concept, but I use the word *planning* more often because it implies having a sense of agency, a feeling that one can take some control of the direction of one's life. I will alternate between the two in this book.

In selecting this terminology, I have tried to move away from the words *career* and *career planning* to a descriptor that better communicates the broad concept of life roles and how they intersect. In my teaching over the years, I found that many of my students—women in particular—identified with Super's expanded concept (probably because many of them were living multiple roles even while still graduate students). But when they entered real-world practice, they found that most clients and many other practitioners used career to mean occupation or job. The concept of career development as lifelong patterns and processes rather than mere occupational choice was liberating to them.

A Sense of Agency

I was reluctant to abandon the word *planning* because much in the early career development literature suggests the importance of planning in one's life. One of the most important concepts in Super and Overstreet's (1960) study of ninth-grade boys was that, while they were not ready for choice behavior, they were ready for "planfulness." Some of the psychological literature suggests that the ability to plan, to have what some call "a sense of agency"—a feeling of control over what happens in one's life—is usually linked to psychological health. There are important cultural value differences in how people view their fate or destiny, but in Western culture this concept of control has been an important part of empowerment counseling, especially with women, racial and ethnic minorities, and those in poverty who are outside the opportunity structure and feel there is little they can do to improve their lives.

Although I still believe we can help clients and students in a changing society to plan through greater self-knowledge, environmental information, and knowledge of the decision-making process, increasingly we know that we cannot predict lives or anticipate the random events—positive and negative—that influence opportunities and life choices. Nancy Schlossberg (1991) and Schlossberg and Robinson (1996) state that "non-events"—the times when we don't get a job, are not elected to office, do not get a promotion, do not have a child—also have a powerful impact on our lives and those around us. It seems to me that it is helpful to think in terms of patterns over a life span, that is, spiral movements of a kind of circle of life, rather than in terms of the traditional ladder of success. Although at times we plan and gain a sense of empowerment from doing so, it may be more realistic to understand that the patterns of our lives develop and require living with ambiguity and uncertainty. Planning (part of the logical, rational paradigm) ultimately plays a smaller part.

Moving Toward Integration

The movement toward wholeness and connectedness has become quite prominent in counseling and career development in the last decade. Indeed, it is part of the new paradigm. When I began ILP, I was focused on the integration of work and family and the roles and relationships of women and men. Although these issues are still important, I have realized that life in a postindustrial society has many more aspects that need to be brought together. I realized that my worldview was not inclusive enough.

I used the term *integrative* at first to communicate the connection between work and family, but I soon realized that other parts of our lives needed to be included too. I was struck by the fact that for years professionals have been talking about the connection between education and work or work and learning and even about work and leisure but seemed reluctant (and still do, in education at least) to talk about work and family. Even in the mid 1990s, models of career guidance in schools and career development in colleges and businesses tend to exclude or minimize family during the career planning process. This may be a consequence of our focus on Western linear thought, but it is an increasingly inappropriate practice, especially when counseling people of ethnic minorities and non-Western cultures.

The concepts of wellness and wholeness are beginning to take on more credibility in the 1990s, but suspicion of the term *holistic* remains, especially in academic psychology, with its logical positivist tradition. It is not a word widely used—and that's an understatement—or wasn't until multicultural counseling became more recognized. I believe we need to do a better job of seeing the connectedness; we need to see things steadily and see them whole. Some authors and career professionals have begun to write about spirituality and work. Others connect the rational and the intuitive. Still others (myself included) focus on the integration of women's and men's lives. Those working in the area of wellness emphasize the connection between body, mind, and spirit—the development of a kind of wellness wheel that includes physical, intellectual, emotional, spiritual, social, and career development. Futurists call attention to the link between the local, national, and global that is embodied in the motto, "Think globally, act locally." Although there is a growing body of literature on diversity and multiculturalism, few have connected that aspect of life with career planning. ILP attempts to include many of these pieces.

ILP Principles

Integrative Life Planning is a comprehensive concept designed for career professionals—including counselors, career specialists, advisers, adult educators, organizational development specialists, and human resource managers—to assist young people and adults in learning a life planning process that is holistic in nature. The process may be viewed from six perspectives. First, it is a way of seeing self and world that takes into account both personal development and the contexts in which we live; local, national, and global change; work, family, education, and leisure changes; cultural changes and the changing roles of women and men; the relative importance of various life roles (that is, learning, loving, working, relaxing); the need for reflection on one's own developmental priorities for mind, body, and spirit; and the importance of change itself, both personal and social.

Second, while work has been the focus of our lives for generations, especially in the United States, ILP offers a model that incorporates emerging knowledge in the fields of career and organizational development, gender roles, multiculturalism and diversity, and social and personal change into a unified framework for practice. The focus on valuing diversity and inclusivity is one of the aspects of ILP that makes it unique. The ILP concept suggests ways in which professionals can examine various aspects of their own lives and integrate them into a more meaningful whole, as well as develop skills and strategies for using the model with students, clients, and employees. It also recognizes that such approaches may be most useful for those who are beyond Abraham Maslow's (1962) survival level of needs, that is, from the physiological to the safety, belonging, esteem, and self-actualization needs.

Third, the integrative model involves examination of the society, the organization (especially the work organization), the family, and the individual, and it considers relationship goals in human development as well as achievement goals and community goals. It presents a context of societal changes that makes new approaches necessary, and it provides an expanded framework for career development, career planning, and human resource development.

4. Fourth, the ILP model explores a number of connections and links. It examines the links between work and family and the two-earner family in order to exemplify ways in which integrative planning can occur. Rather than assuming the existence of an ideal family, it recognizes the multiple family types that exist in the United States and suggests that ILP can be relevant for all of them. Other life roles in addition to family and work are explored, but since to work and to love remain life's two major experiences, emphasis is given to how these roles are carried out in the family and the workplace.

5. Fifth, ILP introduces spirituality, meaning, and purpose as key aspects of life planning that are often ignored in traditional career planning. Yet these are especially important to cultural and ethnic groups in which spiritual concerns are central. The rational logical career planning models of the past followed the reductionist Newtonian tradition and gave only a limited place to the spiritual aspect of human development, especially in relation to work.

6. Finally, ILP emphasizes helping people manage change and understand their life choices, decisions, and transitions in a societal context. ILP suggests that we can all be change agents in our own lives, in the lives of others, and in the larger society. It is important to understand how our personal choices and transitions affect our local and global communities. Because work, family, learning, and leisure are major parts of and contribute to community, I believe that if we understand our personal development, male and female issues, cultural diversity, the transition process, and social change, we will also achieve more effective communities. The ILP concept's broad foundation comes from a wide body of literature, both quantitative and qualitative, from diverse fields of knowledge.

The Six Critical Tasks

The Integrative Life Planning concept is now organized into six critical life tasks that in my view are central to career development and decision making. These tasks have been ignored or given little attention in career development theory and practice. Yet they address the critical issues that humans face at the end of the twentieth century and appear likely to continue to be important in the new millennium. Chapters Three through Eight are devoted to describing each critical task, which I introduce briefly as follows:

Critical Task 1: Finding Work That Needs Doing in Changing Global Contexts

There are so many needs and issues as the world becomes a global village that it is almost impossible to include all that might be relevant. I have identified some that seem most important to me. The issues I have selected are those that reflect the work that needs to be done in the local and global setting. I hope that my readers will identify those issues that are most relevant to their populations and communities and then help them understand how these issues affect their choices and decisions about work.

Critical Task 2: Weaving Our Lives into a Meaningful Whole

Career development for both women and men has been changing around the world but perhaps most dramatically in the United States. Since the 1970s, more attention has been given to the importance of gender in careers and the differing career socialization of men and women for various life roles. The internal and external factors that affect the life planning of women and men are different in some ways, similar in others. The BORN FREE concept, which formerly focused on gender, career, and social change, is part of ILP's foundation. The purpose of the BORN FREE concept, process, and training model is to expand life career options for men and women. It is a framework now being "re-visioned" to reflect culture and community as well. It is generating considerable cross-cultural interest through a global electronic network called BORN FREE International (BFI). (The BORN FREE concept is described further in Chapter Two.)

Holistic life planning—which includes mind, body, and spirit, as well as social, intellectual, physical, emotional, and career development—seems somewhat incongruent in a society that puts so much emphasis on working. Nonetheless, there is growing recognition that our lives do not compartmentalize conveniently and that what happens in one part of our lives affects the other parts. There is also recognition that paid work may not be as central in the future as it is today with the changing workplace roles. Men and women are beginning to feel that work cannot meet all their needs and are expressing a desire to balance work and other life roles—to see "work within a life"—to become more integrated people. Because it is difficult if not impossible for human beings to develop in all these areas at once, they need help in prioritizing according to their unique individual, family, work, and community needs and values.

Critical Task 3: Connecting Family and Work

As I've already made clear in this chapter, I believe that much more attention needs to be given in the career development field to male-female roles and relationships and the connection between family and work. A small portion of the extensive literature on work and family is summarized in this book. Although many types of families are mentioned, the emphasis is on two-income households and single-parent families, which have become dominant family types in the United States today. Other households—including those made up of blended families, extended families, role-reversal families (with husband as homemaker and wife as income producer), and single adults—are also important but not the main focus here.

Gender-role dilemmas that arise as people move beyond their ascribed roles of provider and nurturer can cause considerable stress in families and in the workplace. Career professionals need a greater understanding of work-family conflicts, single-parent stress, and caregiver stress (when adult children care for elderly parents). They need to know how to facilitate mutual planning and partnerships. By *partnerships* I mean those relationships in which each partner treats the other with respect, is flexible when negotiating roles, and enables the other to choose roles and fulfill responsibilities that are congruent with his or her individual goals and the partners' mutual goals for their relationship, the family, and the community.

Critical Task 4: Valuing Pluralism and Inclusivity

An informed awareness of all kinds of differences—racial, ethnic, class, religious, gender, age, disability, geography, and sexual orientation—will be essential in the future. Already in the works, diversity training in business, multicultural counseling courses and curricula in universities, political action for change, and programs to reduce bias and discrimination represent a constructive response to the human relations issues facing society. It is my belief that we must help people learn not only to understand but also to accept, value, and celebrate diversity.

Developing positive interpersonal relationships on and off the job is an important component of the broad concept of Integrative Life Patterns.

Critical Task 5: Exploring Spirituality and Life Purpose

The exploration of spirituality is a critical task central to the lives of many that is often missing in the career development literature. I link spirituality with meaning and purpose, the core of the self that gives meaning to life. It relates to the search for self-actualization, personal values, wholeness, and a sense of community. I use the term *spirituality* to mean a yearning for a higher power, something larger than oneself, a need to give back to society, contribute one's talents toward community improvement, and achieve a sense of connectedness with others. Our logical, rational approaches to career development have put little emphasis on the place of the spiritual in life, even though many cultural groups accord it a central position. Yet as career professionals, we can play important roles in helping others explore meaning and purpose in their lives, including the value of money and the meaning of materialism in relation to one's own life and that of the community.

Critical Task 6: Managing Personal Transitions and Organizational Change

The critical task of managing personal and social change is one of the most important. There are several models that career specialists can use to help their clients think about and successfully negotiate the transition process. Clearly, transition counseling will be an important field in the future, not only for outplacement or school-to-work situations but for transitions made at all stages of life, including middle and later life planning. It will be a challenge to career professionals to help people in transition integrate the most important parts of their identities in their own contexts at different life stages, such as the second adulthood after age forty-five that Gail Sheehy (1995) describes. Clients also will need to be taught the relationship of decision making to transition making, utilizing new decision models such as H. B. Gelatt's (1989) Positive Uncertainty to help prepare people for the change and instability they may face in the new millennium. Changes in organizations also will affect individual and partner career decisions and work and life values as workplaces implement new structures, policies, and forms of work.

Equally important in transition counseling will be helping people become agents for change. An already rich body of literature on organizational dynamics and systems change explores this theme. Individuals can be change agents in their own lives, in their interpersonal relationships, and in their institutions, thus affecting their larger communities especially as they relate local work to global contexts.

Conclusion

By its nature, the Integrative Life Planning approach to career development is comprehensive, interdisciplinary, and inclusive. As a systems approach, it connects many parts of lives and society. No counselor, career professional, or career planner can be expected to absorb the whole concept at once. All will have to select the central tasks that are most important or meaningful at a given time and work with them. As each task is accomplished, it connects the varying dimensions of human life: *identity* (ethnicity, race, gender, class, age, ability, beliefs, and sexual orientation), *human development* (the social, intellectual, physical, spiritual, emotional, and career), *life roles* (love, labor, learning, and leisure), and *context* (society, organization, family, and individual). These are the pieces of the Integrative Life Pattern quilt. Let us turn now to the theoretical base and knowledge trends that underlie this concept.

Chapter Two

Tracing the Interdisciplinary Origins of ILP

> *So many theories focus solely on the individual and do not take into consideration the dynamic relationship between the individual and society. Career success is a vague concept that varies significantly depending on the person defining it. For example, my father defined it through his professional work while my mother defined it through her volunteer work and homemaking. I didn't know what it meant for me. Although there are no full-blown theories of career development for women, I think that the developmental perspective and a feminist empowerment model would have given me confidence to examine my needs and desires and move from the position I was in to one of growth and positive discovery.*
> —Female counseling graduate student

The ideas that Integrative Life Planning embodies are drawn from several disciplines in addition to career development and vocational psychology. ILP is a quilt that tries to synthesize many patches. It is difficult to write about professional knowledge and practice across so many disciplines; yet I chose to explore other fields in order to view the world and my field through a larger lens.

Portions of the section "The Gender-Role System" were adapted from Hansen (1984). Used by permission of Jossey-Bass Inc., Publishers.

The academic world is organized by subject and discipline, yet the current thrust for more collaborative, interdisciplinary programs may be a belated recognition that the old fragmented disciplines approach to teaching and learning is no longer useful.

This chapter offers a brief review of authors whose concepts, philosophical thoughts, and professional practices have contributed to my thinking. These people might be regarded as "co-quilters." They offer theory and research from the fields of career psychology, adult development, gender roles, gender and feminist psychology, and multiculturalism. They provide concepts from organizational psychology, spirituality, transitions, and futurism that are presented in more detail in other chapters. Because the different ILP themes often cut across more than one source, it is not always possible to attribute the precise origin or influence. Where it is evident, I will indicate the source in this chapter. However, it is probably best to see ILP as my synthesis of multiple influences.

Career Development and Adult Development

In the past two decades, a new synthesis between career development and adult development has been made with the recognition that human development occurs over life stages rather than stopping after adolescence and that career is more than just an occupation or a one-time choice. A review of the theories of these two fields begins this chapter's discussion.

Career Development

Super's (1951) theory of career development over the life span has had a powerful impact on theory and practice in career counseling and human resource development. Super's early studies triggered movement away from the narrower field of vocational psychology to the broader perspective of career development. Especially unique were the following concepts:

- *Career patterns:* Patterns of vocational and career choices change over time and life stages.
- *Life patterns:* Women and men have different life patterns.

- *Career maturity:* There are vocational and developmental tasks to be mastered at different life stages, including growth, exploration, establishment, maintenance, and decline (now termed disengagement).
- *Life roles:* Six basic roles (child, student, worker, homemaker, leisurite, and citizen) are played out in each person's life. (See Figure 2.1.)

Super's Life Career Rainbow, which he created in the 1980s, depicts what he called the roles and theaters of life, as well as personal and situational determinants in each person's life. He pointed out that roles may vary within the lifetime of any person and at different developmental stages. Super's rainbow forms the basis for an activity that can be useful as a counseling tool, especially with adults.

The culmination of Super's work was the Work Importance Study (WIS), a cross-national study conducted in ten countries over an eight-year period. *Life Roles, Values, and Careers,* which presented this comprehensive international work, was published posthumously in 1995 with his co-editor, Branimir Sverko of Croatia, and his son, Charles Super. Researchers from Australia, Belgium, Canada, Croatia, Italy, Japan, Poland, Portugal, South Africa, and the United States collaborated on the study, which Super himself began after his retirement. The studies support the continuing universality of the fulfillment of personal potential as a life goal that transcends boundaries of status, gender, and culture. In the powerful and poignant preface to the work, Super comments:

> The central thread of the tapestry that is this volume is the observation that the various roles each contain distinctive challenges and distinctive opportunities for the fulfillment of values. The roles, and a person's ability to fulfill them, shift with development, with age and stage. . . . The process of career can be told as science, as this volume aims to do, or it can be told as narrative or life history, as we close this preface. The roles shift. The focus of life shifts. The challenges and rewards, the sources and uses of energy—all these are altered. Because the WIS book was not finished, I invited my son, a developmental psychologist, to become the third editor as the work—indeed, my life's work—neared completion. This too is a study in the importance of work [pp. xx–xxi].

Figure 2.1. Super's Life Career Rainbow.

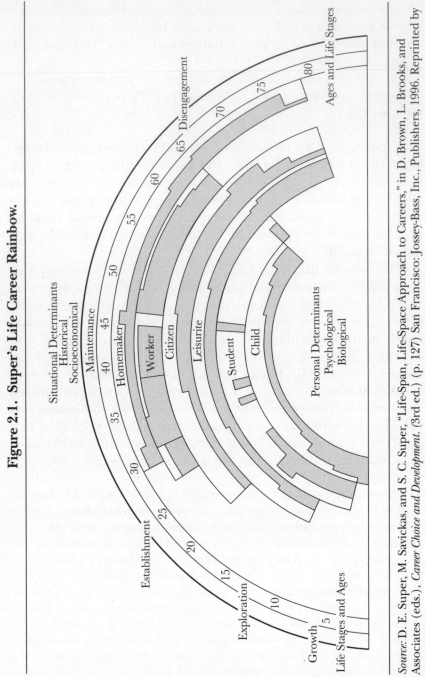

Source: D. E. Super, M. Savickas, and S. C. Super, "Life-Span, Life-Space Approach to Careers," in D. Brown, L. Brooks, and Associates (eds.), *Career Choice and Development.* (3rd ed.) (p. 127) San Francisco: Jossey-Bass, Inc., Publishers, 1996. Reprinted by permission.

The impact of Donald Super's work cannot be expressed adequately in a book of this nature, but his contribution to ILP, to theory and practice with regard to life choices, roles, and decisions, and to the importance of work in life has been immense.

Adult Development

The field of adult development, which blossomed in the 1970s and 1980s, complements the life-span career development theory and developmental psychology. Few would argue that life stops at adolescence or midlife. The growing emphasis on counseling at midlife and later attests to the importance of this topic today, especially as the population continues to age, and demographic indicators show that the fastest-growing population is aged eighty and over. Researchers too numerous to mention have studied different stages in the lives of men and women and found that individual differences in adults increase with age. A rich and relevant body of literature has emerged on adult transitions, a topic discussed at some length later in this book.

Integrative Research

A recent study that is closely related to Integrative Life Planning investigated the interrelationships between work, love, and learning in adult life, studying both men and women from a framework of life events or life markers (Merriam and Clark, 1991). The researchers created a questionnaire on work, love, and learning in adulthood and distributed it to adults across North America through graduate and continuing education faculty. Their final sample consisted of 405 adults, most of whom were white, female (27.7 percent of them were men and 72.3 percent were women), and ages 20 to 62 (the average age was 37.6 years). A well-educated group, 88 percent had some college and 39 percent had graduated college.

Three broad patterns of interaction between work and love were revealed: (1) in the *parallel pattern,* the two areas of love and work are intertwined and change (or constancy) in one area is reflected in the other; (2) in the *steady/fluctuating pattern,* one area remains steady while the other fluctuates and the steady area acts as a stabilizer and a source of personal identity; (3) in the *divergent pattern* change is frequent and self-initiated and love and work appear to exist independent of and often in opposition to one another. The authors found that "each pattern has a different stabilizing factor that creates a sense of organization and harmony" (p. 211). In relating work and love to learning, they established that the most significant learning occurred when things were going well in both domains of work and love. The four major discoveries of this study were of (1) three distinct patterns of interaction; (2) a stabilizing factor in each pattern; (3) a lack of gender differences; and (4) the role of learning in the development of capacity to work and love (pp. 210–212).

This qualitative study, like ILP, looked at people's lives from an integrative perspective and may be useful to counselors and human development professionals interested in how the lives of these educated adult women and men intersect.

Another study that moved away from the old linear paradigm, this one of adult women, investigated connections in people's lives. Grace Baruch, Rosalind Barnett, and Caryl Rivers (1983) took a psychological perspective as they examined new patterns of love and work for women today. This was a random survey of about three hundred Caucasian women in different life patterns, including never married, married without children, married with children, and divorced with children. All the never married and divorced women were employed, as were half of each of the other two groups. The researchers looked at how women experience certain areas of their lives and their life satisfaction from a framework of mastery and pleasure and concluded that there is no "one size fits all" lifeprint. These works are but two examples of research that has attempted to link various aspects of life roles.

Developmental/Contextual Theories

Another emerging characteristic of the psychological literature, especially in vocational psychology and career development, is a focus on context, particularly cultural context. This new emphasis is especially important in a field that traditionally looked inward to the intrapsychic rather than outward to the external. A considerable body of literature now embraces a *developmental-contextual approach* to career development, acknowledging the limitations of earlier theories and offering new conceptualizations. The developmental-contextual approach focuses on the development of the person in context and avoids the overemphasis on the intrapsychic and intrapersonal for which psychology and counseling so often have been criticized (Vondracek, Lerner, and Schulenberg, 1986; Vondracek and Schulenberg, 1992). A multicontextual model of counseling, bridging brevity (brief counseling) and diversity, sees the link between contextualism and development as a way to offer a more interactive, relational worldview (Steenbarger, 1991, 1993). Support for the contextualist worldview has come from a multicultural theorist, Derald Wing Sue (1991), who would probably argue that it is one of the cornerstones of multicultural theory.

E. P. Cook's (1991) annual review of practice and research in career counseling and development emphasizes the developmental-contextual themes found in the literature. The review highlights approaches and interventions related to "work within a life" and stresses the need for individuals to function as "integrated psychological beings" (p. 99). It also cites the literature on multiple roles and points out how multiple roles impact on the lives of both women and men. This framework is also consistent with the development of ILP.

Gender-Role Theory

The importance of gender roles as one dimension of Integrative Life Planning will become evident throughout these pages. Some writers and researchers omit the gender variable, refusing to acknowledge its importance. However, even if I acknowledge that it is not always the defining issue, I assert that it is important in career development of both women and men. An extensive body of literature on male and female gender-role socialization contributed to the development of ILP, and the impact of gender and the power of gender are the basis for some themes of this book. The BORN FREE program, created in the late 1970s as a concept, a process, and a model, also provided part of the theoretical foundation for ILP (Hansen, 1979).

The Gender-Role System

A gender-role system is at the core of our cultural norms and affects both women and men. This system is the network of attitudes, feelings, and behaviors that result from the pervasiveness of gender-role stereotyping. It is clear that every culture has its gender-role system and ascribes certain roles to men and women (Chetwynd and Hartnett, 1977). Three important factors in the system are the following:

1. *The male and female stereotypes.* Based on a person's gender, one of two different series of personality traits is assigned. The male stereotype is characterized by dominance, independence, aggressiveness, and problem-solving abilities; the female stereotype is characterized by subordination, dependence, passivity, and greater subjectivity in approaching problems.

2. *The segregation of "men's work" and "women's work."* This is the allocation of different types of activities considered necessary or appropriate for the sustenance or improvement of living—that is, the division of labor—by sex. This division of labor is still very much with us in the 1990s, despite progress in some occupations.

3. *A higher value on the male.* The characteristics and traits associated with men are considered more important and valuable than those associated with women.

Although society has undergone important changes in the past fifteen years, few would dispute that stereotypes still exist, that socialization patterns change slowly, that segregation between the sexes still exists in the workplace (despite some adjustments), and that a higher value is still attached to what men do than to what women do.

Some Definitions

We are all aware of the meaning of the term *stereotype*—that is, a process of assigning certain habits, expectations, and abilities to people solely on the basis of their group membership, in this case, male and female, independent of their individual attributes. However, some specific types of stereotypes and related terms that may be less familiar to readers are reviewed in the following paragraphs.

Gender-role stereotypes are beliefs about the general appropriateness of various roles and activities for women and for men. *Gender-trait stereotypes* are psychological characteristics or behavioral traits believed to characterize one sex more than the other; thus gender-trait stereotypes undergird both the gender-role stereotypes and gender roles themselves (Williams and Best, 1982).

Gender-difference stereotypes are perceptions of "typical" characteristics and behaviors of males and females, or views of what the sexes "are like." *Gender-role orientation* consists of the attitudes we have learned through our socialization about masculinity and femininity and masculine and feminine roles. *Gender-role ideology* describes a normative view of appropriate behavior of males and females—that is, what they "should" do (Kutner and Brogan, 1976).

Socialization is the process by which behaviors, roles, attitudes, and beliefs are transmitted to the next generation. Socializing agents, including the family, schools, religious institutions, television, the workplace, and peer groups may have stereotypical beliefs about gender-appropriate characteristics. *Career socialization* consists of the lifelong series of differential processes and experiences through which women and men are prepared for the educational, vocational, and life-role options considered appropriate for them based on their sex, race, or class (Hansen, 1979). As we examine the career development of women and men, it is important to keep these concepts and definitions in mind. They provide one of the foundations on which both ILP and BORN FREE were developed.

The BORN FREE Program

One of the most important emphases of Integrative Life Planning is the interrelationship of gender and career. Most of my professional life over the past twenty years has been devoted to studying the impact of gender on life roles and choices and related gender-role issues. This resulted in BORN FREE, a national program whose goal is to reduce career-related gender-role stereotyping and expand options for and improve relationships between women and men.

The BORN FREE concept represents an important piece of my personal quilt. My first real awareness of the relationships between gender and career occurred after I had received my doctorate and was appointed assistant professor at the university. While in high school and college, I was deeply involved in writing editorials about racism and prejudice—about "brotherhood," as we called it then—and my consciousness of gender issues was limited until the mid 1960s and early 1970s. At that time, my awareness was heightened by the women's movement, the increased participation of women in the workforce, my experience as a teacher and counselor with adolescent girls and boys, and my experience as one of the few women professors in a largely white male environment.

I knew that I did not want to make an either-or choice between marriage and career, which was the choice suggested to many women of my generation and accepted by the few female professors I had had. Because of this, some professors did not take their women students seriously and the halls of academia were not a particularly welcoming environment for female faculty. Delving into the gender-role and socialization literature heightened my awareness of my need to be a whole person and my conviction about the strong connection between the personal and professional, particularly between gender and career. An even more powerful influence was my children; as the mother of a daughter and a son, I directly experienced the gender-role stereotypes they brought home (which my husband and I worked hard to eliminate).

Out of this growing awareness—or concurrent with it—came the BORN FREE program. BORN FREE is a research and training program designed to expand life career options for girls and boys and men and women from kindergarten through postsecondary/college educational levels. It builds on the expanded definitions of career and is unique in its focus on both sexes. An indirect intervention targeted primarily to educators and parents, its main contribution has been being one of the first gender-equity programs to link three areas: career development, gender-role socialization, and social and educational change.

BORN FREE has two meanings. Literally, the term means that we humans are born free of stereotypes but then learn them through our socialization and so must unlearn them. But the words are also an acronym for exactly what the program is about: to Build

Options for both women and men; to Reassess the Norms through which we have all been socialized; to Free Roles of both men and women in work and family; and to do this through Educational Equity, that is, the development of awareness and action plans in educational institutions of all kinds and levels. (Figure 2.2 shows the BORN FREE logo.)

Several assumptions underlying BORN FREE are based on the changes occurring in the lives of men and women and society that will be emphasized throughout this book. These are the following:

1. Both women and men are seriously limited in their career development by the pervasive gender-role stereotyping and socialization in society. Just as there is a female stereotype, there is also a male stereotype. (See Chapter Four for more on this.)

2. No one individual or group is to be blamed for these barriers to development because we are all products of our socialization; this is the way most societies evolve. Men and women need to work together as partners to solve the problems not only of career-related gender-role stereotyping but also of other societal barriers.

3. Students are affected at every level of the educational spectrum. Educators and parents need to become aware of the

Figure 2.2. The BORN FREE Logo.

inhibitors at home and in school that limit as well as of the facilitators that support career development.

4.   Through systems interventions and action plans developed by both men and women, educators and parents can help create more humane learning environments to expand opportunities for males and females at all educational levels.

As indicated, BORN FREE is a *concept*, a *process*, and a *model*. The concept has focused on the three substantive areas of career development, gender-role theory, and educational and social change. The process has been one of collaboration, consultation, and training and teaching participants the principles of change and organizational change. The model shows how institutional change occurs and how one can be a change agent in one's home institution. BORN FREE was influenced by my commitment to educational and social change—a perspective not always compatible with the objectivity sought in the natural and behavioral sciences.

Having spent most of my professional life teaching counselors to be change agents for human development after having grown up in a low-income family in a small midwestern town, I am acutely aware of the social, political, economic, and other environmental factors that affect our life options and all aspects of our lives. The strong emphasis on teaching educators and parents to be change agents is a unique characteristic of BORN FREE. We all know that the best ideas or programs can be sabotaged by people who resist change; the principles of organizational change and the change process were employed not only to address resistance but to gain system support for BORN FREE strategies and interventions.

One of BORN FREE's goals has been to achieve a ripple effect. In other words, people trained would return to their home institution and train others, with their students being the ultimate beneficiaries of our efforts. There is considerable evidence of the impact on the participants; the strength of the multimedia materials BORN FREE offers; the attractiveness of the concept of linking career, gender roles, and social change; and achievement of the desired ripple effect. Yet there is still much to be done not only to improve equality between men and women but also to improve equality between people of all races and ethnic groups, the physically challenged, and other groups in the mid 1990s. To this end,

BORN FREE now is being "reenvisioned" and updated to emphasize a more total concept of culture.

BORN FREE has been widely disseminated for fifteen years through teacher education, counselor education, women's centers, media projects, and human relations and gender-equity programs and projects, and several evaluations of products and participant attitudes have been conducted. Yet there is much evidence that the problems of stereotyping, prejudice, and discrimination still continue. In the 1970s we used the term *sex-role stereotyping;* the current preferred term is gender-role stereotyping. In this book, I will refer to *sex* as the biological condition of being male or female and *gender* as the ascribed roles.

Theories of Women's Development

Much of the thinking behind ILP has evolved from the emerging literature on female development and, more recently, on the development of the "new male." Also important have been the now-extensive discussions of work and family (Hansen and Rapoza, 1978). Although it is impossible to address all the literature in a book of this nature, it is important to call attention to that which supports the integrated, connected, and gender-role development of men and women. A few of the theories and studies developed by women are discussed here.

A new approach to understanding the psychology of women was introduced in the mid 1970s (Miller, 1976). The experiences of certain women were studied in the search for knowledge about such issues as authenticity, domination and subordination, self-esteem, power and self-determination, conflict, and affiliation and attachment. Although it did not consciously address race and class issues, Miller's study identified forces that affect all women. This new self-in-relation approach was a landmark in the conceptualization of women's lives.

The concept of self-in-relation has dominated much of the research on women in the past twenty years. One of the first self-in-relation theories offered a view of women's voices as representing an ethic of care. It challenged the applicability of Kohlberg's stages of moral development to women and triggered many quantitative and qualitative studies of the lives of adolescent and adult women (Gilligan, 1982).

A related study of women in New England colleges and communities analyzed the development of "self, voice, and mind" to describe six "women's ways of knowing": *received knowledge,* acquired from listening to the voices of others; *subjective knowledge* that is one's inner voice and *subjective knowledge* that is a quest for self-determination and revised self-concept; *procedural knowledge* that is rational and objective and *procedural knowledge* that is both fragmented (identified with men) and connected (identified with other women); and *constructed knowledge,* which integrates women's voices. The authors use the metaphor of voice and silence to illustrate that the truest knowledge is that acquired through women's own experiences and their stories (Belenky, Clinchy, Goldberger, and Tarule, 1986).

Theorists at the Stone Center in Wellesley, Massachusetts, have developed the self-in-relation concept further. They assert that women's self-concepts are focused on relationships more than on achievement and on connectedness more than on autonomy and offered a self-in-relation theory of women's development (Jordan and others, 1991). This theory is explicated by several researchers, including Jean Baker Miller (1976), on themes in women's lives such as women's sense of self, empathy, mutuality, mothers and daughters, dependency, power, depression, work inhibitions, eating patterns, and implications for therapy. Their perspective can be summed up as follows:

> Our culture has overemphasized the agentic, individualistic, competitive, lonely qualities of human life; and women have suffered, as their valuing of relationship, their immersion in caring and open need for connection have been denigrated. . . . And of course women should enjoy the freedom and be encouraged to develop and exercise their creative, intellectual, and self-expressive abilities for their own pleasure as well as for others' benefit. . . . The reconciliation of self-expression and relational enhancement is particularly important for women since so much of our sense of ourselves takes shape in relational contexts. Feeling connected and in contact with another often allows us our most profound sense of personal meaning and reality [Jordan and others, 1991, p. 289].

It should be pointed out, however, that not everyone agrees that women's lives are defined (or should be defined) in relation.

Some challenge what they call "difference feminism" (that is, the perpetuation of gender-differences theory), charging that rather than empowering women it is a means to maintain the status quo and ignores one of the most important aspects of women's lives—economics (Pollitt, 1992).

With a postmodern perspective, other feminist theorists have taken the position that gender differences have been overemphasized. They suggest that gender is an ideological construction of reality that was created by human societies which, because it was constructed, can also be deconstructed (Hare-Mustin and Maracek, 1990). They challenge traditional psychology's construction of sex, psychology, and individual differences on two premises: (1) differences between men and women largely are made and gender is not a natural category of essential differences between the sexes and (2) how we define gender difference, that is, what we interpret gender to mean, makes a real difference. The authors state, "What we make of gender and how we define male and female have an influence on how people see themselves and the world. The meaning of gender also has an influence on behavior, social arrangements, and the organization of such crucial social institutions as work, reproduction, child care, education, and the family" (p. 5).

Hare-Mustin and Maracek call for a new approach to psychology, gender, and differences and suggest that "a feminist constructivism can be crafted that will give a central place to women's lived experience" (1990, p. 195). Like Belenky and colleagues, they reject the old logical positivist paradigm as the only way of knowing and seek a more open-ended approach to knowledge, acknowledging both the subjective and objective, and greater acceptance of uncertainty about the basis and methods for interpreting human experience. These theories have common ground in that they recognize the exclusion of women from mainstream psychology, the interpretation of women's lives primarily in relation to men, and the need for new inclusive psychologies for postmodern times as well as new methods of developing them.

Theories of the Development of the "New Male"

The field of psychology has been severely criticized because it has been developed largely by men about men and then applied to other groups, such as women and ethnic minorities. Much of the traditional vocational and career development theory focused on male subjects and was written by male theorists (with a few exceptions, such as Anne Roe). Until recently, most career development textbooks were written by men; recent editions contain a separate chapter or paragraph on women and other "special populations." Indeed, the new emphasis on diversity is a welcome contrast to this.

The focus in this section will be on perspectives and knowledge about the new male, taking into account the gender-role system and men's roles, which are in an early stage of transformation. It should also be acknowledged that much of the new literature on men has been written by white heterosexual men and does not include men of other races or sexual orientations. Fortunately, this is beginning to change, and both men and women of all backgrounds are finding their voice. With men, as with women, it is important to remember that there are more within-sex differences than between-sex differences.

The Male Stereotype

As BORN FREE points out, a male stereotype exists just as a female one does. Stereotypical characteristics associated with men and masculinity are aggressivity, independence, unemotionality, objectivity, dominance, ambitiousness, worldliness, leadership, assertiveness, analysis, strength, sexuality, knowledgeability, physicality, success, aptitude for mathematics and science. That is, male stereotypical characteristics are the reverse of the female stereotype (Cook, 1985). Williams and Best (1982) concluded that male and female stereotypes are consistent across cultures.

A difference between the female and male stereotypes is that the male stereotype is more positive and is rewarded with what is valued in society: money, status, and power. Although we hope there is a diminishing of stereotypes in society, we know that much labeling and judging on the basis of gender, race, ethnicity, age, class, and sexual orientation still continue. The stereotype of the black man or the gay man may be as or even more limiting than the stereotype of the white man to those who don't conform to norms of what a "real man" should be. An important function of counseling and education is to help men move beyond the stereotypes, to understand the power of their socialization and to unlearn and relearn male roles.

Men's Career Development

Just as women's lives are traditionally defined by family, men's lives are defined by work. Some career researchers on male psychology have pointed out that for men "vocational success equals self-esteem." For men, especially American men, success in the work-place is the major criterion of overall success (Skovholt and Morgan, 1981). Awareness of this has been heightened in the 1990s, as the men who have lost—through downsizing—jobs that they expected to have throughout a lifetime find themselves without the work that has been the primary source of their identity for years. Further, the prospect for most of them of finding another job with equal pay and status is unlikely.

When men are outside the opportunity structure (which is true for many ethnic minority males), there is a strong potential for low self-esteem, anger, and violence. In the United States, this idea was brought out repeatedly in the media in the aftermath of the O. J. Simpson murder trial in fall 1995 and during the Million Man March in early 1996. The importance of paid work in men's lives has been a constant theme in the literature of vocational psychology as well as in the popular press. The exclusion of many men of color from equal education and opportunity and their overrepresentation in the prison population continue to be major problems for which solutions are needed.

Joseph Pleck (1981) conceptualized a new theoretical framework for examining men's lives. He analyzed male sex-role identity and presented a new paradigm of male sex-role strain, challenging "the myth of masculinity." New directions in research on men and masculinity were presented in another book on changes in men's lives that addressed such topics as reformulating the male role, men and fathering, male and female relationships, and sexuality, race, and gender (Kimmel, 1987).

Men's socialization toward work and its limiting effects have been described by several authors (O'Neil, 1981). Men experience gender-role strain during early, rigid, male sex-role socialization and when they learn how to deal with the changes in women's roles. Six patterns of gender-role conflict for men emerge from personal and institutional sexism and sex-role conflict and strain: (1) socialized control, power, and competition issues; (2) restriction of sexual and affectional behavior; (3) obsession with achievement and success; (4) homophobia; (5) restriction of emotionality; and (6) health problems (see Figure 2.3).

Other Literature on the New Male

Several psychologists, researchers, and social critics have begun to look at men's lives in some new ways. They have examined not only occupational careers but also men's roles in work and family, the consequences of male socialization, midlife shifts and preretirement, men and leisure, men and their fathers and men as fathers, men in two-earner families, men and power, men and violence, and so on. Among early counseling and psychological analyses of "the new male" were two special journal issues on counseling men and counseling males (Skovholt, Schauble, and Davis, 1980; Scher, 1981). Both present an excellent overview of issues related to men's traditional roles, their development in work, family, and parenting, and their relationships to other men. Since the early 1980s, studies of the new male increasingly have appeared in psychological journals.

Important issues of male socialization and sexuality also have been addressed, focusing especially on counseling adolescent males (Coleman, 1981). In *Finding Our Fathers,* Samuel Osherson (1986) confronts the issues of "men's unfinished business" with their fathers by keeping a journal, recording crises and insights in his own life, and making a longitudinal study of the lives of a large number of men at midlife at Harvard. Interviews with these men reveal the painful and profound consequences of and frustrations and yearnings about their relationships with their fathers. Both the personal and the professional perspective are displayed in these interviews as illustrated by this provocative quote: "Many of the male-female skirmishes of our times are rooted in the hidden, ongoing struggles sons have with their fathers, and the varying ways grown sons try to complete this relationship in their careers and marriages. Yet despite their importance, fathers remain wrapped in mystery for many men, as we idealize or degrade or ignore them. And in doing so we wind up imitating them, even as we try to be different" (p. ix).

An overview of men's issues from a counseling and men's development perspective was created by Dwight Moore and Fred Leafgren (1990). This work includes discussions about black, Latino, and Asian male development by men from these ethnic groups. Problem areas are identified, but more important are the problem-solving strategies and interventions for men in conflict that are suggested.

There has been a proliferation of articles and books on the male sex role and the emerging men's movement over the past ten to twenty years. Much of this literature suggests that men are beginning to discover the disadvantages and limitations of the rigid male-sex role prescriptions. Some of this literature appeared in the 1970s. Books by political scientist Warren Farrell, who wrote *The Liberated Man* (1974) and *Why Men Are the Way They Are* (1986), and Herb Goldberg, who wrote *The Hazards of Being Male* (1976), were popular. More recent works include Robert Bly's *Iron John* (1990) and Sam Keen's *Fire in the Belly* (1991), which, along with similar works, brought greater public attention to the male gender role. But despite their having given visibility to the men's movement, not all of these perspectives are appreciated by feminists.

The new knowledge about women and men is beginning to have an impact on how we view the development and roles of both sexes. Although much of the gender literature is interpreted as "women's issues," the literature just cited indicates a growing interest in how both men's and women's lives are changing. These are central themes in ILP and will be discussed further in Chapter Four.

Multicultural Theories and Knowledge

Multicultural issues raised in the 1960s lost some ground in the American consciousness during the 1980s but have reemerged with apparently increasingly divisive racial attitudes. It seems clear that new approaches to living and working in the twenty-first century will need to include educating laypeople and professionals in multiculturalism and diversity. Such training will have to emphasize the multiple dimensions of diversity.

Figure 2.3. O'Neil's Patterns of Gender-Role Conflict.

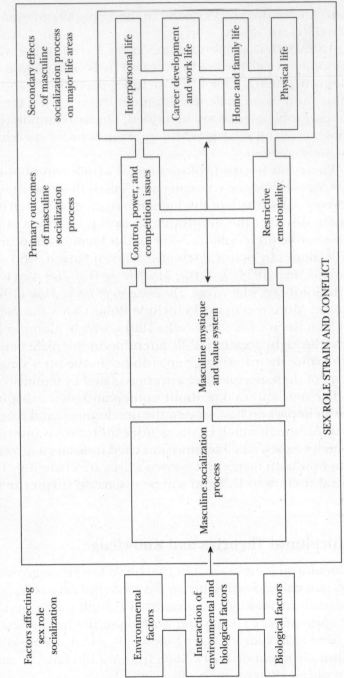

Sex-Role Patterns and Conflicts and Their Effects

Psychological Patterns and Conflicts Developed During Men's Sex-Role Socialization

Fear of femininity
Fear of emasculation
Fear of being vulnerable
Fear of failure
Low self-esteem
Obsession with success/achievement
Work stress and strain
Homophobia
Limited body awareness/sensuality
Restricted sexual behavior
Restricted communication patterns

Restrictive emotionality
Treating women as sex objects and inferiors
Socialized competitiveness that restricts self and others
Socialized power needs that restrict self and others
Socialized dominance needs that restrict self and others
Socialized control needs that restrict self and others

The Psychological Effects of Male Sex-Role Conflicts and Strain in Four Life Areas

Interpersonal Life
Limited intimacy with other men, women, and children
Marital conflict
Fear of aging
Fear of retirement
Loss of heterosexual interest
Lack of confidence

Career Development and Work Life
Overwork
Success bind
Career ladder bind
Work stress and strain
Type A behavior
Role conflict
Breadwinner bind
Fear of unemployment
Fear of failure

Home and Family Life
Role overload
Sexual dysfunction/dissatisfaction
Family violence (child and wife abuse)
Inabilities in active and positive parenting
Overt/covert subordination of women and children
Fear of failure

Physical Life
Health problems (ulcers, hypertension, coronary heart disease)
Drug, alcohol, and food abuse
Early death

Source: J. O'Neil, "Male Sex Role Conflicts, Sexism, and Masculinity: Psychological Implications for Men, Women, and the Counseling Psychologist. *Counseling Psychologist, 9* (2), 61–80. Copyright © 1981. Reprinted by permission of Sage Publications.

Eurocentric Theories

Most counseling and career development textbooks continue to present the major theories in the field (for example, Rogerian, Psychodynamic, Behavioral, Existential, Cognitive-Developmental) but have begun to point out how these theories are limited because they emerge from a single Western tradition. Often based on assumptions and studies of white male subjects, these theories have been criticized as inappropriate or insufficient for the diverse populations to which they are being applied. In most cases, the authors try to address this issue by adding a few chapters or parts of chapters on special populations: racial and ethnic minorities, gays and lesbians, women, people with disabilities, poor people, the elderly.

One of the few texts to approach counseling theory with multicultural theory in the foreground is a volume focused on Developmental Counseling and Therapy (DCT) by Ivey, Ivey, and Simek-Morgan (1993). Multicultural content is integrated into the core of the book, the first part of it. The second part of the text goes on to discuss traditional counseling theories. This is in refreshing contrast to the majority of texts, as already discussed. A new work by several authors delineates a theory of multicultural counseling and therapy (MCT) with critiques of the theory by leaders from specific racial-ethnic groups. The theory has a strong focus on connectedness, spirituality, wholeness, and indigenous healers (Sue, Ivey, and Pedersen, 1996).

Multicultural Theories

It is probably accurate to say that there is no full-blown theory of multicultural counseling and development, although, as indicated, Sue, Ivey, and Pedersen (1996) have begun to formulate one. Yet there is a significant body of professional knowledge on counseling people of color and particularly on the largest ethnic minorities in the United States, namely, African Americans, Asian Americans, American Indians, and Latinos. Emerging theories relate to racial-cultural identity development. They are part of what Paul Pedersen (1991) calls "the fourth force" in counseling and psychology (augmenting the psychodynamic, the behavioral, and the humanistic).

Many authors writing about multicultural counseling and multicultural career development, often from minority populations themselves, call for movement away from an emphasis on the Eurocentric knowledge base of the past to include a pluralistic knowledge base, the latter characterized by holistic approaches to helping and healing, focusing on the communal and family rather than the individual, and on integrated rather than linear worldviews.

A problem with the term *multiculturalism* is that people define it in different ways and it is difficult to know exactly what they mean. Early definitions tended to emphasize race and ethnicity and some of the early and the current theorists prefer to limit the definition to those variables (Ponterotto, Casas, Suzuki, and Alexander, 1995; Locke, 1992; Sue and Sue, 1990). But others argue that multiculturalism must include all kinds of oppressed groups, not only people of color, but those oppressed because of gender, class, religion, disability, language, sexual orientation, and age (Arredondo, Psalti, and Cella, 1993; Trickett, Watts, and Birman, 1994; Pedersen, 1991).

Multicultural trainers have disagreed on whether to use the universal or *etic* approach, which emphasizes commonalities or universals across groups and is inclusive, or the culture-specific or *emic* approach, which highlights the unique characteristics of specific populations and their special counseling needs. Atkinson, Morten, and Sue (1989) define multicultural counseling as any counseling relationship in which the participants represent differing ethnic or minority groups or in which "the counselor and client(s) are racially and ethnically similar but belong to different cultural groups because of other variables such as sex, sexual orientation, socioeconomic factors, and age" (p. 37).

Fukuyama (1990) takes the universal view, pointing out there is a growing body of literature that describes characteristics, values, and techniques for working with specific populations that are different from the dominant middle-class white male culture. These are groups that also have suffered from oppression, discrimination, prejudice, and neglect and often need assistance with such issues as identity development, self-esteem, and empowerment. Fukuyama suggests that this inclusive approach might also be called "transcultural" counseling.

In contrast, Locke (1990) makes a case for the narrow, focused view that takes into account both individual characteristics and unique cultural group membership but suggests that being too inclusive "waters down" the ways we address the problem. Other leaders have argued for a narrow definition but advocate focusing on concepts such as stereotypes, prejudice, discrimination, racism, assimilation, acculturation, culture, and so on rather than a "groups" approach (Vontress, 1991).

Racial Identity

Among the most significant concepts in multiculturalism and multicultural counseling is that of racial identity, developed by William Cross (1971); Janet Helms (1984), who introduced the concept of both black and white identity development; Atkinson, Morten, and Sue (1989), who introduced minority identity development (MID); and Sue and Sue (1990), who described racial-cultural identity development (RCID). Helms's model grew out of what she perceived to be a deficiency in cross-racial models of counseling, which she summarizes as an overemphasis on minority clients as the service recipients and majority professionals as the service providers; a view of minority clients as "so deviant that the counselor must possess the wisdom of Solomon and the patience of Job if he or she is ever to establish a cross-racial relationship"; and a lack of mechanisms by which to account for the interactions between the two (or more) cultural perspectives, the counselor's and the client's, implicit in counseling relationships" (p. 153). Thus she developed a model for predicting the interaction between various potential pairings of counselor and client, including cross-race and same-race interactions. The model is based on an assumption that all people go through a process of developing racial consciousness that leads to a final stage of acceptance of race as a positive aspect of themselves and others.

Helms (1984) describes the four types of racial identity attitudes (originally presented by Cross, 1971) as *preencounter, encounter, immersion/emersion,* and *internalization.* Black identity stages are different from those of whites. There are also within-race differences as well as between-race differences. The stages of black identity move from denigration and denial to euphoria, idealization, acceptance of, and identification with being black. White stages, she suggests, move from contact (becoming aware that blacks exist) to disintegration (whites acknowledging being white), reintegration (becoming hostile toward blacks and more positive toward whites), pseudo-independence (gaining intellectual acceptance of and curiosity about blacks and whites), and autonomy (actively seeking "opportunities to involve herself or himself in cross-racial interactions because he or she values cultural diversity and is secure in his or her own racial identity") (Helms, 1984, p. 156).

Gender Aspects of Multicultural Counseling

Although it is important to understand that race may be the most salient aspect for people of color, I contend that gender is a central aspect of every culture and cannot be ignored. Much of the current multicultural counseling literature has been written by men, with women's names increasingly appearing on articles but not as often on books. This is beginning to change as leaders challenge the lack of literature on ethnic women, the narrow and limited portrayal of them, and the stereotypical references to them in multicultural textbooks (Arredondo, Psalti, and Cella, 1993). An extensive text on ethnicity and identity in counseling and psychotherapy for women addresses this gap (Comas-Diaz and Greene, 1994). Hansen and Gama (1995) analyze these issues in some depth—discussing such topics as the omission of discussion of gender in much of the literature, important topics to include when gender is the focus, cross-cultural dilemmas when traditional cultural values and universal values collide—and interventions to assist counselors with these issues. They also suggest strategies for counseling and research.

In this book it is not possible to discuss adequately all the groups that fall into the broad definition of multicultural counseling; it is not a "groups" approach. This volume focuses on race, culture, gender, and class. Although examples of other dimensions will be given, the primary dimensions discussed are these. Multicultural topics are discussed in more detail in Chapter Six and are integral to my thinking about Integrative Life Planning.

Spirituality

As mentioned earlier, the topic of spirituality or spiritual development has long been neglected in the career development literature, although it has been a part of certain counseling theories.
The term *spirituality* is sometimes used synonymously with purpose
and meaning. It is in the last decade that spirituality has become a
word more centrally associated with career. Although a number of
theorists and practitioners from the fields of psychology, sociology,
career development, and counseling have included aspects of spirituality in their theories, most of the time it has not been very visible. Besides the obvious ones who have done so, such as Carl Jung
and Joseph Adler, such theorists include Abraham Maslow, Viktor
Frankl, Carl Rogers, Lawrence Kohlberg, Carol Gilligan, Gordon
Allport, Erik Erikson, and a number of practitioners and popular
writers such as Janet Hagberg, Richard Leider, and Richard Bolles.
Some of these are discussed in Chapter Seven. I regard the aspect
of spirituality, meaning, and purpose as one of the most important
components of ILP.

Other Roots of ILP

Other fields of knowledge also have provided a base for Integrative
Life Planning. These include work and family, transition theory,
organizational development, and futurism. They are not discussed
here but are found in several chapters of this book or are included
in specific chapters. For example, references to futurism and futurists occur throughout; work and family theory and issues comprise
Chapter Five. Relevant literature on adult transitions, organizational
change, and leadership is incorporated into Chapter Eight.

Conclusion

I hope that this brief overview of the professional knowledge that
influenced my thinking and the development of ILP will help
counseling and career specialists to review the influences on themselves and open them to new ways of thinking and knowing.
    Let us now turn to the first theme of the Integrative Life Plan-
ning quilt, the global transformations that inform the local context in which career professionals will soon be working.

Chapter Three

Critical Task 1: Finding Work That Needs Doing in Changing Global Contexts

*Integrative Life Planning is the concept most useful to
me as I try to examine the tapestry of my life. I've often
made decisions on an intuitive level, so it's no surprise
that I can't always explain the hows and whys of my
decision-making process to others. ILP is a tool that
can be used to generate understanding for the idea that
everything is connected and impacted by everything
else. How that impact occurs is defined individually;
that it occurs can be accepted universally. One thing I
know is the importance of having hope, hope for the
possibility of a future that is better. It is a faith in our
world's continued evolution toward a cooperative
existence in which all is respected and valued.*
—Inner-city public school teacher

In this chapter I present the first critical task of Integrative Life
Planning: to understand the external context within which we as
career professionals do our work. ILP focuses on the multiple
aspects of human development and calls for counselors and career
professionals to become genuine agents of change to improve the
human condition. The first task is thus to delineate the external
context because it has been ignored in much of the professional
career development literature.

If we are to help career clients from diverse settings increase their awareness of their life possibilities beyond their local boundaries, they will need to gain a sense of the changing global context. This idea has been reinforced for me many times when I have participated in international conferences. For example, in the summer of 1995, I spoke at a conference in Stockholm, Sweden, whose central theme was career guidance and social context. Most of the presenters, myself included, attempted to relate the issues of career guidance (a term used in Europe to encompass career counseling and career development) not only to our own national settings but also to global settings (see Exhibit 3.1).

Thinking and Acting Globally and Locally

One of the most original and enduring slogans of the twentieth century was the one used by the World Future Society in 1980, "Think Globally, Act Locally." Although this is still good advice, from an Integrative Life Planning perspective it might be changed to "Think *and* Act Globally *and* Locally," for it is no longer necessary or desirable to separate the two.

Living in today's global society, we know the dramatic changes that have been brought about by the computer chip, for example; there are now lasers, computer networks, satellite communication, and transnational information systems. Political and economic systems are changing, too. New international alliances have been formed through organizations such as the European Union and economic pacts like the North American Free Trade Agreement (NAFTA). In addition, new recognition of natural and human ecology has made us more aware of our connections across boundaries. What used to be national problems are now international problems.

A provocative article written from an organizational development perspective lists 10,233 global challenges that confront humanity. These represent what may be called *the work that needs doing* (Johnson and Cooperrider, 1991). According to the authors, global social change organizations (GSCOs) should be created to focus on people-centered paradigms of service and technologies of empowerment. The authors recommend engaging in an innovative process of transnational cooperation to bridge traditional

Exhibit 3.1. Picturing the Global Village.

What would the "global village" look like as a community of, say, a thousand inhabitants? According to Donella Meadows (1992), if the world were a village of a thousand people, it would hold 584 Asians, 124 Africans, 95 Europeans, 85 Latin Americans, 55 Russians, 52 North Americans, and 6 Australians and New Zealanders. The inhabitants would have some difficulty communicating, as they would speak such languages as Mandarin (165), English (86), Hindi/Urdu (83), Spanish (64), Russian (58), and Arabic (37). And that's just half of them; the others speak Bengali, Portuguese, Indonesian, Japanese, German, French, and an additional two hundred languages.

Religion in this village is represented by 329 Christians (187 Catholics, 84 Protestants, and 31 Orthodox), 178 Muslims, 132 Hindus, 60 Buddhists, 3 Jews, 132 without professed religion, 45 atheists, and 86 of other religions.

Of the thousand inhabitants, two hundred receive 75 percent of the income; another two hundred receive only 2 percent of the income. Seventy own an automobile (some of these own more than one). Clean drinking water is available to about one-third of the 670 adults, half of whom are illiterate. There are five soldiers, seven teachers, one doctor, and three refugees who fled their homes due to drought or war. Of the village budget of $3 million, $181,000 goes for weapons and war, $159,000 for education, and $132,000 for health care. Nine hundred of the villagers fear the nuclear weapons buried below the village, weapons that are owned by the other hundred.

These figures put the world's population into perspective and provide additional ideas for the work to be done. They also add a graphic picture of the contexts in which the challenges of the future must be carried out.

Adapted from Donella Meadows, "If the World Were a Village of 1,000 People ... " In J. D. Hale Sr. (ed.), *The Old Farmer's Almanac*. Dublin, N.H.: Yankee, 1992. Reprinted with permission from Donella Meadows and *The Old Farmer's Almanac* © 1992, Yankee Publishing, Dublin, N.H.

barriers to stewardship and sustainable development of the planet. The big picture they present offers a very idealistic view of these organizations. GSCOs would be committed to serving as agents of change for a healthier and sustainable world; making innovative social-organizational arrangements to enable human cooperation across previously constraining boundaries; promoting values of empowerment, egalitarianism, and people-centered forms of social action in the accomplishment of their mission; and functioning across two or more countries without primary loyalty, identification, or reliance on national governments. Writers such as Hazel Henderson (1995, 1996) and Matthew Fox (1994) sound a similar theme.

This chapter examines ten global and local needs that form the context of ILP. These ten needs are the constructive use of technology, preserving the environment, understanding changes in the workplace, understanding changes in the family, reducing violence, advocating for human rights, accepting changing gender roles, valuing human diversity, exploring spirituality and purpose, and discovering new ways of knowing.

These needs affect our lives and professional practice in the area of career counseling and career development. I see these needs as the work that needs doing around the globe. Seeing the big picture is essential to the purpose of the Integrative Life Planning concept. The profound changes and often troubling issues in society require us to think in new ways about the totality of our lives—our work, families, education, nation, and the global village that is rapidly becoming our community. Although we may see that reality through different lenses and never gain consensus on the most important needs, there are some universal concerns that career professionals can help to address, especially if we are committed to being change agents in our local and global communities.

By career professionals, I mean all those involved in helping others make life choices and decisions. I include counselors, human resource personnel, career specialists, organizational specialists, managers, adult educators, agency staff, college advisers, paraprofessionals, and others. However, throughout this book I will use primarily the terms *career counselors, career professionals, career specialists,* and *life planning specialists.*

Understanding Changing Global Contexts

Before exploring the ten ILP needs, it is important to examine the global, societal, and individual changes that make new approaches to career development necessary. I have to admit that when I was growing up in a small, mostly white midwestern town, I wasn't thinking globally, except in identifying with my Norwegian ancestry and in wanting to understand the United Nations, the North Atlantic Treaty Organization, and the racial issues that even then were prominent. But through many international and intercultural experiences, I have had unexpected opportunities to look at the world through a wider lens.

As counseling and career professionals, we do not usually begin to help a person by introducing global issues. Unless we are conducting training and workshops that focus on larger organizational or systems issues, we usually start with that person's problems. But it is my contention that the changing nature of our global community requires us to recognize shifting boundaries and wider human contexts. It is precisely because we have been somewhat insular and idiosyncratic in our perspectives—both regionally and in the United States as a whole—that we need to see the world more broadly. I believe that several global issues are relevant to helping our various clients make life choices and decisions. You may have your own list. The issues I discuss in this chapter are not meant to be definitive but to stimulate you to think about those contexts that are being transformed in your own work, that is, to identify your own list of needs that are most important to get your students, clients, and employees to think and act globally and locally in preparation for the twenty-first century.

The world has changed a great deal since the 1960s. The global village of the mid 1990s is quite different from what the world was back then. A number of global issues have been identified by demographers, futurists, social critics, political scientists, economists, management consultants, educators, and professionals in other fields. The issues we choose often depend on the discipline through which we view the world as well as our own personal values, which cause us to attend to certain issues more than others.

The lens through which I view the world is an interdisciplinary one that includes perspectives of psychology, sociology, education, career development, adult development, multiculturalism, and futurism; my own cultural background as a second-generation Norwegian American; my experience as a woman who thrived in the work environment of academia for more than thirty years and enjoyed an equal-partnership marriage during a similar time period; the vantage point of rewarding if unanticipated international study and lecturing in Western and developing nations; and a lifetime commitment to social justice and human rights issues. Although some of the global issues I discuss are on the lists of many futurists (for example, Robert Theobald, 1987; Rushworth Kidder, 1987; Peter Drucker, 1989; John Naisbitt and Patricia Aburdene, 1990; and Hazel Henderson, 1995), others are unique to my perspective. The point is that my personal quilt has pieces from many sources of knowledge, as do the quilts of the people we try to help, as we all try to break away from the fragmentation and reductionism of society to achieve integrative thinking and acting.

The political, social, and economic scenes present dramatic evidence every day of the changing contexts in which we live. A case in point was the fall of the Berlin Wall on November 9, 1989, and the rapid changes in the Eastern European countries that followed. The breakup of the Soviet Union had viewers around the world glued to their televisions. The world has seen the difficulty of boundary-shifting, of moving from closed market to free market economies and from totalitarianism to democracy and it has recognized the truth of the observation that "the world is coming together and flying apart at the same time" (O'Hara, 1992). Ethnic violence, environmental pollution, and tribal conflicts in some regions of the world are counterbalanced by regional and national alliances in others. As career professionals observing the international scene, we cannot ignore the fact that we and those we help may be affected by the global problems and that we can play some part in addressing them.

To frame the global quilt of Integrative Life Planning, I identify several macro issues or needs relevant to counseling, career, and human development professionals, needs that I believe embrace major issues of the work that needs doing. Within each I will identify an example on the micro level that illustrates the connection between the global and local issues that affect our clientele. The first critical task is to identify work that needs doing across global boundaries.

Promoting the Constructive Use of Technology

With the advent of the computer and satellite communication, we have become increasingly aware of the need for all citizens of the world to be technologically literate, that is, not only use and understand the new technology but also evaluate its potential and its limitations. *Network* has become one of the most important words in the Information Age (and in the career field), with computer networks, team networks, personal and collegial networks, and job search networks of all kinds. Although most professional helpers are not in high-tech occupations, most of us are affected by technology in our work and everyday lives.

In the future, we will rely on computers and television to meet almost all of our service needs; we will be affected by computer technology to complete whatever transaction we might be engaged in. Presentations are being given with the aid of sophisticated software, making teaching and learning much more lively. Resumes, curriculum vitae, and dissertations are all on disks; academic degrees are available through electronic mail. Satellites, interactive teleconferences, distance education, presentation software, and the World Wide Web provide new modes of teaching, learning, and communicating. Indeed, while writing this book I communicated from my home office and, like many professionals, increasingly handled my business correspondence via e-mail, voice mail, computer, and fax.

Although robotic technology has existed for years, we are just beginning to understand the positive and negative impact of robots on our industries and space research. Some futurists suggest that robots will be the preferred candidates as space pioneers because certain space environments—Jupiter and Venus, for example—are inhospitable to humans (Cornish, 1994). Similarly, genetic technology and genetic engineering are opening human possibilities (through DNA research and research in such areas as in vitro fertilization, postmenopausal childbirth, and longevity) while also raising ethical questions. The Infotech Society—defined as computing combined with telecommunications and networking—is expected to have a profound effect on work and workers in the year 2010 (Hines, 1994). Many of the high-tech innovations have "high-touch" implications for people and for counseling and human development professionals, including implications for employment, unemployment, families, and careers.

In *The End of Work* (1995), Jeremy Rifkin envisions technology (especially computerization) replacing jobs such that large numbers of people will not have work as we know it. What is needed, he suggests, is a rethinking of work in the global economy, of what will happen when the global labor force feels the effects of technology and many traditional jobs will cease to exist. He predicts shorter work weeks, a new social contract, and increased emphasis on what he calls the third sector or the social economy, work done in the volunteer sector, serving the nonprofit community.

Some of the negative effects of technology have been pointed out by social critics such as Neil Postman (1992), who writes of "technopoly," the surrender of culture to technology. Postman describes technopoly as a self-perpetuating and self-justifying system in which technology is granted sovereignty over social institutions and national life. He calls technological innovation "a burden and a blessing" (p. 5). His concern is that while technology represents progress, it takes us away from important traditional concepts. He warns against the tyranny of machines over human beings but also suggests that if technology is placed within the context of our larger human goals and values, it can be an especially valuable instrument. To counteract the tyranny of technology, Postman offers the image of the "loving resistance fighter" who has a healthy skepticism about the impact of technology, supports a new idea-centered and cohesion-centered curriculum based on "the ascent of humanity," and admires technology but does not regard it as the highest form of human achievement (p. 185). In short, technological literacy must be combined with admiring skepticism and caution about how it is shaping our lives and our culture.

Preserving the Environment

New-paradigm thinking about preserving the planet is evident in the work of theologian Matthew Fox, economist Hazel Henderson, and Danish career guidance leader Peter Plant. In his treatise *The Reinvention of Work* (1994), Fox criticizes the analogy of the universe as a Newtonian machine and our bodies and minds as machines as well. He suggests that we need to see the universe and the planet as the center of our work and understand the necessity of people doing good work to contribute to the wheel of justice and compassion in the world. Respect for all living things, with everyone engaging in the "great work" of preserving the earth and all living systems, is essential. In the future, work will have important new characteristics. It will be environmentally friendly; interdependent (rather than competitive). It will promote a planetary worldview rather than individualism or nationalism; aim for harmony with the environment rather than attempt to control it; not accept economic determinism; and seek creativity and values beyond technology alone.

Concern about human development, economics, and the environment has been linked by environmentalist, economist, and futurist Hazel Henderson (1995). She is especially critical of traditional economics and the Western emphasis on gross national product (GNP) or gross domestic product (GDP) as the central means of measuring global or national growth or health. She calls for assessments that take into account the impact on the environment and human beings. Thus, she has developed a broader-based scale that she calls Country Futures Indicators to reflect "other indicators of progress toward society's goals" (p. 146). She has beautifully integrated human and environmental issues in her call for a new world order that she names the Age of Light.

Peter Plant, a career guidance leader in Denmark and the European Union, brings an international "green" perspective to career counseling. In Stockholm in 1995, he introduced the concept of "green guidance," an ecological model for counseling and career professionals. ("Career guidance" is used in Europe as an umbrella term covering career development and career counseling.) Plant arrived at his model by identifying four "waves" through which career guidance has passed in the past century.

First came the psychometric testing era, which emphasized selecting the "right" people for the "right" occupation. Second was the person-centered approach, in which the career professional sought potential in each person; attended to differences of gender, race, and culture; and directed the person to economic possibilities. Third, career guidance became a market facilitator between client and employer, even providing assistance in obtaining training. Plant characterizes these waves as too unidimensional; furthermore, they perpetuate the status quo rather than promote change. Green guidance is conceived of as a multidimensional approach that focuses on broad aspects of the environment rather than on economics.

Plant (1995) suggests that the challenge of green guidance is to provide a human and environmental ecology in an ethical way. Undergirding principles for this approach include having clients consider the environmental impact of vocational choices, using ethical accounting principles to assess the organization or environment in which one might like to work, and using cultural reflexivity to reflect the consequences of one's choices.

Although the green movement has existed for many years, serious attention to issues of environmental degradation seems only to have begun coming to the fore. In the United States, such environmental champions as Vice President Al Gore, the Sierra Club, and numerous green organizations are campaigning for near-extinct species, resolution of pollution and nuclear waste storage problems, animal rights, control of acid rain, an end to deforestation, attention to the hole in the ozone layer, global warming, resource depletion, and other causes aimed at preserving Mother Earth.

Environmentalists have written about biodiversity and the need for sustainable development, assuring that economic growth is balanced by environmental protection and attention to human and natural resources and wildlife conservation on the planet. One of the most compelling among these writers is Harlan Cleveland (1993), who describes the global environment not as separate parts but as parts of an integrated "global commons." The world's populations are responsible for the health of the commons, he suggests, because the environment's health is essential to their own. Cleveland highlights the seriousness of the problem as follows: "The poor and the rich, we are cooperating to destroy—in different but mutually reinforcing ways—the environment we share. It is the acts of individuals that produce the pervasive threat to the global environment; the problem is precisely the behavior of innocent voters unwilling to tax pollution, innocent peasants cutting down trees, innocent couples having more babies than they can raise to be healthy and productive, innocent citizens thinking that government regulation and corporate responsibility are not for 'people like us'" (pp. 9–10).

Understanding Changes in the Workplace

Across cultures, people are being confronted with changes unimagined twenty years ago. The expectation of low unemployment, job stability, job security, and one career for life has been replaced by high unemployment, job insecurity, and a revolution in the nature of work and the workplace.

Changes in Work

We are seeing dramatic changes in the nature and availability of work, patterns of employment and unemployment, and the connection between work and family. Leaders in England, Denmark, Hungary, the United States, and other countries are seeking answers to questions about how to prepare youth and adults for work when the future of work is so uncertain. There is great concern about the increasing numbers of unemployed and underemployed youth and adults as a result of economic recessions, scarcity of work, and organizational restructuring. It has been estimated by the International Labor Organization that there are 870 million unemployed in the world, about a third of the world's population (Reichling, 1995).

Traditional patterns of work are changing. The old work pattern of fitting into one job for life is being replaced by the phenomenon of individuals having many occupations in a lifetime. The former pattern of choosing a job, getting established in it, and retiring from it is diminishing. The workplace is no longer a monolithic entity made up primarily of white male workers but a multicultural entity with increasing numbers of women, ethnic minorities, and people with disabilities.

Many writers have identified the uncertainties of the future and the changing nature of work as something we will have to live with. In Great Britain, sociologist Anthony Giddens (1991) describes the global and local factors affecting self-identity as individuals engage in life choices and life planning. The world, he states, is characterized by chaos; it is running out of control. In contrast, at the beginning of the last century, people believed that as they learned more about themselves and the world they would be more likely to control those forces. He describes a "risk society" in which the three important trends are globalization, detraditionalization (that is, traditions are changing around the world), and social reflexivity (that is, individuals have a different kind of experience of the world as they are forced to deal with many different sources of information, process them, and adapt them to their lives—use information to construct a life). He believes that "reflexivity" enables people to write their own biographies—the narratives of their own lives—and to live with greater uncertainty.

According to another British theorist, career development must be much more closely linked with public policy, with greater cooperation between career practitioners and public and private agencies (Watts, 1995). Partly because of the revolution in work, Watts suggests that a new definition of career is needed, that career planning will have to play a much greater role in the future, and that the notion of career development over the life span will be essential as societies and individuals continue to change. He also points out that the old model of education preceding occupation will no longer hold because frequent occupational changes will require retraining and lifelong learning.

A distinct feminist perspective is brought to the changing nature of work and its impact on women and children by Agneta Stark (1995). A professor in the School of Business at the University of Stockholm, Stark makes a strong case for giving greater attention and status to "caring work," the child-care, kin-care, and nurturing occupations. Stark points out the irony that whether women are working for wages or working at home, society regards them as "drainers" (people who use resources) rather than "sustainers" (people who produce resources). Like Hazel Henderson, Stark is critical of the omission of caring work from assessments of national progress.

In the United States, many career and organizational development leaders are redefining work and work patterns. Workers are described as *contingent workers, contract workers,* and *portfolio persons.* Other terms include *dislocated workers, white-collar unemployed, permanent temps,* and worst of all, *throwaway workers* (Figler, 1992). One management consultant, William Bridges, described the dejobbing of America in *JobShift* (1994b) and in a national teleconference in 1993 titled "Where Have All the Jobs Gone? Career Planning for the Twenty-First Century." His projections for tomorrow's workplace would mean major transformations in society. Basically, he suggests the following:

1. The work organization of the twenty-first century will put less emphasis on jobs and greater emphasis on tasks and assignments within organizations.

2. Although workers will perform tasks, they will also need to create tasks (for example, projects). Everyone will be an entrepreneur.
3. The location of work will change. Workers will be conducting their work at home, on planes, in hotel rooms, and in other settings. (This is already occurring.)
4. Everyone will be a temporary worker. People will change jobs several times. The nature of work itself will include frequent transitions, with contracts and consultancies the norm. Many people will experience stress because of the insecurities that accompany having to live with so many changes and their often negative impact.
5. We will all forget about jobs and look for work that needs to be done. We will be "vendor-minded" (our own marketers), look for unmet needs—such as new technologies and new interfaces—and create change.

Like many other career and organizational consultants, Bridges (1993, 1994a, 1994b) stresses the importance of flexibility, adaptability, and lifelong learning. He raises important questions: How will people handle the insecurities of a dejobbed society? What social side effects may be generated by the disappearance of jobs? How will we raise children to be ready for dejobbed work lives? And how will people handle the transition to a dejobbed work life?

Some critics challenge Bridges's view, charging that his scenario represents a managerial view with no regard for the impact of change on workers and unions or corporate responsibility. They also suggest that most workers, especially unskilled or temporary, are not trained to be entrepreneurs and would have to be trained to succeed in the kind of self-directed, uncertain work world Bridges envisions.

New Roles for Human Resource Development

On the positive side, many human resource development (HRD) programs, although now often focusing on outplacement for downsized workers or performance assessment for managers and executives, have recognized that greater productivity is related to happier workers whose human needs are attended to. Early emphasis was on such workplace initiatives as flex time, cafeteria benefits, job sharing, tuition reimbursement, career planning workshops, work and family task forces, decentralized decision making, total quality management, total resource utilization, and high-performance work teams. HRD programs seek to meet worker needs and the needs of the organization; they strive for a humanistic use of all individuals where they are happiest and most productive in the organization. New work structures—such as the "shamrock" organization, with three kinds of workers: professionals, contract workers, and contingent workers (Handy, 1996); transactional careers (Mirvis and Hall, 1994); self-directed careers (Hall, 1996); and programs for valuing diversity (Walker, 1996)—will also mean new roles and training for human resource specialists. Unlike some HRD programs, which now perform outplacement and appraisal for the company, future HRD efforts may focus on the human needs that were the original focus of human resource development, as well as the new relational goals Hall identifies.

The New Psychological Contract

The lack of job security has led to major changes in the relationships between employee and employer. Some believe that the old contract between the two—"You work hard for me, and I'll pay you reasonable wages and provide security and benefits"—no longer exists. Indeed, a lifetime job with benefits, succession hierarchies, and a ladder to climb—especially for managers—no longer exists in many work organizations. Such contracts are being replaced with new work patterns and work ethics (Goman, 1991).

In *Healing the Wounds,* David Noer (1993) describes the pain of survivors in companies that have been downsized. He chronicles their difficulty in dealing with loss and the fear of losing their own job security, as well as finding new meaning and direction in revitalized and empowering organizations.

Understanding Changes in the Family

Increasingly, people are recognizing that there are pluralistic family patterns in many western countries. While it is not the only reason for the changes in family structures, the tremendous influx of women into the labor force has been one of the dramatic trends of the twentieth century. Perhaps this change has been most profound in the United States where different types of families are extremely common but not always accepted, especially by those who espouse what are popularly called "traditional family values."

Single-Parent Families

There is legitimate concern in American society about latchkey children because of the rise in single-parent families. The grim reality is that many of the female-headed families live in poverty and do not have a choice about whether to work for pay or stay at home with the children. The Department of Labor indicates that by the year 2005 women will comprise 47 percent of the labor force, although the growth in their participation will be less rapid in the period from 1992 to 2005 than it has been over the past decade (U.S. Department of Labor, 1993). It is significant that the largest increase in women workers has been in the twenty-five to thirty-four age group, which are the prime childbearing years.

Two-Earner Families

While labor market projections do not include data about changes in family patterns, such changes are well documented in other sources (for example, Browning and Taliaferro, 1990; Hage, Grant, and Impoco, 1993) and especially the family literature. Although exact figures differ, it appears that the traditional "nuclear" married-couple family, with father employed, mother at home with two children, is diminishing, accounting for only 10 to 15 percent of family types.

Two-earner families have increased dramatically; the year 1980 marked the "tipping point" when such families became the dominant type, accounting for 50 percent of all families (Bernard, 1981). However, not all two-earner families are equal partnerships. Bernard points out that the primary family pattern in agrarian times was the husband and wife working together on the farm. With industrialization, men went to work in the factories in urban areas and started earning wages. This pattern has actually existed only for 150 years. The role of the good provider received its death knell, perhaps, when the Bureau of the Census removed the label "head of household" from the census form and the two-earner family became the majority pattern.

Other Family Patterns

Single adults without children comprise another kind of family. There are also extended families, in which several generations live together, share income, rear children, and share living costs. This pattern is common among ethnic minorities. Also common are blended families, in which divorced or widowed persons remarry and "blend" their families. These families are also called "restructured" or "stepfamilies."

There are also gay and lesbian families; they may be single-earner or two-earner and may or may not include children. There are unemployed families, including those on welfare. There are role-reversal families, where the husband does the housework and the wife is the wage earner. The latter type at one time was so unusual that it made newspaper headlines, and the "househusband" became the topic of a book. But in the mid 1990s it is a much more common phenomenon, especially as a growing number of white-collar men in their forties and fifties have become victims of corporate downsizing and find themselves at home, without jobs, unable to find comparable pay and status and are making involuntary career shifts, followed by temporary work, part-time contracts, and consulting. Still another family type is that of grandparents raising grandchildren. Over one million households are headed by single grandparents, raising 3.3 million grandchildren. They have a median income of $18,000 annually (Schlossberg, 1995). Figure 3.1 illustrates the various types of families in the United States.

Working Families

It is fair to say that working families are a common part of the American scene today and are likely to remain so for a long time, even if family structures change. In spite of efforts by conservative groups to return women to the home and their traditional roles of the 1950s, it is clear that the old "exchange theory" of family patterns—where the wife exchanged household services for the husband's services as provider—has diminished and that new patterns of work and family have become dominant. Much attention is now being directed to the issues confronting the new families, such as child care, stress, career development, role conflict, family devel-

Figure 3.1. Family Types in the United States.

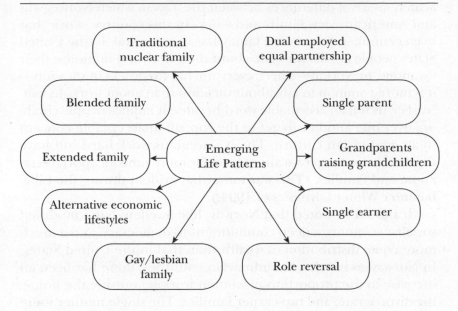

opment, mental health, family and medical leave, balance and overload, and public policy.

Understanding Work and Family

Rosabeth Moss Kanter (1977b) was one of the first to raise the question about the separation of work and family, calling it "unnatural." This accompanied the former role separation of men "owning" the providing role and women the nurturing role. In the 1980s, there was a beginning recognition of the linkage between work and family, but public attention to some of these issues for a while had lessened. Although the Family and Medical Leave Act was passed in 1993, it moved the United States only a short distance toward providing such benefits to families; we remain far behind other industrialized nations and have a long way to go in giving priority attention to human and family needs.

As a Fulbright scholar in Norway many years ago, I became acutely aware of differences between the ways in which Norwegians and Americans view family and work. In this country "work" has been central; in Norway the family has been central. In the United States people are likely to talk about their work and minimize their vacations. In Norway—where everyone has five weeks of vacation—it is more common to talk about vacation than about work. In fact, "career" is not an acceptable word because it implies people climbing over one another to get to the top, an unacceptable concept in an egalitarian culture. The Norwegians work hard but have shorter hours, longer vacations, and far more time for sport, recreation, and families. (This was somewhat evident during the Lillehammer Winter Olympics of 1994.)

It should be noted that Norway, like Sweden, has a modified socialist economy, a deep commitment to democracy, and a much more equal distribution of wealth than that in the United States. In Norway, as in other Scandinavian countries, there has been an increase in the proportion of women working outside the home, the divorce rate, and two-earner families. The single mother there has many more benefits than in the United States.

The need for society to accommodate pluralistic families in democratic societies should be a given. Family lifestyles should be chosen and not forced. Thus, the work to be done in this area is to change childbearing practices and socialization messages so that people can choose their preferred pattern.

Reducing Violence

Violence in its most extreme form is war; the antithesis of violence is peace. Violence is a prominent issue across cultures, whether in developed or developing nations, and it was a major theme at the United Nations' International Women's Conference in Beijing. Our collective conscience is particularly disturbed by the increase in ethnic violence in the 1990s as groups fight over shifting boundaries and engage in inhumane practices. Violence against women (and against men as well) exists across cultures but is addressed more in some cultures than others; for example, such indefensible traditions as infanticide in China, bridal dowry murders in India, and clitoridectomies in certain African countries still exist.

After domestic battering became a public issue in the United States, several countries followed this country's lead, created battered women's shelters, and passed laws on domestic violence. The Senate Judiciary Committee hearings on charges of sexual harassment brought by Anita Hill against Clarence Thomas in 1993 raised the nation's consciousness about sexual harassment. In 1995, the O. J. Simpson case once again focused attention on issues of battering and domestic abuse (and how they are often trivialized).

The spectrum of violence, from verbal to sexual abuse, sexual assault, rape, and murder is condoned in varying degrees worldwide. The United Nations Convention to Eliminate All Forms of Discrimination Against Women (CEDAW) speaks against all kinds of violence against women (United Nations, 1983). In South Asian and African countries, in particular, the convention has been tested in the legal system, with outcomes still uncertain. The International Women's Rights Action Watch (IWRAW), located at the Hubert Humphrey Institute at the University of Minnesota, was created to monitor implementation of the convention. With the support of the Clinton administration, the United States began to consider the possibility of ratifying it, but the election of an anti–United Nations majority in Congress and the move to the political right have made prospects for its ratification dim. Yet counselors of women know that various forms of violence affect women physically and emotionally and impede their career development.

Violence against children has become more common in the United States as guns become increasingly available. Children—especially young black males—killed in schools and on the street has become an all too frequent phenomenon. Random violence occurs in workplaces (post offices, fast-food restaurants, abortion clinics, and offices), in educational institutions (as when a transient murdered five students at the University of Florida), and on highways and subways. The bombing of the federal building in Oklahoma City on April 19, 1995, which killed innocent children and adults, was a wake-up call to the United States because through it we recognized that terrorism can be committed by violent Americans as well as foreigners. Besides evoking incredulity, such events make us realize that violence is possible in our own workplaces.

Thus far, I have not even touched on the violence against children in Africa or Bosnia-Herzegovina. I have not mentioned children as victims of sexual abuse or the violence against gay men and lesbians. Men are also victims of violence in wars and in gang warfare. By now it should be obvious why counselors and other helpers must be aware and available to treat victims of violence of all kinds; they also need to be at the forefront of prevention programs. Career counselors assisting people in positive life planning are part of the systems that can help reduce the choice of violence. Certainly lots of work in this area needs doing globally and locally.

Advocating for Human Rights

Violence and human rights are clearly cross-cultural issues. They are both local and global. We need only look at the rising rates of homicide and other crimes in our U.S. communities to see how near to us these concerns are. The ethnic cleansing in Bosnia, Somalia, and Rwanda are examples on a global scale. A look at the regular prisoner lists maintained by Amnesty International and the frequent violations of the United Nations Convention on Human Rights in Beijing and other places offer other examples.

Human rights is a core issue affecting human development and all who work to facilitate it. The barriers to human development have been given considerable attention in the United States, although we, too, have a long way to go in some areas of human rights. Indeed, the Congress attempted in 1995 to pass laws hurting the most vulnerable among us and undo the gains in equal opportunity realized through affirmative action and other such initiatives. Constitutional protections, special executive orders, and past legislation have gone a long way to protect the rights of specific groups. There have been the Civil Rights Act of 1964, the Women's Educational Equity Act of 1972, the Equal Opportunity Act, the Americans with Disabilities Act of 1990, and the Older Americans Act of 1991, to name a few.

As recently as 1996, Britain ruled against allowing gays and lesbians in the military. Some Middle Eastern countries refuse even to acknowledge that homosexuality exists and certainly do not recognize the rights of gay people. We have our own homophobia in the United States. Although some progress has been made on equal rights for the gay and lesbian population, the "two steps forward, one step back" experienced by gays in the military indicate that there is a long way to go even to begin to assure equal treatment. Some states attempted to pass laws denying gay people basic rights to housing, education, and employment because of their sexual orientation until the Supreme Court declared such laws unconstitutional. Domestic partner ordinances in some states have begun to open up opportunities for gay and lesbian couples, but these people continue to fight for opportunities in equal employment, housing, and civil and military rights. Perhaps most controversial is the push to legalize same-sex marriage and the Defense of Marriage Act. Clearly, there is still much work to be done.

Across cultures, considerable discrimination exists based on disability and social class. Some cultures try to avoid talking about either of these subjects, while others have taken actions ranging from creating special institutions for people with various disabilities to passing laws to assure that they are "mainstreamed" into regular classrooms in schools. People living in poverty also may be outside the economic opportunity structure. There are some indications that when one is examining issues of race, gender, and class, it is socioeconomic status that is the major determining factor in questions of access and opportunity. A recent publication dealing with the intersection of race, class, and gender provides an excellent integration of these topics (Rothenberg, 1995).

Another group that was silent and neglected for a long time is the elderly population, which is now the fastest-growing population in this country. However, older people have asserted their rights since passage of the Older Americans Act in 1991, and lobby groups for this population, such as the American Association of Retired Persons (AARP) and the Gray Panthers, have made their force felt. Yet older workers are among those most negatively affected by the corporate downsizing of the 1990s.

While the United States has been recognized for leadership in some areas of human rights, much remains to be done. It is a telling reminder that most Western countries have greater representation of women in government leadership positions than we do. (For example, in most Scandinavian countries, women make up almost 40 percent of the membership in Parliament. Gro Harlem Bruntland, the prime minister of Norway and herself a woman, appointed women to eight out of twenty positions available in her cabinet.)

Developing countries too have elected women prime ministers and presidents, such as Khaleda Zia of Bangladesh; Chandrika Bandaranaike Kumaratungh and her mother Sirimavo Bandaranaike, president and prime minister, respectively, of Sri Lanka; Benazir Bhutto of Pakistan; and Tansu Ciller, former prime minister of Turkey. Career counseling and human development professionals who work with women and other underrepresented groups need to be aware of this continuing political footdragging as they try to promote human development and human rights. That many human rights issues, including access, prejudice, and discrimination, also affect human careers should by now be obvious: this is fertile ground to sow.

Promoting Economic Opportunity

Issues of economic opportunity are truly global. Although most democratic cultures proclaim the right of all citizens to a decent standard of living or quality of life, most societies fall far short of this goal. The increasing numbers of people who are homeless, hungry, and living in poverty remind us how far we have to go in achieving the goals of democratic societies and in advocating for a decent standard of living for all.

Many people argue that the United States is becoming more of a class society divided between the haves and the have-nots. Although progress has been made through laws to advance equal educational opportunity and reduce various kinds of job discrimination, the mid 1990s seem to have brought a political climate of blame, in which the most vulnerable are affected as laws reduce assistance to people on welfare, college students, and the elderly. It has not gone unnoticed that, while the future of these groups grows ever bleaker, corporate CEOs, chief administrators, professional athletes, and television entertainers continue to be given disproportionate shares of the society's wealth. A particularly confrontative and ironic article in *Newsweek* pictured CEOs of large corporations who have enjoyed increases in what were already six-figure salaries after laying off thousands of employees. The article cited the backlash that has occurred among ordinary citizens as "corporate killers" fire workers en masse and increase their own and stockholders' profits (Sloan, 1996).

Many have argued for a fairer distribution of wealth in the United States but few remedies appear on the horizon. One country that seems to have achieved a balance in this regard is Norway. Most of the population there is middle-class; there are few people at either end of the wealth spectrum. The high tax structure helps to pay for the social safety net available to all. Besides the discovery of oil in the North Sea, another reason for this 90 percent middle-class phenomenon is Norway's egalitarian philosophy in all aspects of society—a fundamental aspect of human rights.

Although we as career professionals cannot "solve" the economic issues, awareness of them on both a global and local level—and the ways in which they affect the populations with whom we work—is imperative.

Addressing World Population Issues

World population issues are a significant human rights concern. The right to make decisions about one's own body is a right many women around the world are denied. In the United States and in many developing countries, there is deep concern about children having children and the consequences of babies being born into the world without adequate care, nutrition, parenting, or the prospect of a positive future. The result may be starvation, environmental problems, and political instability, according to Timothy Wirth, State Department official in charge of population issues. He points out that people mistakenly confuse the issue of abortion with issues of population control. He sees family planning as a way to slow the growth of the world's population and avoid a world population crisis (Sternberg, 1994). Issues of pregnancy, reproductive freedom, and a woman's ability to control her own life and future are among the many needs that cross cultures. Their importance in counseling and career and human development cannot be overstated.

Accepting Changing Gender Roles

The roles of women and men are changing around the world, as are their relationships. How much has changed depends on a variety of factors—the historical status of men and women in a culture, the place of religion in the culture and its influence on gender roles, the social and political climate, the extent to which women participate in the political system, the education (and basic literacy) of women, the health care conditions (particularly availability of contraceptives and sex education), and the laws regarding marriage and property.

If one were to put countries on a continuum of change as far as the rights of women are concerned, they would probably end up in different places depending on the item or condition being considered. The Population Crisis Committee (1988) compared the status of women in ninety-nine countries based on a number of criteria, including marriage and children, education, health, social equality, and employment, and found that different countries ranked at the top for many of the criteria. The top-ranking countries overall were Finland, Sweden, the USSR, Norway, and the United States. While the United States ranked highest in education, it tied for fourth overall with Norway, with 22 points out of a possible 25.

A great gap existed between the leaders and certain developing countries. Bangladesh, Saudi Arabia, Egypt, Syria, and Nigeria ranked lowest, with scores of from 5.5 to 8.5. Other South Asian and African countries ranked among the lowest based on political and legal, economic, and family equality issues.

A number of recent reports on the status of women in Russia and Eastern European countries (for example, Russia, Czechoslovakia, and Poland) reveal that women have lost ground in their quest for equality.

The Conference on Equality Between Women and Men in a Changing Europe, an important conference on gender roles sponsored by the Council of Europe, was held in Warsaw, Poland, in March 1992. Participants agreed that for democracy to advance there must be equal status between women and men. The conference concluded with the following recommendations (Estor, 1994):

1. Equality between women and men is crucial for democracy and the realization of human rights.
2. Because of political changes in Europe and the fact that women have lost ground in the quest for equal sharing of power, the challenge for the promotion of equality is great.

3. Social and economic changes must be directed toward more equality between women and men in their participation in the labor force, in training, in work-family situations, and in compensation.

4. The human rights of women and men regarding free and responsible determination of their own relationships and family planning should be strengthened. (As frequently happens, there was considerable debate on this one.)

5. The Council of Europe and its member states should fully integrate equal rights for men and women into any cooperative and technical assistance programs they sponsor. The council should use legal documents to promote equality (for example, inclusion in the European Convention on Human Rights), information and awareness, and other strategies and mechanisms for equality.

This is one example of ways in which but one part of the world is addressing gender issues and changing roles. Scandinavian countries also have been working on issues of *likestilling* (equal status of the sexes) for many years. They approach the topic from the male and the female perspective, not only from the female perspective. Several countries are noting the connection between work and family. When Japan passed an equal opportunity law in 1987, the government produced a document that discussed "Harmonizing Work and the Family." This topic has inspired considerable research and discussion in the United States in the last decade. (This subject is discussed further in Chapter Five.)

As pointed out in Chapter Two, the emerging men's movement and the growing literature on the "new male" in some Western countries has also sparked interest in gender issues. The career development and changing roles of both women and men in work, family, and society—central themes in Integrative Life Planning—are subjects in which career professionals must be well grounded.

The patriarchal social systems in which we live have been passed down by generation after generation throughout history; nevertheless, relationships between men and women have not always been of the dominant/subordinate type. In early societies, relationships between the sexes were sometimes matrilineal or egalitarian. Indeed, because patriarchal systems were created by people, they can also be changed; strong cases can be made for equal relationships between women and men, as the men and women who have created such relationships will attest (Eisler, 1987; Lerner, 1986). But attitudes passed on through socialization change slowly. The work to be done in this area will continue for generations.

Valuing Human Diversity

It is easy for people of any nation to think that their culture is unique and unchangeable. The conflicts in Bosnia-Herzegovina provide a tragic example of what happens when ethnocentrism goes awry. As we label ourselves the richest or strongest power in the Western world, it is not uncommon for many Americans to become insular, even provincial, in their view of the world; such feelings are all too evident in some of the political candidates' positions during election season. In my classes, I often cite the figures for the global village to remind students where we Westerners fit in the larger scheme of things (see p. 51).

Celebrating Domestic Diversity

The need to celebrate both within-culture and cross-cultural diversity is perhaps greater than any other. My lifelong interest in civil rights has affected many areas of my life. One of the most important events occurred around 1990 when I was president of the American Association for Counseling and Development (now the American Counseling Association). The slogan I chose for the organization was "Global Visions: Celebrating Diversity, Creating Community," a theme that was carried out in many of the association's branches and divisions during the year. Although the efforts touched only the tip of the iceberg, they produced some action and cohesion. Members were asked to become more aware of all the dimensions of multiculturalism—race, culture, gender, class, beliefs, disabilities, sexual orientation, age, and ethnicity. They were asked to seek to understand how these issues affect counseling and human development; to help increase the participation of underrepresented groups in our organization; to accept our uniqueness while celebrating our differences; to work toward greater inclusiveness of those outside of the opportunity structure; to work toward gender equality through reduction of violence; and to work together, men and women as partners, to address and solve personal and societal problems. Thus, they were asked to examine their own professional roles to become proactive agents for change in their own settings. Through expanded efforts since then, diversity has become a much more central concern of the organization and its approximately sixty thousand members.

The global events of the 1990s have caused considerable growth in the recognition of the importance of pluralism and multiculturalism in education and in business, and particularly in counseling. Learning how to deal with difference and manage diversity has become a central goal of corporate organizations and educational institutions around the world. Whereas for many years counseling techniques were believed to be applicable for all (usually when viewed through white male eyes), in the 1990s efforts to address multicultural issues have moved from the periphery of counseling and career counseling to the mainstream. Indeed, thanks to the encouragement of professional counseling, psychological, and career development associations, career counselors today must take courses in multicultural counseling and specific populations—and *not* special populations—to gain certification.

The state of our world, nations, and neighborhoods requires that we become more aware of the diverse races, cultures, and ethnic groups that enrich our globe and challenge our professions. Although individual differences have been the cornerstone of the counseling and psychological professions, we have not always been able to address the differences that divide us or the humanity that unites us.

Professional counselors and career specialists too are a diverse group. Learning to accept our uniqueness and celebrate our differences provides a continuing challenge. It also means becoming aware of our own biases and prejudices and how they manifest themselves in career counseling and human services work.

Celebrating International Diversity
A great challenge in many societies today comes from the influx of new refugees and immigrants. The ethnicity of the immigrants

is different in each. In Norway, for example, Pakistanis and Bangladeshis have entered the country in large numbers, initially working in such sectors as the transit system and the restaurant business. In Germany, Turks have migrated—not always to a welcome reception. In the United States, the ethnicity of the immigrants depends on the region of the country. In the Southwest, Mexican migrant workers and other Latinos seek a better life; in Florida, Cubans and other Caribbeans are refugees and immigrants; in California, Latinos and Asian Americans are dominant; and in the Midwest, refugees from Laos, Cambodia, and Vietnam have accounted for large numbers, such as the Hmong people who have settled in Minnesota and Wisconsin.

Carolyn Williams and John Berry (1991) are among the psychologists who help us understand the refugee and immigrant experience. They describe how these groups experience "acculturation stress" as they attempt to deal with life in new cultures. They point out that refugees may have feelings of loss—of status, family, and homeland. When they are not accepted yet expected to acculturate, they may suffer great stress that can lead to mental health problems.

Williams and Berry point out that reaction to a new culture depends on several things, including the reason the group migrated (whether voluntarily or involuntarily); the dominant culture's view of minority cultures; and the attitudes of the minority's members about their own culture and what they want their relationship to the dominant group to be. It seems clear that counseling and career professionals must understand how these issues affect populations in their local and the global communities. Helping immigrants and refugees find a welcoming environment and work for a living wage is thus certainly part of the work that needs doing.

Exploring Spirituality and Purpose

There is considerable evidence that people around the world are seeking a new sense of meaning and purpose in their lives. Furthermore, they do not necessarily seek spirituality through formal religion, although many express their spirituality through religion. They search for something outside of themselves, something larger than themselves to give them a sense of purpose and meaning. Long neglected or minimized, the theme of work and spirituality is finally coming into its own.

Richard Leider's (1985) book *The Power of Purpose* offers many ideas and activities to help people reflect on why they get up in the morning and do what they do all day. More recently, Leider and Shapiro (1995) elaborated on meaning and purpose from the midlife years on. The authors identify "four deadly fears" that keep us from living a good life: fear of living a meaningless life, fear of being alone, fear of being lost, and fear of death. They note that the first can be eased by work, the second by love, the third by creating ties to a community, and the fourth by the motivation to live with a purpose. They also offer a formula for a lifestyle rich in purpose: begin with your talents, add your passions and your environment, multiply these by your vision, and you will wind up with your own way to put your hoped-for future together.

Many readers are surely familiar with one of the early books on purpose and meaning, that is, Victor Frankl's (1963) description of his experience at Auschwitz. He told how his ability to engage in "imaging" of his wife and their relationship and to visualize the lectures he had given students helped him to live through the horrors of the concentration camp. It also served as the basis for a new school of therapy called Logotherapy, finding meaning in one's experience.

Spirituality and its relationship to work is a relatively recent concern in the field of counseling and career development. The Association for Religious Values in Counseling (ARVIC), which has existed as a division of the American Counseling Association for some years, recently changed its name to the Association for Spiritual, Ethical, and Religious Values in Counseling (ASERVIC). Similarly, the National Career Development Association (NCDA) some years ago created a Special Interest Group (SIG) on the topic of spirituality, which has grown in numbers as counselors increasingly want to learn how to deal with the issues of spirituality and purpose. In the mid 1980s two career development leaders in Minnesota, Janet Hagberg and Betty Olson, spurred greater interest when they presented professional programs describing how spirituality affected their own personal career journeys. Although such subjects have not been part of the mainstream counseling and career development literature (except for many multicultural counselors and counselors who work in religious or pastoral settings), they are extremely important to many people. The issues seem to be especially important to women and ethnic minorities for whom the larger search and the spiritual path have always been a central part of their lives. Perhaps spirituality has been downplayed because it can't be measured, whereas in fields like psychology and counseling measurement is supreme. But considerable attention is given to this aspect of development in Integrative Life Planning. While there are few road maps for how to help people with their spirituality, there are some models and strategies.

Discovering New Ways of Knowing

Questions of what we know and how we know it are central today in the minds of many researchers, especially feminist psychologists, multicultural leaders, women's studies faculty, and faculty in disciplines other than psychology. "New ways of knowing" are being articulated by people such as astronaut Edgar Mitchell, who had a profound experience in understanding the universe when he walked on the moon. Later, he founded the Institute for Noetic Sciences (*noetics* is the study of new knowledge), "in which women and men from many fields are exploring new frontiers of the human mind and ways of knowing," as he put it in the institute's first bulletin. "I was troubled," he went on to explain, "by the startling extent to which our perceptions, motivations, values and behaviors are shaped by unconscious beliefs which we acquire from early experiences and from our culture."

In many fields we recognize that there are new knowledge paradigms. Leaders in their respective fields include Peter Drucker (1989, 1996), management consulting; Rushworth Kidder (1987), ethics; Mary Catherine Bateson (1989), anthropology; Oliva Espin (1994), psychology; Lillian Comas-Diaz and Beverly Greene (1994), psychotherapy; and Robert Theobald (1987), futurism. The literature of many disciplines reveals movement away from neutrality and objectivity and toward commitment and subjectivity and a recognition that the scientific method is not the only path to truth in the social and behavioral sciences.

Although psychology and counseling have been dominated for years by quantitative research methods, there is emerging interest, even in some areas of educational psychology, in new ways of knowing, that is, qualitative methods of research. These methods may be field-based, subjective, hypothesis-finding rather than hypothesis-testing and may permit researchers to become involved with or part of the group they are studying. Elizabeth Gama (1992) points out how natural it is for counselors to use qualitative methods but also emphasizes the utility of both quantitative and qualitative methods, depending on the topic studied. Although qualitative methods long have been used in such fields as anthropology and family social science, they still are not fully accepted as mainstream in psychology. More and more students, women and ethnic minorities in particular, are asking for training to help them answer the large field-setting questions in gender and cross-cultural research.

As already mentioned, researchers in New England are among those who have studied women in several colleges and communities. In *Women's Ways of Knowing*, Belenky, Clinchy, Goldberger, and Tarule (1986) define six ways in which women perceive reality. Following in the tradition of Jean Baker Miller (1976) and Carol Gilligan (1982), they use innovative methods to define women's true voices. The fact that a number of leaders in the helping professions (for example, counselor educators, family therapists, social workers) are adopting methods other than empirical ones may help to facilitate change. For example, the current conceptualizing in psychology (and career psychology and counseling) about the use of narrative and storytelling as legitimate forms of research may help broaden the tools and methods of counseling and psychology (for example, Cochran, 1990; Jepsen, 1992; Cochran and Laub, 1994).

Although a few journals have begun to accept qualitative studies, there is still a bias toward the quantitative. Despite the fact that key leaders in the American Educational Research Association have become advocates of qualitative research for certain kinds of studies, there is still considerable resistance to their use. The journal *International Journal of Qualitative Studies in Education* and the book *Qualitative Methods in Family Research* (Gilgun, Daly, and Handel, 1992) are excellent resources for researchers and practitioners interested in alternative ways of knowing and in learning the methods used in this growing field. Gama (1992) also presents a cogent argument for the use of qualitative research in counseling psychology.

Of course, I realize that research methods may not be the primary interest of many of the counseling and career professionals who are reading this book. Nonetheless, if you use theoretical and conceptual perspectives to guide your practice, it is important that you be aware of this controversy and able to ascertain the origins and types of knowledge on which you are drawing. There is much work to be done in this area by both producers and users of knowledge. This topic is only briefly dealt with in Integrative Life Planning, but the very assumptions and concepts on which ILP is based make it congruent.

Conclusion

Do the global needs and tasks described in this chapter resemble the needs in your local community? Do they resemble the needs of your clients? Just as it is not possible to deal exhaustively with such broad topics in a book of this scope, neither is it possible for career professionals to address all these needs in working with their respective populations. Obviously, priorities will have to be explored and set in conjunction with your clients' personal needs and contexts, as well as community needs. I have touched on these global issues to stimulate thinking about how they might affect counseling and human development strategies in the future (you will note an obvious emphasis on social justice needs). Their exhaustive scope is indeed evidence of the amount of work to be done locally and globally. Countries are at different stages in dealing with these issues. As the preceding discussion makes clear, these are universal human issues that need to be attended to not only by counseling and career and human development specialists but by citizens and professionals in all fields alike. They are the global needs that require thinking and action but also our local application. They are a global quilt of potential change.

Chapter Four

Critical Task 2: Weaving Our Lives into a Meaningful Whole

The gains far outweigh the losses I felt from the changing roles of women and men. I have felt a sense of wholeness in being able to use my talents and abilities. I feel independent, and yet I feel perfectly free to be dependent on my husband for some things and interdependent for others. I have felt economically self-sufficient, and I have had a marriage where I felt like an equal partner.
—Forty-nine-year-old woman returning to college

The second critical task of Integrative Life Planning is to encourage the holistic development of human lives. This chapter provides career and counseling professionals with a knowledge base for assisting their clients, employees, and students in this process. It discusses several areas of wholeness that ILP embodies, including the life roles of labor, love, learning, and leisure; some of the influences on career socialization and development of women and men; and the concepts of self-sufficiency and connectedness as viable frameworks for career specialists to understand the holistic development of both sexes.

The pieces of the ILP quilt sewn together in this chapter have to do with whole persons and ways in which they struggle with multiple identities, potentialities, and dimensions. Career professionals can help men and women move beyond traditional stereotypes and gender-role socialization toward equitable relationships and a more complete development as human beings.

Holistic Development

To some, holistic development may not a seem realistic goal. So much of society is still focused on fitting people into jobs without regard to other parts of their lives and locked into stereotypical male and female behavior. It may seem naive to suggest that holistic life planning—which includes the development of the body, mind, and spirit together with the career—is possible. *Holistic* certainly has not been an acceptable word in traditional academic environments.

Yet the concept of holistic development is central to Integrative Life Planning. ILP seeks to determine how counselors and educators can assist young people and adults to learn a life planning process that is holistic in nature. It seeks to help counselors demonstrate awareness of these major areas of development so that they can help clients or students see the connection and understand when certain areas are ignored, out of balance, or need work.

Work has been the central focus of most people's lives for many years, but Integrative Life Planning incorporates changing contexts, career development, life transitions, gender-role socialization, cultural diversity, and social change into a unified framework. It also asks how spirituality, or a sense of meaning and purpose, fits in with the rest.

Although ILP is designed mainly to help career counselors and other career specialists assist clients in their life decisions, it is a model that can be used by other helpers to examine various aspects of their own lives and integrate them into a meaningful whole. One of my basic assumptions is that people who help others make career decisions need to go through a process of reflection on their own career development. Though all should have the right to develop their full potential and obtain satisfaction in many areas of life, those who are at survival level probably will have to gain some measure of economic independence before they can fulfill higher needs, as suggested by Maslow's (1962) hierarchy of needs. It would be unfortunate, however, to think of ILP as something appropriate only for middle- or upper-income persons. One of my students introduced ILP to low-income women students with considerable success. Each drew a Circle of Life (see Chapter Nine) to represent her experience, clearly revealing an understanding of and need for holistic life planning.

The Holistic Concept in Integrative Life Planning

Obviously, traditional ways of delivering vocational guidance are not sufficient for the integrative approach, because they assume that people do not change and that society does not change, that occupational choice is the outcome, that there is one job for life, and that logical, rational decision making should be the strategy. Thus, the focus is on choice rather than process. In contrast, ILP looks at not only occupation but also other parts of one's life. In Integrative Life Planning, the word *integrative* suggests an emphasis on the various domains of human development—social, intellectual, physical, spiritual, emotional, and career/vocational (SIPSEC). These are also called the six areas of human wellness. Figure 4.1 illustrates this Wellness Wheel.

Integrative also suggests the integration of mind, body, spirit, gender, and time (that is, our past, present, and future). It suggests that we do not make occupational or family choices in a vacuum. To integrate is to put pieces together in ways that make sense to the individual. As stated in Chapter One, *life* is an inclusive term that encompasses four basic roles: loving, learning, labor, and leisure, or the Four Ls.

The term *pattern* suggests a nonlinear series of interrelated roles, decisions, and choices, not all of which produce desired results. I use the term *pattern* alternatively with *planning*, which evokes a much more linear, rational process. However, for a whole host of reasons, most people cannot logically plan their choice of partner or life careers with any degree of certainty; this seems more true today than ever. H. B. Gelatt (1989) says there is a need for what he terms positive uncertainty in career decision making, for reason and intuition, for process as well as choice. Creating a *life plan* is different from *planning your life*. There are plans and there are random factors for which one cannot plan, and sometimes these alternate in people's lives with both anticipated and unanticipated effects. Nevertheless, planning is important because it

Figure 4.1. The Wellness Wheel.

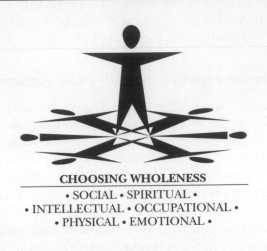

CHOOSING WHOLENESS
• SOCIAL • SPIRITUAL •
• INTELLECTUAL • OCCUPATIONAL •
• PHYSICAL • EMOTIONAL •

Source: Minnesota School Counselors Association. Reprinted by permission.

allows a sense of control over one's life, which is a feeling of empowerment that is conducive to good mental health. There are also transitions, both voluntary and involuntary, that affect people's lives and livelihoods, their emotional, economic, and social well-being, and their work, family, and leisure patterns. ILP aims to help people understand the patterns in their lives, the larger changes in society, and ways in which they can change themselves and bring collective talents and energies to bear to help solve the problems of the local, national, and world community. (See Chapter Three for more on global needs.)

Holistic development refers to our need to be whole people, not half-persons. Holistic development refers to integration within ourselves as individuals and in all aspects of our development: holistic in the roles we take on or choose not to; holistic in our total development as men and women, away from the socialized gender roles that limit us; and holistic in our ability to have a better perspective on time, that is, to see the connection between our past memories, our present experiences, and our future hopes and dreams.

Identity Dimensions

The dimensions of *identity, development, roles,* and *contexts* are described in Figure 4.2.

Identity dimensions refer to the multiple identities all people have: their race, ethnicity, gender, social class, age, ability, sexual orientation, religion, and so on. Although little attention has been given to the identity dimensions, the multicultural movement and the women's movement have increased awareness. Counselors are urged to help clients consider how important all of these factors are at different times and how they affect life planning.

It has not always been recognized that all people have multiple identities that may take different priorities at different times in their lives. People who have experienced some kind of oppression may feel that the experience made one dimension of their identity more important in their lives. For example, being gay may have different meanings to different gay people. To a gay white male politician who has not come out but is quite happy with himself, sexual orientation may not be the most important part of his identity. Another man who is openly gay and has experienced harassment and considerable pain may seek support from gay resource centers to strengthen his identity. In another example, when a white woman in one of my classes was asked her ethnicity, she said she was American and never thought about her Irish ancestry. In contrast, a Native American student said, "Being Indian *is* my identity." The point is that, in a society that values linear thinking, people tend to think in terms of single characteristics rather than recognizing that multiple identities are a strength and should be respected. How we view the different dimensions of our identity influences the extent of our holistic development.

Developmental Domains

Developmental domains are difficult to address. In our schools and colleges intellectual development is given the greatest emphasis, with physical development a close second in some schools. Over the last few years the health and wellness movement has caused more women and men to become aware of the need to keep physically fit through such sports as jogging, walking, cross-country skiing, golf, tennis, aerobics, swimming, bowling, and so on.

Figure 4.2. Integrating Identity, Development, Roles, and Contexts.

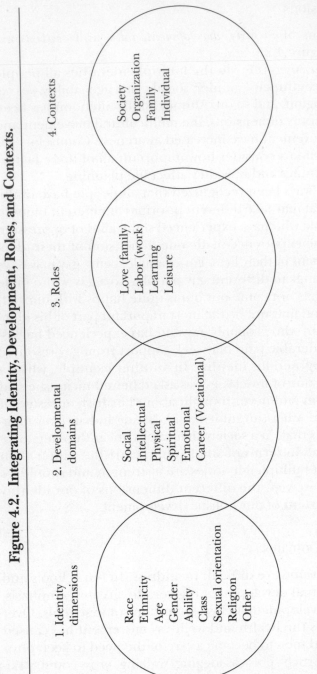

1. Identity dimensions

Race
Ethnicity
Age
Gender
Ability
Class
Sexual orientation
Religion
Other

2. Developmental domains

Social
Intellectual
Physical
Spiritual
Emotional
Career (Vocational)

3. Roles

Love (family)
Labor (work)
Learning
Leisure

4. Contexts

Society
Organization
Family
Individual

Consider

- Changing values regarding life roles
- Dimensions, domains, roles, and contexts of human development
- Love, labor, learning, and leisure priorities
- Societal, organizational, family, and individual goals and values
- Developmental tasks and priorities at different life stages
- How dimensions, domains, and roles can be integrated in individuals, couples, families, and community

Social and emotional development is presumed to occur at home and in the larger society. It is often minimized in schools where the focus is on cognitive rather than affective skills, especially with the "back to the basics" educational reform movement of the 1980s and 1990s. In this more conservative political climate, there may well be an attempt to stop schools from addressing certain issues altogether, including violence, sexual harassment, racism, sexism, and other barriers to personal development.

In addition, both the career and the spiritual aspects of personal development continue to be neglected. Attempts to infuse systematic career development programs into schools have not been very successful, and, in most schools and colleges, the programs are still piecemeal, focused primarily on jobs, occupational information, and placement. Our public schools are afraid of the word *spiritual*, partly because they confuse it with religion. But greater attention has been paid to spirit and meaning in work with adults, as more and more adults seek help in their search for meaning and purpose in their lives.

Life Roles

The expanded framework of Integrative Life Planning also invites examination of *the roles* and *contexts* of our lives. The life roles are the Four Ls: Love (family and parenting), Labor (work), Learning, (education, both formal and informal), and Leisure (activities engaged in apart from work).

The life role concept is drawn largely from the work of Donald Super (1980), introduced in Chapter Two. As already indicated, love and work are considered the two major arenas of life but learning is becoming increasingly important, especially as adult education and lifelong learning become more popular options. There is considerable agreement that paid work, which provides economic security and a standard of living, is essential before other roles can be fulfilled with satisfaction.

Because learning has become a concept of importance throughout our institutions—as in the Learning Organization, the Learning Society, Continuous Learning, and so on—it is referred to throughout this book and will not be discussed in depth in this section.

Work Role

Others have conceptualized the work role in quite different ways from Super. Fox (1994) relates work to community and includes inner work on self and outer work on society, which leads to what he calls the "Great Work" of the universe. His call for the reinvention of work includes a deeper commitment by both women and men to the reorganization of the structures of work in ways that make people feel they matter. He also calls for work to be more spiritual, based on a larger meaning or purpose, not just to fill a job but to benefit society or the community by giving back with one's unique talents. Like others he also suggests that we need to create new kinds of environmental work.

It is important to make a distinction between jobs, which may be on the road to disappearance, and work, which, if defined differently, will continue to be available in abundance. Unpaid work in family and community should also be included in the redefinition of work. Fox says that "work comes from inside out. Work is the expression of our soul, our inner being. It is unique to the individual; it is creative. . . . It is that which puts us in touch with others . . . not so much at the level of personal interaction but at the level of service in the community" (p. 5).

When our work lacks dignity, so do we. When we are out of work, "unemployment" takes on new meaning and "underemployment" may be viewed differently as well. Fox's vision of the work role is where mind, heart, and health come together "in a harmony of life experiences that celebrate the whole person" (p. 2). The other side of the issue is that of workaholics. Fox's solution to the crisis in work is to treat the purpose in work, to redefine it and the way we create it, compensate it, let go of it, and infuse it with play. These broader definitions of work fit well with the kinds of work identified in Chapter Three that need to be done.

Leisure Role

The leisure role is discussed in this section, but a full review of the considerable literature on the subject is beyond the scope of this book.

Although there is a large body of literature on leisure in the behavioral and social sciences and counseling and career development fields, there remains some controversy on how to define

it and research it. Howard and Diane Tinsley (1986) have theo-
rized that leisure experiences affect the physical and mental health
of individuals and are important sources of need gratification.
Some scholars also cite the changes in the workforce that are
affecting work and leisure, such as the increasing participation of
women, immigrants, and part-time workers (Kanungo and Misra,
1984). A recent study at the University of Stockholm using a scale
measuring total workload showed that women with children typically spend ninety hours a week in paid and unpaid work, while
men spent only sixty. In addition, women found it harder to relax
at home than men did, so that just coping with stress took a toll on
women's general well-being (Clay, 1995).

As might be expected, Super (1986) discussed leisure in relation to life roles and self-realization. McDaniels (1989) has argued
that career must include leisure—that is, career equals work plus
leisure—and that the three concepts provide a more holistic framework. He includes the new volunteerism as work in his definition,
but he does not include family in his formula. Leisure counseling
has emerged as a specialty in the counseling field, but the changing nature of work and the workplace may affect the focus of
future studies of leisure as well as the nature of leisure counseling.

It is important to note that little has been found linking leisure
to gender roles. Yet, the leisure role often is determined by other
roles. For example, overloaded "supermoms" may not have much
discretionary time for leisure activities. Men who are workaholics—
whose work is their life—may not worry much about family or
leisure, because after hours they may engage in networking activities, such as sports or other events to gain further advancement
(and that may be their leisure activity).

In a study that focused on women and outdoor recreation,
Loeffler (1995) defined leisure variously as "free time" from job
and life maintenance (the opposite of work); activities chosen by
an individual for relaxation, diversion, self-improvement, or social
participation; and a state of being, with meaning derived from the
experience or activity, a holistic view, and work and leisure not perceived as opposites. She also defined "life context constraints" on
leisure and "gender-based constraints." Although her study focused
on women and sports, her approach is applicable to women's
career development and life roles. Women with children who carry

full workloads and then do the "double shift" at home do not have much time for leisure activities, no matter how these are defined.

Obviously there is a strong connection between leisure and work. In a society in which the work ethic is so strong and work is considered central, leisure has not been a priority. How do people spend their time away from paid work? Do they have a choice in the matter? How do they choose their priorities? How will the changing workplace and work types affect the connection between work and leisure in the future?

The ways in which we spend our leisure time depend on our values, our work and family patterns, and the time and money we have. If we have little money, we are likely to spend leisure time on activities that do not cost much, like watching a sunset or hiking on a nature trail. If we believe in saving for the children's education or other purposes, we may use little money for recreational activities. If we have a lot of money to burn, we may be conspicuous consumers who live high on the hog in everyday life and in leisure time. Indeed, in our materialistic society, influenced by advertising (which makes us think what we want is what we need) and the socialization of individuals, we learn to work and then spend. For example, we are pressured to buy the most advanced technological products—computers, videos, CD-ROMS, and so on—and then to spend our leisure time "surfing the Net."

There are conflicting reports on whether leisure time in the United States has increased or decreased. Some suggest that leisure time has declined by a third since the early 1970s (Schor, 1991). In contrast, a recent three-year study of three thousand couples between the ages of thirty-five and forty-nine with two children and annual incomes of $40,000 or more found that they are having more fun and spending less time on work-related activities (Hamlin, 1995). It reported that while average Americans are getting older, they are working less and playing more. The study did not consider gender differences in leisure time activities. It did not examine the family households in which men increasingly are doing the household chores such as cooking, gardening, or shopping—as in my own household—or dispute the many studies that show that women still carry most of the household work.

Balance in our various life roles is something few achieve and many aspire to. In fact, balance used to be something that women alone sought, but an increasing number of men today are also seeking it. The Center for Creative Leadership, Greensboro, North Carolina, described Larry Grant, a manager who was seeking more balance in his life and raising questions whether men have to make the choice "to love or to work." With the new psychological contract between worker and employee and more contingent workers in downsized corporations, men like Larry may have more time to seek that balance (Kofodimos, 1986).

When it comes to balance, I have to plead guilty—to not always having it. The leisure piece of my personal quilt for a long time was quite small. Although an egalitarian marriage has given me much opportunity to share roles with my husband—and for thirty years we have done a great deal of sharing—the demands of a professor's life have not allowed much time for leisure, with work brought home most evenings. During the child-rearing years, balancing work and family was about all I could manage. Although all four of us love sports and arranged for ski trips and other vacations, all too often my work dominated. My husband and I both fortunately had some flexibility in our schedules (he as a sales engineer, I as a professor), but my work often spilled over into other areas of our lives. The area that suffered most was friendships. As I fulfilled the roles of parent, wife, and professor, there was almost no time left for the role of friend, which I deeply regret. In our "couples society," it seemed that most of our social life was with coupled friends. Now that our adult children are out of college and working, I have more time for friendships but find that the former friends are well established in their own social patterns with husbands, partners, families, and other friends and not as available as they once were. The structures of work and our own compulsive motivations sometimes keep both women and men from giving priority to those things that are most important in life.

Nevertheless, while elusive, balance is a value that many are seeking today and one that may be more achievable in the future as work and family structures change.

Life Contexts

ILP suggests that we human beings need to be aware of our life contexts: as individuals, families, organizations, and in the larger society, what I call SOFI. Part of our task as human beings is to determine our priorities among the Four Ls and the larger context. In summary, ILP encourages professionals in counseling and human development to help clients to consider several issues. When individuals consider these issues they should be able to begin the process of integrative life planning by identifying those which are most relevant to their own situation at their stage of life and with regard for family and community.

- Changing values about life roles at different life stages
- Relationships between work, family, learning, and leisure
- Potential conflicts between family and work and their intersection
- Priorities among love, labor, learning, and leisure, and the ways they change over time
- Values and priorities about individual, family, organizational, and societal goals
- Importance of gender in career and life planning
- Developmental domains, identity dimensions, and priorities at different life stages
- The ways in which identities, roles, contexts, and domains can be integrated for individuals, couples, families, and communities

Holistic Career Development of Women and Men

Let us now take a look at the gender factor in career development and life planning. Gender-role conflicts are a part of societal discrimination and contribute to ongoing sexism. We are just beginning to acknowledge the damaging effects of gender-role socialization on men.

Like Hare-Mustin and Maracek (1990), I believe that the deconstruction of gender with less emphasis on gender differences is called for. But the current reality is that career socialization remains different for men and women. Both are stereotyped, although the male stereotype is valued more and tends to bring more of society's rewards. Just as women's lives have been limited by expectations of the family role, men's lives have been limited by a focus on the work role. If both are to have more holistic lives, each needs the opportunity to achieve in both life roles: self-sufficiency (usually expressed through work) and connectedness (usually expressed through family).

To move toward a holistic view of career development, we must understand influences on the career development of both sexes. In the following section, I examine selected aspects of the changing life patterns of men and women and their different career socialization.

Career Development of Men

In some ways, to talk about men's career development in a holistic sense is an anomaly. Because men's careers have been seen to be linear with a focus on autonomy and separation, the very concept of thinking about career as more than occupation and including other life roles may seem foreign. Yet an examination of new directions in men's careers and life planning is an important part of ILP.

The traditional career development literature, with its focus on men, is not the primary emphasis here. With few exceptions, most of the traditional career development textbooks have been written by men and about men, although recent editions are likely to contain a separate chapter or paragraph on women and other "special populations." In this section, the emphasis will be on new perspectives and knowledge of "the new male." However, I recognize that even this new literature has been written mostly by white men about white men and does not always apply to others.

Chapter Two described the literature on the new male. The work of scholars in the men's movement gives us a somewhat different picture of contemporary men and a better understanding not only of why they are the way they are but, perhaps, how some of them are changing or may change.

Influences on Life Planning

In the past more attention has been given to the female stereotype than to the male stereotype. But as the BORN FREE program maintains, both women and men are limited by gender stereotypes. Since both sexes are affected in negative ways, both need to work together to reduce the inhibitors and increase the facilitators of their career development.

Socialization and Stereotyping

As O'Neil (1981) has pointed out, men have experienced gender-role strain and conflict because of the male stereotype. (See again Figure 2.3 in Chapter Two.) According to O'Neil, the patterns of men's lives emerge from what he calls the "masculine mystique," which is very destructive to them, often resulting in damaged health and shortened lives.

O'Neil makes four recommendations for professionals who counsel men: (1) assess the degree to which gender-role conflicts limit their emotional, interpersonal, and physical lives; (2) develop educational and preventive programming to help men who are experiencing gender-role conflict, including information about the restrictive effects of male socialization; (3) provide consciousness-raising experiences to explore their fear of expressing their "femininity" and gender-role conflict patterns; and (4) educate the public about the oppressive and destructive effects of gender-role socialization for both women and men.

Male Role Conflict

In this section I am especially indebted to my colleague, Tom Skovholt, who has influenced my thinking on factors affecting men's development in many ways.

Skovholt (1993) defines another aspect of male socialization that causes conflict: the 180-degree role conflict. What he means by this is that men at an early age learn to be aggressive and are socialized to believe in violence and war. Yet, at the same time, they are asked to be intimate partners, spouses, and fathers, that is, to learn nurturing skills. Skovholt suggests that this creates a basic incompatibility in men's lives. With reference to the early socialization of boys to grow up to be warriors, Skovholt observes: "Combat demands that young males be able to do a number of complex difficult tasks: be hardened emotionally so trauma does not weaken the person, be able to exert themselves physically to the maximum extent, be able to follow orders even if the order is frightening to the individual, and be able to inflict physical harm on other human beings. This approach, however, has costs because these attributes and skills are opposite of what female partners often want in a contemporary marriage, defined as a lifetime partnership of intimate equals" (p. 3).

Skovholt's thoughtful discussion of this phenomenon increases our awareness of the costs of male socialization and the consequences for both men and women. If we expect men to develop more holistic lives, we will need to make major changes in their socialization and the expectations we put on them at home, in educational institutions, and in the larger society.

Vocational Success and Achievement

I already have alluded to the vocational success factor in men's development. They are socialized early for careers and vocational roles; their success later on is judged by their achievement as worker and provider. The male norm is to be autonomous, strong, and analytical. These expectations put a tremendous burden on those boys and men who do not fit the mold. Skovholt describes this as another of the dilemmas facing men, especially now that there are also expectations for them to be equitable partners in new work and family relationships. Perhaps as changes continue to occur in the workforce, men will be relieved of the vocational-success-equals-self-worth burden and, through shared roles, gain greater esteem as a result of more time spent with and more satisfaction from the family.

Being a nontraditional man in a traditional field of work can be difficult, as my husband learned when he tried to carry out his part of our equal-partner marriage. He took the children to the dentist and doctor and shared in the cooking and household work. He cared for the children many times when I was away on business trips. Some of his customers in the construction industry could not understand how he could "let his wife work" or go away so frequently. Because he has a strong sense of self (and a good sense of humor), and because he was committed to our equal relationship, he was able to put up with the comments. He has often said that it has been great having a professional wife and two incomes, but that it was certainly not the norm among the people with whom he worked.

Influence of School Norms and Structures

How and what we teach boys in school affects their attitudes toward gender roles. Although there is evidence that boys get more attention, are called on more often, and generally are reinforced more positively by teachers (Sadker and Sadker, 1994), there is also evidence that boys have more disciplinary and reading problems and are referred more often to counselors and psychologists. In high school they are encouraged to be aggressive in sports activities and may act out through acts of vandalism, reckless driving, and other "macho" behavior (Skovholt, 1978). Thus, boys do not "have it so good" either.

Restricted Emotions

A number of writers have called attention to the restricted emotional expressiveness of boys and men. Society still gives a strong message that boys are not supposed to cry or show emotion—except perhaps anger—even at funerals, although this appears to be changing somewhat, as some male leaders now demonstrate emotion in public. Because boys limit their expressivity in childhood and adolescence, it is harder for them to show emotions as adults, especially as partners in intimate relationships. Indeed, although divorced women experience a loss of income and lifestyle, divorced men experience the loss of one of the few people with whom they can express their emotions.

Referring again to my personal quilt, I feel fortunate being married to a man who is able to express his emotions. Although my husband grew up in Norway (a country of people known for their stoicism), served in the Norwegian military, and was educated as an engineer (a group that is supposedly made up of nonverbal types), he is one of the most open and expressive men I have met and is not afraid to shed a few tears while watching a television program or a movie.

The Women's Movement

There can be little doubt that some men have difficulty dealing with the women's movement. Much literature since the 1970s has criticized the traditional dominant-male, submissive-female relationship; many feminist books have attacked patriarchy, male privilege, sexual violence, misogyny, and sexism. A relatively new men's movement in the United States, called the Promise Keepers, is a religion-based program to help men bond with each other and keep their biblical promise to protect their wives and families. While some observers applaud the opportunity for men to be more expressive, others express concern that the underlying goal is to keep women in subordinate roles.

Several of the books mentioned in Chapter Two emerged from the men's movement and in a sense are a response to the literature of the women's movement. Whether men have a fear of femininity, a fear of women in power, a fear of women taking over positions that were formerly held by men, or fear of loss of dominant status, they cannot engage in broader life planning until some of the dichotomies and conflicts between women and men disappear.

Workplace Changes

Although the expectation that men will be successful workers remains widespread, there is also a new understanding that the changing workplace may not allow that to happen. Downsizing and layoffs are hitting older men hard, especially those in their late forties and their fifties. The old career pattern of "work before all" may not continue as more men in this age group lose their jobs and are unable to find equivalent positions. There is a kind of paradox here: on the one hand, a tight job market and job losses make men anxious as they compete for a piece of a seemingly smaller pie; on the other hand, the consistent evidence that adults, male and female, would like to spend more time with their families may help them to see opportunity out of crisis and take advantage of the new status by acting on their family values. Of course, this assumes they have a reasonable standard of living and income that allows them to do so.

Career Development of Women

I wrote my first article on the career development of women in the United States more than thirty years ago. At that time there were no textbooks on the topic. Career development research was based on men's lives.

At the time, I was counselor in a university high school attended primarily by academically gifted students. I became concerned about what seemed to be a gap between the attitudes of the teenage girls I worked with and the reality of women's lives in the broader society. These girls personified some of the literature in its suggestion that, although girls in junior high school still have high career aspirations, by the time they get to high school some of their goals disappear. I found that many of my students talked about college but did not link it to a career. Because my own experience growing up had led me to value education, I did not want my female students to foreclose on their options. As a woman who did not follow the norms of my generation—that is, marry by age twenty-one, have children, stay at home—I was more achievement-oriented than most of my contemporaries while refusing to make the either-or choice between a traditional career and a family.

Changes in Women's Lives

Over the years, there have been profound changes in the lives of the high school students I have counseled, in my own life, and in the roles of women and men. Changes also have occurred in the field of career development and counseling, that is, in what we know, what we think we know, and ways of knowing. Shortly after I became a professor at the university, I set up an innovative course on the career development and counseling of women and then had to create my own textbook for it as well (Hansen and Rapoza, 1978), as none was available.

Today, the literature on women's psychology and women's career development is much more abundant than in the 1970s. A comprehensive body of theory and research is now available on all aspects of women's development, at all ages from youth to old age, from traditionalist to feminist perspectives.

Some of the older studies dealt with such issues as the effects of working mothers on children and examined such factors as self-concept and self-esteem, locus of control, attribution of success and failure, achievement motivation, and expectancies and aspirations. Early studies also looked at gaps in women's career development, such as lack of work orientation, role models, self-efficacy, achievement in mathematics and science, economic independence, and managerial skills. Many of these studies tended to present women in a way that limited their options, devalued their contributions, inhibited their development, and prevented them from utilizing their potential in getting the world's work done.

Women, Employment, and Role-Sharing

Recent statistics on women and employment in the United States contain both good news and bad. Women are the ones most damaged by poverty. Women have broken the glass ceiling over middle management, but they hold only 2 percent of the top executive positions. The number of women in medicine, finance, business, accounting, and law has increased impressively, and some progress has been made in dentistry and veterinary medicine. But in science, particularly the hard sciences such as physics, women comprise only 4 percent of the positions. There are still limited numbers of them in the engineering fields, although the gap is closing (Friedman, 1989). And in government and politics, although women have made progress at the local and state levels, the United States lags far behind many Western nations in the percentage of women in high government positions. Despite some progress toward equity to varying degrees in various nations, sex segregation is still a common phenomenon across cultures.

In terms of employment, women who have moved into mainstream jobs find themselves just as likely to be "downsized" as their male counterparts. In the psychological literature, it appears that gains have been made in the portrayal of women; they are more visible and there is movement toward gender equality. In the workplace, too, gains have been made, yet women have a long way to go in gaining equal access to the positions they merit in business, industry, and government and in high-skill, high-wage industries, crafts, and trades.

Influences on Life Planning

The recent literature on women's psychology and development is voluminous. I focus here on the most salient factors affecting women's opportunities to live more holistic lives that include the roles of worker, mother, and partner. Some of these have changed over time, but others seem as present in the 1990s as they were in the 1970s.

Economics and Poverty

Economic issues continue to be among the most significant in one's well-being. It is well known that unmarried women with children are disproportionately represented among people living in poverty. A 1985 study documented the fact that, in economic terms, after divorce the quality of men's lives increases while that of women diminishes considerably (Weitzman, 1985).

Although divorce has negative effects on both partners, women who have not previously worked outside the home and have few skills and little experience suffer most both socially and economically. It is estimated that one out of every five children will live in poverty at some time during their lifetime, including those in intact families. A woman from a middle-class family in Los Angeles described her fall from a reasonable standard of living to one below the poverty line after she went on long-term disability and her husband's business failed. They lived at the subsistence level, their children crying from hunger, with no health insurance. They resorted to filing for bankruptcy. The pain this woman felt is expressed in the following quote: "My dominant feeling became one of numb amazement as I was forced by circumstances to see that without money, a person simply doesn't matter. . . . I thought I was well-informed, but I was not at all prepared for the violent, demoralizing effect of poverty. I had no idea how it would feel to have no food in the house, no gas to drive to buy food, no money to buy gas, and no prospect of money. How it would feel not to matter to the larger world, and to know that my smart, funny children also do not matter" ("Without Money," 1991, p. 27A).

I myself grew up in a working-class family and for the first eighteen years of my life lived in an apartment located on an alley. But I never experienced hunger. There are many homeless and jobless families today who do experience hunger, and their increasing numbers affect not only blue-collar families but white-collar and professional families as well. Although we professionals cannot do much about the economy (except by voting), we need to be aware of the central place of economics in helping people not just survive but lead more fulfilling lives. We also must not overlook the fact that education can accomplish both those goals: help the disadvantaged first obtain jobs and then work their way out of poverty.

Socialization and Stereotyping

A case has already been made for the power of socialization and the pervasive stereotyping that persists in society. Women are usually portrayed as emotional, sensitive, expressive, compassionate, tactful, gentle, security-oriented, quiet, nurturing, tender, cooperative, eager to please, dependent, sympathetic, helpful, warm, vain, intuitive, domestic, sensual, artistic, and literary; in sum, they embody the reverse of masculine characteristics (Cook, 1993).

Although society is trying to reduce the pervasiveness of these stereotypes, they persist. We can all cite traditional male fields that women have entered (and vice versa). Yet several studies carried out in the 1980s and early 1990s reveal continuing stereotypical attitudes among adolescents, both in occupational preferences and in gender roles (Hansen and Biernat, 1992).

Self-Esteem and Self-Efficacy

An early study by Smith (1939) indicated that girls' self-esteem diminishes with age. Although findings over time have not been consistent (Bower, 1991), recent studies of adolescents indicated that girls do have lower self-esteem than boys but that boys' self-esteem may also lessen with age (American Association of University Women, 1990). The AAUW study indicated that African American females had more positive self-concepts than their white peers; it was hypothesized that this was the result of their having strong mothers as role models, who taught them that there was nothing wrong with them but something wrong with society. Other studies, such as that by Epperson (1988), have shown that even female high school valedictorians think less positively of themselves and develop less self-confidence as they progress through college. Epperson's study also suggested that subtle sex bias in schools has effects later on work life. Case studies of women seeking treatment for depression or seeking counseling in midlife provide some evidence of self-esteem issues.

Another aspect of self-concept is self-efficacy, an area in which research has mushroomed in the last fifteen years. Self-efficacy theory refers to the expectation or belief that one can successfully perform a given behavior. Research by Hackett and Betz (1981) and others has revealed gender differences in career aspirations and achievement. They postulate that low or weak expectations of self-efficacy constitute one internal barrier to women's career achievement. They suggest that female socialization experiences, such as strong involvement in domestic, nurturing activities; low exposure to female role models; high levels of anxiety; and lack of encouragement or active discouragement in nontraditional pursuits (such as math, science, and engineering) have negative effects and produce lowered self-efficacy in girls and women.

Female Identities and Work Motivation

Today most women in the United States work at paid jobs (about 60 percent of them), and the rest do unpaid work in the home. Most women, like most men, work out of economic necessity. Yet we know that women's motivation to work varies. Some women may prefer to be home with family but are the provider or co-provider; some in role-reversal families are the main source of family income; some women work to gain self-fulfillment; some work to meet a societal need. During World War II women went into the factories to contribute to the war effort while men went off to war; when the war was over, most women dutifully returned to the home. My mother was one of these. One of the greatest incongruities for me was that this traditional, dependent housewife, who had worked only a short time as a beautician before marriage, went to work as a welder during the war. She gave up her job because it was the patriotic thing to do but said, years later, "I really missed having a nice paycheck coming in each week."

Although women, like men, have aspirations and expectations, in the past many took on the stereotypical role of homemaker and nurturer. Others had a different vision and wanted to have multiple roles, to be able to achieve outside the home as well as inside it. Still others followed their sexual orientation and developed lesbian relationships, creating their own patterns of work and intimacy (Dupuy, 1993). Swiss and Walker (1993) cite the various patterns of women's lives as fast-track superwomen, part-time and temporary workers, risk takers, entrepreneurs, and full-time moms.

Women's desire to work outside the home or to carry out certain life patterns also has been affected by the ideal sex roles projected for them over time. Lindberg (1989) conducted a qualitative study of women's self-esteem and identity with seventy-seven female volunteers attending the Michigan Women's Music Festival and a second group taking a course in human relations in a large university. She defined female identity development as "the process by which a woman identifies and values herself as a female self and how that process is influenced by the social-psychological context of how culture and society perceive that gender" (p. 1).

Lindberg found that the self-concepts believed to lead to psychological well-being have changed over the decades. In the 1930s, it was agreed that the ideal mental health pattern was acquisition of a masculine identity by males and a feminine identity by females. Furthermore, the ideal gender-role characteristics were highly sex-typed. In the 1940s, although the same sex typing prevailed, sex typing was considered detrimental. Thus, these views were not as widely held as earlier. In the 1960s and 1970s, an emphasis on androgyny suggested that a person with both high masculine and high feminine characteristics would have high self-esteem (Bem, 1974). Lindberg points out that society devalued the feminine half of the androgyny concept. By the 1980s, the research had come full circle, and again the instrumental/masculine person had characteristics most closely related to self-esteem and mental health (Lindberg, 1989). An important question cited by Lindberg was, How do women live in the world as men have defined it while creating the world as women imagine it could be? (Raymond, 1985).

Educational-Occupational Structures

Although considerable change has occurred in higher education—in access, testing, scholarships, flexibility, schedules, support services, and increased representation of women and minorities—change does not come easily; inequities persist. It is true that women account for more than half of the undergraduate and graduate populations in U.S. colleges and universities. They also have increased opportunities to complete degrees, participate in athletics, and gain greater visibility through women's studies programs and an emphasis on women in many disciplines. The percentage of women faculty has increased at the assistant professor level, but at the full professor level the percentage remains small.

In some institutions of higher education with sexual harassment policies, grievance committees cannot keep up with the caseload. Women seeking to move up the academic ladder tell stories of bias, harassment, and discrimination. Although class action suits have had many positive outcomes, the search for equality in higher education continues. Work done by Bernice Sandler (1986) and the American Council on Education Center on the Education and Status of Women reconfirms that colleges and universities often create a chilly climate for women.

Similarly, the structure of the workplace, while changing in some respects, still maintains barriers that limit women's participation and advancement. Women tend to remain clustered in non-professional (often clerical or word processing) jobs, with only a small percentage in what have been traditionally male occupations. And the pay gap still exists, with women earning about 70 percent of what men do. That inequity is exacerbated for disabled and minority women.

A number of books about women and the workplace have provided both anecdotal and quantitative data about women's recent experience in work. Hardesty and Jacobs (1986) portray women's experience in business as full of hidden forces that propel them upward, only to hit the glass ceilings that limit their advancement and increase their disillusionment. The authors dispel some of the myths that women bring to the workplace and document the reasons why many women drop out of the corporate structure and become entrepreneurs.

Swiss and Walker (1993) provide additional documentation of the difficulties women still face in the workplace. In their study, 902 women from Harvard business, law, and medical schools reported the dilemmas they faced as they tried to combine a career and families. They reported that the primary factor limiting their careers and triggering workplace hostility and prejudicial behavior was the announcement that they were pregnant. Workplaces demonstrated little awareness of the needs of women, children, and families. The authors called this phenomenon "The Diana Penalty," from the Roman myth of the goddess Diana. They suggest that all kinds of talented modern Dianas face contradictions and barriers in the workplace because of their gender and particularly because of their desire to fulfill both the achievement and maternal roles. Thus, in addition to the glass ceiling, they identified the "maternal wall" that existed for many of the women in the study and resulted in loss of jobs, unforeseen changes in professional responsibilities, roadblocks to arranging maternity leaves, barriers to job reentry, deteriorating work relationships, and resentment or even outright hostility from other professionals. This study seems congruent with Betz and

Fitzgerald (1987), who found that the most important barrier to women's career development was the belief that women could not fulfill both the maternal and career roles.

Health, Age, and Timing

Whether a woman marries, has children, and remains healthy all affect her life role opportunities. It is an important fact that the largest proportion of women entering the workplace are those between twenty-four and thirty-four, which are the prime child-bearing years, and that over 60 percent of women with children eighteen and under work outside the home. This number is expected to reach 70 percent by the year 2000. In spite of these realities, it is still often suggested, especially among white populations, that women should not work after they have children. In my generation it was assumed that college-educated women, like other women, would stay home when their children were young and certainly if there was more than one child. Yet I withstood the pressure of a mother and a father who had only an eighth-grade and a high school education, respectively, and could not understand why at twenty-eight I had not settled down to the "serious business" of life. In their eyes I really "arrived" only when I married (past age thirty) and even more so when I had my first child (at thirty-eight) and my second (at forty). Such later-life births were not as common then as they are today! Marrying later and having children later in life have had some advantages, particularly since my husband and I were fortunate to have relatively good health and relatively healthy children whose illnesses were mostly the typical childhood variety.

Violence Against Women

This summary of the influences on women's life planning would not be complete without at least a reference to the violence that they face daily. Sometimes this violence manifests itself in racism, sexism, ageism, and so on. At other times it appears as sexual harassment, sexual abuse, physical abuse and battering, rape, and even murder. The topic cannot be adequately discussed here, but there can be little doubt that violence inhibits women's development because it disempowers them and makes them feel they have little control over their lives. A sense of agency and internal locus of control is important to all people's feelings of empowerment. Career professionals and counselors, within the limits of their training and competencies, have a responsibility to help women understand how violence may have affected their career development and to assist them in moving beyond it.

Other Factors

Many other factors influence women's life career planning: physical health and eating disorders, mental health such as depression and addictions, and issues of power and gender. Although the foregoing is not an exhaustive discussion, it calls the helping professional's attention to the variety of factors that can keep women from achieving their potential and living fulfilled, holistic lives.

Gender-Role Agency and Communion

An important aspect of wholeness and the ILP quilt is what I call *self-sufficiency and connectedness*. I believe that, as women's and men's relationships change from dominant/subordinate to equal partnerships, and as professionals become more aware of the career development and life roles of men and women, a new integrative framework can facilitate the holistic development of both self-sufficiency and connectedness.

David Bakan suggested in 1966 that people order their reality in two ways: *agency and communion*. The *agentic* he describes as rational, analytical, autonomous, logical, competitive, and self-directed; the *communal* is expressive, subordinate, emotional, nurturant, cooperative, and integrative. Bakan was one of the first to link the agentic with males and the communal with females and to suggest that a major developmental task for both is to work out an integration of both types of characteristics in their lives.

Bakan's formulation has stimulated considerable research on the development and life patterns of women and men in the past three decades. Jeanne Block (1973), in her study of cross-cultural and longitudinal perspectives on conceptions of sex role, suggested that a balance between agentic and communal behavior is optimal. In discussing the socializing influences on the development of sexual identity, she observed that traditional male and female socialization tends to reinforce traditional sex roles. She says: "If our social aim can become, both collectively and individually, the integration of agency and communion, the behavioral and experiential options of men and women alike will be broadened and enriched and we all can become more truly whole, more truly human" (p. 526).

Another researcher pointed out that the agentic style is typical of the empirical research conducted at universities, characterized by fragmentation, isolation, objectivity, and rationality (Carlson, 1972). Communal style research, in contrast, may involve the researcher in the topic being studied, may be subjective, involves qualitative patterning, and is integrative. She also suggested that it is insufficient to study women's lives only with empirical methods and encouraged research on women that is communal in nature.

Other literature that reflects the agency-within-communion philosophy includes Jean Baker Miller's *Toward a New Psychology of Women* (1976) and the more recent work from the Wellesley Stone Center on self-in-relation, *Women's Growth in Connection,* by Jordan and others (1991). All believe that women's lives can be studied most effectively within the context of relationships.

Pamela Aasen (1990), one of my doctoral students, tested the Stone Center self-in-relation model in her dissertation on women's life planning. She studied the topic by examining a number of variables that affect women's lives. According to Chekola (1975), life planning is the process of integrating desires and intentions into a set of life goals. This set of life goals, or life plan, motivates and directs one's behavior. Aasen states: "Life satisfaction and well-being depend on the pursuit and actualization of one's life plan. Life planning is an active ongoing process in which an individual engages for the purpose of living a meaningful, satisfying, and fulfilling life through establishing, pursuing and accomplishing work, relationship, and life style goals" (p. 5).

In her path analysis causal model, Aasen explores the interrelationships between relationship support for life planning; self-support (the ability to overcome barriers to one's life plan); resistance (from significant relationships); self-efficacy; self-esteem; past and present planning; past and present integration of plans for work, relationships, and lifestyle; goal accomplishment; and life satisfaction. Aasen's study provides an excellent model for helping women look at their lives in a relational and nonlinear way to connect work, family, and lifestyle.

Gender-Role Dimensions

Psychological literature in the past reveals a tendency to think of male and female as opposites. Many similar words and phrases have been used to describe these gender-role dimensions. Although I do not wish to perpetuate this dichotomous thinking, for clarity purposes I have put together a list of the traditional gender-role dimensions in Exhibit 4.1. The bottom of the exhibit moves away from the dichotomies and toward the model of women and men as equal partners that is involved in Integrative Life Patterns.

The topic of gender-role dimensions has not been central in education, career counseling, or the emerging field of futurism. But because we order our world through hierarchical structures and specialties that separate us from one another, we are unable to maintain an integrated view. The male (left) side of the exhibit is the one that has been valued more highly in American society, though the yin and yang have been viewed as complementary. One of the goals of men and women as partners is to move beyond the dichotomies of gender roles.

The concept of this kind of partnership can be illustrated by an experience I had in Japan in 1984. After being invited to lecture on career guidance, I was surprised to learn on arrival that my mostly academic hosts really wanted to hear about BORN FREE, the program I had designed to expand career options for both women and men. I quickly revised my notes and included sections I did not believe my Japanese hosts were ready for, in particular the parts about partnerships between men and women. My husband had accompanied me on the trip—something most Japanese husbands would be unlikely to do—and had arranged to visit the factories of two companies with which he did business. Because of my interest in workplaces and personnel, I was invited—although as an afterthought, because women generally are not seen in this capacity—to join him. The only woman in a group of businessmen, I shared lunch with them at a restaurant in a town known as "the city of strong women," the female server informed me, and dinner at a theater restaurant frequented mostly by Japanese businessmen and their male guests.

Exhibit 4.1. Traditional Gender-Role Dimensions.

Agentic (Male)	*Communal (Female)*
Work	Family
Are instrumental	Are expressive
Are providers	Are nurturers
Have ethic of rights	Have ethic of care
Achieve	Relate
Are autonomous	See self-in-relation
Are single providers	Are dual earners
Sex-role system	Sex-role transcendence
Dominate	Are subordinate
Seek separated role	Seek integrated roles
Express yang	Express yin
Live work-family separation	Live work-family integrations
Live fragmented lives	Live holistic lives

At the closing dinner of the conference two weeks later, my hosts asked me to give my impressions of Japan, which I obligingly did. Following my brief comments, my host professor said, "And now, Dr. Hansen, since we know you believe in partnerships, we want to hear from Mr. Hansen." My husband graciously rose to the occasion and did not disappoint. Later, one of my University of Minnesota international graduate students, who happened to be at home in Japan at the time, told me that the partnership that my husband and I modeled had left a deeper impression on my audience than anything I had said. I also learned that a number of younger Japanese couples were developing more egalitarian relationships and that many traditional wives were tiring of their husbands' monolithic work patterns. Recent reports bear out that patterns of work and family are indeed changing in Japan.

Movement away from the dichotomized roles will require new ways of understanding male and female connectedness and self-sufficiency. Economist, environmentalist, futurist, and author Hazel Henderson in *Paradigms in Progress* (1995) examines a new "ecology of love," highlighting the need for people to explore new frontiers in their relationships and new definitions of love, including expanded definitions of caring. She sees changes taking place in three "zones" of human experience:

1. *The Breakdown Zone,* where there is national restructuring in the middle of cultural confusion
2. *The Bifurcation Zone,* where individuals, families, and communities try to reframe their career choices and their values
3. *The Breakthrough Zone,* "where successful adjustments occur and old ideologies give way to new social terrain, new goals, and new criteria for success" (p. 143)

Henderson believes that romantic dyadic love, a concept that became popular in the fourteenth century, has outlived its usefulness. She believes that traditional monogamous marriages produce narrow horizons and broken relationships (often caused when partners evolve personally) and are breeding grounds for incest, battering, and child neglect. She calls for new assumptions and a new global sense of caring for the human family. In part, her solution, as mentioned earlier, is to recognize unpaid caring work and make it honorable.

Henderson is one of those visionaries who sees change occurring and necessary in all aspects of society but particularly in economics. Her position may be described by one chapter title: "Beyond the Battle of the Sexes." Her view on relationships between women and men is especially relevant to the agency and communion paradigm.

Self-Sufficiency and Connectedness

Moving on from gender-role dimensions, I would like to focus on self-sufficiency and connectedness as a metaphor for agency and communion.

The Excelsior Model

A group of female colleagues and I adapted a new version of the agency and communion model in 1990 at the women's gathering of the National Career Development Association (Andersen and others, 1990). It is called the Excelsior Model both because *excelsior* means "the highest level" and because we conceptualized it in Excelsior Springs, Missouri. The model was generated in two days of unstructured discussions in which each team of women participants created their own topics. The five of us were concerned about the need for better models for understanding and valuing gender in a pluralistic society. We called the Excelsior Model that evolved out of our deliberations an "integrative model of development."

We discussed Bakan's (1966) agentic and communal ordering of reality and the more recent work by Miller and the Wellesley Stone Center group. We asked the question, What does the mature woman [or man, or person] in this society look like? We decided to use the term *self-sufficiency* to indicate the agentic and *connectedness* to indicate the communal, recognizing that society still tends to link the former with men and the latter with women. Figure 4.3 depicts our conceptualization of self-sufficiency and connectedness for women and men.

The rectangle represents a way of looking at men's and women's lives. What it says is that there are conceptions of the traditional female and the traditional male, of the ideal male and female (which the model sees as an integration of self-sufficiency and connection in each), and of the disenfranchised male or female (the homeless, poor, and deprived). Agentic men tend to have a high degree of self-sufficiency, often represented through their role as provider, while communal women tend to have a high degree of connectedness, represented through the relationship role. In two-parent families, both go through a process of constant compromise to achieve ideal roles in self-sufficiency and in relationships.

The goals of career counseling are to help men and women assess where they are in these dimensions and, through a systems approach, help both to achieve a high degree of self-sufficiency and a high degree of connectedness. These goals can be achieved directly, by working with clients to enhance self-sufficiency with a high degree of connectedness, and indirectly, by developing environments in which connectedness and self-sufficiency are adaptive for women and men (Andersen and others, 1990). External or environmental inhibitors and facilitators hinder or help people, respectively, achieve self-sufficiency and connectedness. Strategies can be developed to create environments that promote relationships and achievement values in both men and women, empowering to both.

Figure 4.3. Self-Sufficiency and Connectedness for Women and Men.

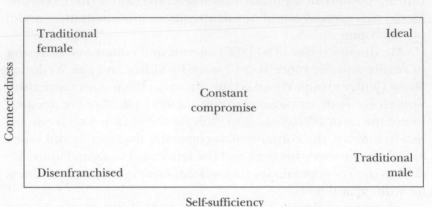

Goals: (1) high self-sufficiency
           (2) high connectedness

Strategies: (1) direct: work with clients to enhance self-sufficiency with a high
              degree of connectedness
              (2) indirect: develop environment in which connectedness and
              self-sufficiency are adaptive for women and men

Source: P. Andersen, L. S. Hansen, J. Lewis, L. Vetter, and P. Wickwire. National
Career Development Association Women's Conference, Excelsior Springs, Mo.,
Oct. 1990.

A Systems Approach

My approach to gender issues always has been a systems one.
Women and men do not live in isolation but in context. A holistic
framework for human development—like ILP—helps move us
away from earlier "either-or" explanations of gender differences
and stereotypes in men's and women's roles to more integrative
ones.

Inhibitors to Self-Sufficiency

Some of the environmental inhibitors to self-sufficiency are the following:

1.   Career socialization by parents, schools, religious institutions, work, peers, and media has perpetuated stereotypes, discrimination, and bias.

2.   Hierarchical and closed institutions, including old boys' networks, keep women from moving beyond the glass ceiling and result in hostile work environments by creating such barriers as sexual harassment, closed systems, stereotypes, promotion barriers, unchanging work cultures, and little support for new work and family patterns. Men who want to share roles and take advantage of benefits available, such as paternity leave and flex time, may find themselves in disfavor and even punished as eccentric for not putting work first in their lives.

3.   Economic recessions affect both men and women through cutbacks in the workplace. Those most recently hired are likely to be the first to be laid off. Both sexes are affected today when so many people have lost their jobs—a loss that may affect their ability to feel connected and agentic. Many young adults, unable to find jobs and still living at home or returning to the formerly "empty nest," are demoralized because the dreams they had upon graduation are not being realized.

4.   The dominant/subordinate organization of society continues to be one of the most fundamental external barriers. In *The Chalice and the Blade,* lawyer and author Riane Eisler (1987) reports on her studies of prehistoric civilizations, some of which she found to be caring, peaceful, and egalitarian. What is needed today, she urges, is a "partnership society," in which women and men are equal in all areas of life. She calls for cooperation over competition, linking over ranking, connection over separation, and partnerships over subordination.

When I met Eisler in Finland in 1987, her book had just been published. I was in Kuoppio speaking about BORN FREE and told her about the ambitious gender equity program, which for years had been working to implement the concept she was talking about. Since then, she and her husband, David Loye, have formed The

Partnership Center and written a practical book called *The Partnership Way* (Eisler and Loye, 1990).

Defining Connectedness and Community

Before describing the inhibitors to connectedness, we need to define again what connectedness is. Women's perspectives appear to have a different focus from men's. For example, among female psychologists who have examined connectedness, the perspectives of Chodorow (1978) and Gilligan (1982) seem especially relevant. Chodorow describes the continuous, fluid, flexible, adaptable characteristics of attachment. Gilligan sees identity defined in relationship, attachment supported by an ethic of care, and the fusing of identity and intimacy. Jordan and others (1991) also see women in relationships (in connection) but point out their need for agency as well. Henderson (1995, 1996) describes connectedness from a worldview perspective.

Men who have directly or indirectly observed various kinds of connectedness include Pleck (1981), work and family; Capra (1982), connectedness of the new physics worldview paradigm; Harman (1988), global mind change; Peck (1987), spirituality as community; Fox (1994), connection to all living things and the cosmos; and Etzioni (1993), the need for both rights and responsibilities and communitarianism.

For me, connectedness is a search for meaning and a sense of being that are linked with community. It begins with a search for who we are in community rather than in isolation. The following communities are important to ourselves and our worldviews.

- The community of women and men, our relationships, and the continuing struggle to work out those relationships, communication, and patterns.
- The community of diverse ethnic and cultural groups in which we learn to value our own uniqueness but also celebrate the diversity of others, regardless of race, ethnicity, creed, appearance, sexual orientation, physical or mental condition, age, or socioeconomic status.
- The community that is our family, our family of origin and our families of choice, which come in all shapes and sizes.
- The community in which we practice our spirituality.

Inhibitors to Connectedness

The primary inhibitors to connectedness are the old paradigms that have dominated our world for centuries—reductionism, fragmentation, separation, specialization, hierarchy, and rationality. Societies, and even academia, are at last beginning to discard the old ways and focus on collaboration, cooperation, cooperative learning, celebrating diversity, and interdisciplinary and cross-cultural approaches to learning. Futurists and physicists (Capra, 1982; Harman, 1988; Ferguson, 1980; Theobald, 1987; Henderson, 1995, 1996) are helping us change, but movement is slow.

Many external inhibitors still limit our search for meaning and wholeness; these include unemployment, poverty, drug abuse, discrimination, crime, and violence. These societal problems keep both women and men from realizing connectedness and self-sufficiency.

Career professionals implementing new life planning models need to address these issues because they are the antithesis of connectedness. Both men and women must work together as change agents in the workplace, educational institutions, religious institutions, agencies, communities, and professional associations to help eliminate these problems. At the same time, the limits on connectedness that are unique in men must be identified and removed.

Facilitators to Self-Sufficiency and Connectedness

Another question asked by the Excelsior Model group was, What does the relationship of the environment and the mature person in this society look like? Figure 4.4 depicts the relationship, showing internal and external inhibitors and facilitators of self-sufficiency and connectedness.

How can career counselors and other helpers intervene to reduce the inhibitors and increase the facilitators so that we can achieve our twin goals of self-sufficiency and connectedness? How can we intervene to change both individuals and society, that is, reduce stereotyping, change sex-role norms, influence lifelong holistic development and socialization, develop more open institutions and organizations, transform cultural norms, and move

Figure 4.4. Inhibitors and Facilitators of Self-Sufficiency and Connectedness.

What does the relationship between the environment and the person (woman, man) in this society look like?

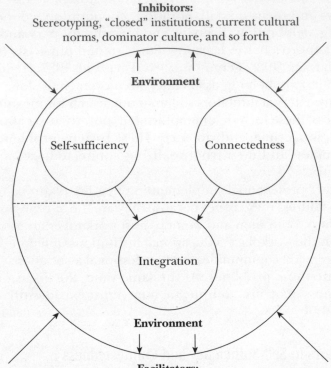

Inhibitors:
Stereotyping, "closed" institutions, current cultural norms, dominator culture, and so forth

Environment

Self-sufficiency

Connectedness

Integration

Environment

Facilitators:
Egalitarian schools and workplaces; partnership culture; public policies and legislation that support freedom of choice, affirmative action, and egalitarian relationships; power and leadership toward a human rights agenda; gender-aware teachers, parents, and counselors; role models for integration of work and family

Source: P. Andersen, L. S. Hansen, J. Lewis, L. Vetter, and P. Wickwire. National Career Development Association Women's Conference, Excelsior Springs, Mo., Oct. 1990.

from a dominant/subordinate society to one of equal partnerships? In the following paragraphs, I review some strategies counselors and other professional helpers can use in various settings.

1.   *Schools and colleges.* We need to work toward less hierarchical and more egalitarian schools and colleges and programs. This means educating teachers, parents, students, administrators, and others about the advantages of a system in which both girls and boys, men and women can develop to the fullest by experiencing both self-sufficiency and connectedness. Although numerous educational programs for gender, racial, and disability fairness were developed in the 1970s, they just touched the tip of the iceberg. Now, in the mid 1990s, there is renewed interest in such programs. Continuing programs about multicultural and gender equity are essential, especially to expand nontraditional options (for example, the hard sciences and mathematics) and to eliminate sex-role stereotyping. A developmental curriculum to prepare children, youth, and adults to develop their potential both for their own satisfaction and the benefit of society and the community should be created. Examples of programs include the national 4-H program called "I'll Take Charge," which integrates the areas of dreams, education, family, work, and lifestyle (Walker, 1989) and the BORN FREE program (Hansen, 1979), which provides training for educators and parents to unlearn stereotypes and relearn new ways of creating humane work and learning environments. In addition, there are programs like those described in *The Kids' Guide to Social Action* (Lewis, 1991). In it, Lewis describes the activities of sixth graders who get involved in action learning by cleaning up a hazardous waste site near their school, enlisting the help of the entire community in doing so. Lewis points out how both community and students benefit when talents and desire to serve are tapped. The "developmental assets" program created by the Search Institute enlists the entire community to help youth increase assets (Benson, 1996). There are also many college-based outreach and intervention programs such as the University of Minnesota Career Connections Program for students with disabilities and the faculty and staff who work with them. Keierleber and Hansen (1992) describe several issues and barriers for adult women and men in university settings.

2.   *Workplaces and organizations.* As pointed out in earlier chapters, the workplace is changing, and it will be part of the task of counseling and career development professionals to prepare workers for the kinds of work environments and work ethics they will confront. As jobs continue to change from the lifelong to the contractual, perhaps men and women alike will be able to reevaluate the place of work in their lives, achieve balance, and more easily fulfill multiple roles (Hall, 1990). Although students still need work experience and skills and job-seeking skills, they also need to be aware of changing work ethics, relationships, communication patterns, work teams, and leadership styles in the workplace. They also need to learn entrepreneurial skills, including how to draw up contracts, do consulting work, and manage change.

In a recent article, Kiechel (1994) states that managers and workers in the new economy will need to understand power and how it is used (and sometimes abused) and obtain the skills to help create more humane work environments that attend to worker needs both on and off the job. They will need to learn to be decision makers and change agents in their own systems.

Organizations that embody these characteristics will help instill in employees a sense of connectedness. Giving people a sense of identification with the larger community and enabling them to contribute their talents to the betterment of it is part of what self-sufficiency and connectedness are all about, for both women and men.

Conclusion

In this piece of the Integrative Life Planning quilt, we have considered what it means for men and women to become whole human beings, examined aspects of life roles important to Integrative Life Planning, reviewed how the influences on women's and men's careers shape their life patterns, and reflected on the meaning of self-sufficiency and connectedness as two central goals for an integrated life for members of both sexes. Holistic development—weaving our lives into a meaningful whole—is a large task and an idealistic goal, but it is worth striving for, even though it may take a lifetime.

Chapter Five

Critical Task 3: Connecting Family and Work

ILP views integrating self-sufficiency, achievement, and relationships as an important goal in life planning. It's not easy. Entering graduate school at my age seemed scary, and I had qualms about being "selfish." I wouldn't have much time for my kids, my mother, my friends, my sister. I feel fortunate, however, that my husband is my biggest cheerleader. As I helped him through school, he now helps me in many ways. He often grocery shops and cooks, especially during exam periods. Fitting with Super's Life Span Theory and Hansen's Integrative Life Planning, I keep recycling, moving back and forth between roles depending on circumstances, chance, family needs, and my needs.

—Returning female student in counseling

The third critical task of Integrative Life Planning is to help clients connect family and work. It is an assumption of Integrative Life Planning that the changing roles and patterns of men's and women's lives require new definitions and descriptions. Some of our individual development theories do not adequately explain the behavior of women and men with one another. The multiple changes cited in earlier chapters—such as the dramatic increase of women in the labor force, the rise of two-income households, and the evolution of work structures and ethics—have created new patterns that do not fit the old norms. Work and family changes are challenging old socialization patterns and stereotypes not only in the United States but also in other Western cultures. New family patterns create high expectations for success in both the career and family domain. They also require new skills in communication and role definitions.

This patch of the ILP quilt is especially important because it represents family patterns that are common in contemporary society yet still not well understood. A growing body of literature since the 1970s provides insight into the connection between family and work. This connection has become more salient with the movement of women into the labor force and the slower movement of men into more active roles in family. It has been reflected by the development of a variety of human resource initiatives to address worker needs. It is important to career professionals seeking to help women and men with the unique issues they face as they negotiate their workplace and family roles.

This chapter examines some of the changes that are occurring in family and work, some of the theory and research on the interaction between the two, how these kinds of relationships are relevant to Integrative Life Planning, and techniques that ILP professionals can use to help clients, students, and employees more effectively manage these changes. Difficulties in separating out the family issues from the work issues resulted in my discussing them together and attempting to see how they interface.

Changes in Family and Work

Chapter Three described a number of family types that now exist in the United States. Although the current chapter focuses heavily on dual-income families, this does not mean that other types of families are not important. Rather, the role and relationship issues in the two-income family are those with which I am most familiar: they are part of my personal quilt. However, people do not remain in one pattern all their lives; their work and family situations may change, depending on their life circumstances and both anticipated and unanticipated events. Many families, even if not dual-income now, may become dual-income in the future or may have been in the past; therefore, the focus of this chapter is relevant to a wider audience than may be apparent at first glance.

Single-Parent Patterns

The number of single-parent households has increased significantly in the past twenty years; they are estimated in the early 1990s to make up about 28 percent of all families. Most single-parent households are made up of women with children, and many are living in poverty. When there is no partner, there is no one to share the joys or burdens of work and family. Recently proposed "workfare" programs, designed to get welfare recipients off welfare, often do not take into account the complexity of these lifestyles. But single parents (including some fathers) do have roles and relationships in both paid work and family, and many have been successful in raising children alone.

A recent study by the Search Institute (Benson and Roehlkepartain, 1993) indicated that one in four youths under age eighteen lives in a single-parent family. On average, youth in these families are more likely than those in two-parent families to smoke, drink, use drugs, steal, and be sexually active; they are also more at risk for vandalism, absenteeism from school, and depression and suicide. This kind of report underscores the need for youth to have significant adult role models in their lives, including male role models. However, the report also points out that there are healthy single-parent families and that "family structure is not destiny" (p. 1). Improving conditions of the workplace and public policy toward child care are as critical or more critical for these families as for families with two partners.

Two-Earner Families

Dual-income or two-earner families became the dominant family pattern in 1980 when the "tipping point" occurred, with over 50 percent of U.S. families identified as that type. It was also when the Bureau of Census removed "head of household" from the census form (Bernard, 1981).

Two-earner families are those with two incomes, including those in which the husband's work is dominant and the wife's is supplementary as well as those in which both spouses have career commitments and are equal providers. *Dual-career families* are one kind of two-earner families; in these, both partners have strong identification with their work, usually extended preparation for it, commitment to it, and expectations of moving up a career path. It is estimated that about 20 percent of all dual-income couples are dual-career couples, and it is this latter type on which much of the literature has focused. Although labor market projections do not offer data about changes in family patterns, such changes are well documented in other sources (for example, Browning and Talia-ferro, 1990; Hage, Grant, and Impoco, 1993).

Changing Family Demographics

Demographic reports on the status of women and men in work and family provide a strong rationale for the need to reevaluate family patterns and restructure the workplace to meet changing needs. The high incidence of divorce is one indicator of the ongoing change. Although the divorce rate has leveled off in the United States, in 1988 there were 4.8 divorced persons for every thousand people compared with 3.5 per thousand in 1970. Although women's participation in work has increased dramatically, the size of families has remained relatively unchanged in the past twenty years, with the average American family having 1.9 children. The size of the family varies enormously depending on ethnicity, however. In the United States, the average white family has 1.7 children; the average African American family has 2.4 children; Mexican American, 2.9; and among Southeast Asian families in the United States, Vietnamese, 3.4; Laotian, 4.6; Cambodians, 7.4; and Hmong, an average of 11.9 children per family (Atkinson, Morten, and Sue, 1993). Many Asians believe the richness of life comes from the number of children. Obviously, the number of children has an influence on the mother working outside the home; cultural norms and attitudes toward male and female roles also play an important part in the nature and extent of their participation in work and family.

As more and more women participate in the labor force, women are having children later in life, although only 2 percent of all births in 1988 were to women over age forty. In the United States, statistics show that more women with newborns and children under six are in the labor force.

As the life expectancy of women has increased to about seventy-eight and of men to seventy-one, concerns about work and family over the life span take on new meaning. It is expected that by the year 2010, the life expectancy for women will be eighty-one and for men seventy-four. It appears that women will continue to outlive men by several years. Already in the over-eighty age cohort, which is growing at a rapid rate, women make up the largest part of the population.

The highest labor force participation among women occurs in those ages forty to forty-four, with 78 percent of women in this age group employed (Commission on the Economic Status of Women, 1991).

In 1988, 57 percent of married women with children were in the labor force, compared with only 30 percent in 1970. Most women work full time regardless of marital status. Statistics also indicate that women continue to be concentrated in low-paying jobs such as clerical work, child care, and retail sales. Although the income gap between men and women continues regardless of educational level, married-couple families have the highest incomes of all types of families.

It is well known that women (and children) are more likely than men to be in poverty, and that older women are more likely to be poor than their male counterparts (Commission on the Economic Status of Women, 1991). According to a Gallup poll conducted for the National Career Development Association (1990), adults of all ages (both women and men) overwhelmingly indicate that family is more important than work. Yet the structures of work and family, along with societal norms, do not allow men and women to act on these values. The Gallup poll also found that more than a third of the respondents felt conflicts between work and family.

Changing Workplaces

A number of changes in the workplace also affect the ways in which women and men are able to carry out their roles in work and family. Corporate attention to human needs is a relatively new phenomenon. The creation and expansion of human resource development programs in the 1970s and 1980s offered one corporate response to employee needs both on and off the job. Perhaps encouraged by the entry of women into the workforce in unprecedented numbers, corporate management has recognized that work affects family, that family affects work, that satisfied workers are more productive workers, and that all the foregoing may affect the bottom line (Naisbitt and Aburdene, 1990).

Most women in Western cultures have long seen the connection between family and work, but men need to see this connection as well. That scenario has changed somewhat since women went to work during World War II; many stayed there, and more have entered in increasing numbers since the 1950s. It has changed further in the 1990s as increasing numbers of men are out of work, spending more time with family, and engaging in child care and household tasks. Rosabeth Moss Kanter (1977b) asks some important questions: Why can't work sometimes fit around family? Why does family always have to fit around work? Answers to these questions are beginning to emerge as employers, managers, and organizations recognize the needs of men, women, and children in diverse family types.

A difficulty in addressing this issue is that much of counseling, counseling theory, counselor preparation, and career development is still focused on helping individuals make a vocational choice or find a job. Although a substantial body of knowledge exists on work-environment fit, and a certain amount of congruence is needed for people to be happy in their work, the larger career development questions such as those posed in this chapter also need to be addressed. Even some of the broad life-role-based concepts of career seem to have vocational choice as their ultimate outcome, and most vocational assessment tools or instruments are based on narrow matching models. I believe that a major task for career professionals is to understand better the interaction between work and family and how both roles can be integrated for men and women.

Research on work and family has been carried out in a variety of disciplines, including sociology, family social science, organizational dynamics, and home economics, as well as psychology, counseling, and career development. Some of it has been linked with

gender-role literature, such as Joseph Pleck's extensive and insightful work since 1973 on the male sex role, masculinity and femininity, and work and family (for example, Pleck, 1976, 1977a, 1981;
Richardson, 1981; Zedeck, 1992; and Voydanoff, 1989).

Selected Theory and Research on Family and Work

It is important to acknowledge that helping clients and employees
understand the connections between their two life roles is much
more difficult than dealing with a single role. It is much easier to
help an individual choose an occupation than to help a couple plan
their lives together, for in the latter case they must consider so many
factors, including their individual career needs, the needs of the
family, the needs and demands of the workplace, the needs of any
children, the need to care for elderly parents and other relatives,
the needs of the relationship, and the needs of the larger community. The following section reviews some of the individual, family, and organizational issues that may influence career counselors
and other career professionals in their practice. Since publication
of the award-winning volume by Kanter (1977b) calling for a
research and policy agenda on family and work, considerable literature has emerged on effects of work on family and effects of
family on work.

Integrative Thinking About Work and Family

Awareness of the reciprocal nature of work and family roles has
been cited as a key issue (Richardson, 1981). What is meant by the
term *role*? It includes the demands, expectations, responsibilities,
and pressures that others impose on us; our own perceptions of
what we think we ought to be doing to play that role; and our
behavior, that is, how we act in that role, whether consciously or
unconsciously. The reciprocal roles of work and family need to be
studied in terms of their mutual influence, mutual causality, and
interaction. I noted some years ago that roles had changed dramatically in families. Instead of "owned roles" (of provider and nurturer) we often have "shared roles" (Hansen, 1984).

How work and family roles interact is based on a number of
factors. Important factors include the nature of both spouses'

occupations; the stage of occupational career they are in; their current aspirations in their occupational career; the ages and stages of their children; attitudes toward and satisfactions in parenting; the quality of the marital relationship; and societal factors, such as the quality and availability of child care, and ethnicity and class factors. Also important is the nature of the relationship (whether equal or dominant/subordinate), and the number of family relationships (Richardson, 1981).

Just as there are a number of family types, different perspectives on family-work issues come not only from Western culture but also from other cultures. Particularly important is that the issues are present in families with a wide range of incomes, lifestyles, occupations, and career stages; thus, family and work issues are present in all kinds of families. Goldsmith (1989) presents new models of family-work interaction. Some of the issues that counselors and career professionals should take note of are marital satisfaction, parenting, self-esteem, child-centered concerns, job involvement, stress, conflict, social supports, absenteeism, and time management.

Early research showed that men did not see connections between their work and family lives, and negative effects of maternal employment on children were presumed (Voydanoff, 1989). Economic aspects of family and work sometimes have been ignored although some research has been done on economic resources and rewards. Recent literature focuses on the structural and psychological characteristics of the work role, work-family conflict, child rearing, and quality of family life—all issues that affect life planning.

Contrary to popular opinion, a number of studies indicate that women's performance of multiple roles as worker, spouse, and parent is positively (rather than negatively) related to physical and mental health. However, how individuals coordinate work and family role responsibilities over the life span is important. Career stages and family stages may be simultaneous or sequential. Obviously, with simultaneous stages, individuals perform both work and family roles over the adult life span; in sequential stages, the extent of participation in work and family roles is variable and shifts across stages in family and work careers (Voydanoff, 1989).

Voydanoff states that work and family research lacks an integrated theoretical grounding, except in studies of role strain and role expansion theory (that is, the effects of role overload and role change). An expanded and useful conceptualization for work and family emphasizes the structure of the economy and the labor force as well as the role of the worker in the economy and the earner in the family. Voydanoff stresses the need to focus on unpaid work in the family and community, work often done by women. She also calls attention to the "sandwich generation," families that must care for both children and elderly family members. This function is often carried out by women in midlife. Integrative thinking such as that of Voydanoff is essential if career professionals are to help working families seek balance, role-sharing, conflict resolution, and quality of life.

Some writers point out that much of the work-family literature avoids discussion of gender, and they call for an analysis of gender issues, including such topics as occupational sex segregation, the earnings gap between men and women, and family structure changes (Voydanoff, 1989). The traditional model views jobs as the property of men (who are not seen to have family responsibilities) and family as the bailiwick of women (whose paid work often is seen as only supplementary); it sees part-time work and parental leaves as being the domain of women. All these views are not in sync with the conditions of modern society.

Pleck (1976) created an especially useful way of viewing the different male and female roles. Asking, "Who is the provider?" (see Figure 5.1), he observes that there is both a traditional female role (nurturer) and a traditional male role (provider) and that there are both work and family tasks and work and family relationships. The female role has changed because as large numbers of women have assumed the work role, they have become both nurturers and providers. The importance of the male in the family has also increased (although much more slowly), so that he has now become both provider and nurturer. With these changes come role conflicts that need to be resolved.

Voydanoff's expanded conceptualization of work-family linkage suggests that further research needs to concentrate on the work-family connection in the context of broad economic trends, to incorporate analyses of unpaid family and community work, to examine the implications of worker-earner role difficulties for families, and to acknowledge the importance of changing family

Figure 5.1. Who Is the Provider?

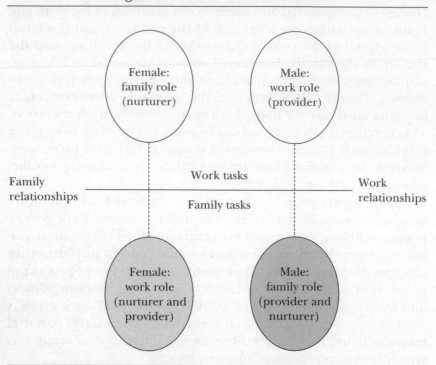

Source: J. H. Pleck, "The Work-Family Role System," Social Problems, 1977, 24 (4), 417–427. Copyright © 1976 by the Society for the Study of Social Problems. Reprinted by permission.

structures for work and family life. She also observes that policy research tends to be gender-linked but does not analyze the effects of family-oriented personnel policies on families and employers. Walker, Rozee-Koker, and Wallston (1987) make a similar point about public policy: it tends to be based on old family structures and is not in tune with the ways in which families in the United States have changed.

Organizational Work-Family Perspectives

An examination of work and family from an industrial/organizational psychology perspective yields still other issues of importance. These issues exist across national boundaries, occurring in such countries as Israel, the United Kingdom, Canada, the Philippines, and Brazil (Zedeck, 1992; Goldsmith, 1989); I have encountered them myself in Sweden, Norway, and Japan.

Industrial/organizational psychologists need to concern themselves more than they have in the past with the work-family domain, and researchers need to acknowledge that there are other parts of workers' lives that need to be taken into account, such as family, leisure, health, personal growth, and community. Although it was assumed for years that work and family were separate spheres, it is important now to assume that there is a natural relationship between the employing organization and the family experiences. Social developments such as the increase in women's employment, new concepts about gender, parenting, and work identity, increased divorce rates, changes in roles of men and women, new concerns about quality of life, and new measures of success all add to this concern (Zedeck, 1992). Certainly this increased awareness on the part of work organizations bodes well for families as well as the success of our work as career professionals.

It is important to study the effects of work on family (this subject has received the most attention) as well as of family on work. Much of the literature indicates that work has a negative effect on family, while the family's effect on work can be either positive (for example, a "shock absorber") or negative (causing absenteeism, lost efficiency, and tardiness). A number of models have been created to describe work-family interaction. Aspects studied on the work side and the family side are quite different. The latter are affective, including marital tension, family-home satisfaction, and child care and housekeeping activities (Zedeck, 1992).

Like Voydanoff, Zedeck suggests that there should be emphasis on unpaid work (in the family) as well as on paid work (in the workforce), with opportunities to study responsibility, self-direction, autonomy, decision making, and the like. Attention should also be given to processes (such as stress, role conflict, and socialization) and the meaning of work and work values in both settings, including the centrality of work.

Corporate Responses

That work and family are legitimate concerns of business is pointed out by the Families and Work Institute (Friedman and Galinsky,

1992). Labor unions, too, are interested in the work-family linkage, often using it as a recruitment tool. Among the reasons for greater corporate involvement in work-family issues are the need for increased productivity (and the belief that satisfied workers are more productive), more working women, more men with employed wives, union pressures, changing values, attempts to break the glass ceiling, increased media attention, and the need for dependent care.

Although there has been some business tension and resistance, corporations have responded with various forms of child care assistance, some elder care, and flexible schedules (for example, flextime, part-time work, work at home, and parental leaves). Generally the larger companies are the ones that have responded most to family needs, offering on-site child care and information about child care, helping parents pay for it, and the like. In 1990 there were fourteen hundred on-site or near-site child-care centers sponsored by employers in the United States.

Although employing organizations have created a variety of programs, program strategies are by far the least preferred means of addressing work-family concerns (Friedman and Galinsky, 1992). Rather, organizations are encouraged to use an integrated systems approach, incorporating work-family issues into the entire system, integrating work-family policies with other policies, and changing the corporate culture to become more generally family-friendly. Among the innovative solutions are Honeywell Corporation's "Success by Six" community effort to help children enter school at age six with greater chance of success; a Johnson & Johnson grant to help child-care programs become accredited; advocacy by American Express, Levi Strauss, and Mervyn's to improve child care through the legislative process; and the Family Care Development Fund created by AT&T. Some companies are also trying to bring together a focus on gender equity, family, and work life (Friedman and Galinsky, 1992). The passage of the Family and Medical Leave Act in 1993, although just a small step compared with those of other industrialized nations, may increase attention on the connection between work and family.

The following summarizes the findings of this research:

- Research on work and family needs to be done on multiple levels, for example, it must examine families, individuals, relationships between genders and cultures, and different types of families and their relational dynamics.

- High family involvement over time does not lead to lower work involvement.
- Gender, family status, and equal opportunity are linked together with both female managers and male managers with children having slower career progression (Hall and Parker, 1993).
- Couples with different styles use different strategies for maximizing the career progression of both: *accommodators* have a joint strategy; *allies* have a cooperative strategy, in which both deemphasize the work or home role; *adversaries* both have a high career orientation and want the other to perform the home roles; and *acrobats* both want to "have it all" (Hall and Hall, 1979).

Criticisms of Work-Family Literature

Although these conceptualizations have been extremely useful in clarifying the link between work and family, the research still has not focused enough on diverse family types (such as blended families, single parents, single people, same-sex families, unmarried partners), subsystems in families, the intrapsychic balance in addition to the balance between work roles and home roles, and family-centered research. Furthermore, the work and family literature has focused too much on two-career families, with the word *career* defined traditionally as a high level of work commitment and progress in a career (Sekaran, 1986).

Greenhaus (1989), an important researcher on role salience, believes that traditional definitions of career exclude too many people and that the topic is too important to focus only on highly involved professionals in dual-career families. He proposes that all the classificatory distinctions be abandoned so that research can study a broad spectrum of couples on a number of dimensions; the research findings will then be applicable to a larger segment of the population. Among areas he suggests for future research are work-family conflict, daily transitions between work and family roles, the role of career orientation (or career salience of each partner), the relationship between two-career status and career accomplishments, and implications of work-family interaction for career growth in organizational settings.

Family-Work Roles and Relationships

The issues affecting two-earner families also have been addressed in the counseling and career development literature. Some of the issues most relevant to life planning, and particularly to Integrative Life Planning, are faced by other types of families as well, although they take different forms. Again, because the two-earner family pattern is the one my husband and I have been in for thirty years of married life, that is the one I know best and the one from which I will draw some examples. What are some of the conflicts and issues the ILP counselor needs to be aware of?

Gender-Role Issues

The abundant career development and counseling literature reminds us that many gender barriers still exist and that they remain sometimes subtly and sometimes not so subtly in work and family roles and relationships. Although lifestyles clearly have changed, attitudes about gender roles cannot change as rapidly. The power of socialization and the ever-present stereotyping of men and women make it difficult for both to implement new roles or to share old ones. These issues emerge in many forms in two-earner families.

Gender-role issues occur during typical family tasks carried out by the earner, worker, nurturer, and provider. My husband and I have shared the provider role (although our incomes have not been equal, since business pays a great deal more than academia). We also shared the nurturing and household roles because we were committed to egalitarian values and were not locked into traditional gender roles. But we still faced some of the dilemmas brought on by following a pattern that was not the norm at the time.

Gender-Role Dilemmas

Gender-role dilemmas can occur within an individual and between a couple and society. As early as 1969, Rapoport and Rapoport identified five dilemmas faced by two-earner families that are very similar to those of today (and many of them match the tensions in my own family). The issues were *overload*, both physical and psychological, especially experienced by the women who often do the double shift of paid and family work; *discrepancy* between personal and social norms, as families discover that their expectations for themselves and their roles differ from societal norms; *identity dilemmas* experienced as both partners attempt to determine for themselves the importance of family and work and to deal with their masculinity and femininity when they engage in roles formerly ascribed to the other sex; *social networks,* that is, when couples select friends with lifestyles, expectations, and norms similar to their own; and *role cycling,* or questions relating to the career and family stages the partners are in and how they affect their family and work roles.

Dilemmas occur when people deviate from traditional gender roles, for example, when women achieve outside the home, use child care services, and share homemaking with men, or when men become active fathers, share domestic responsibilities, and support their wives' personal and career development. These are families in which women no longer exclusively "own" the homemaker role and men no longer exclusively "own" the provider role (O'Neil, Fishman, and Kinsella-Shaw, 1987).

Male-Female Roles

Men's and women's conceptions of sex roles affect their behavior and self-evaluations. Each spouse may face identity questions, such as "How will I maintain intimate relationships over long distances? Will I be able to achieve all my career goals and dreams and also be a competent and caring parent?" Other dilemmas occur when couples deviate from expected roles, experience discrepancies between ideal and real self-concepts, feel restricted or devalued by others, or personally restrict or devalue themselves. O'Neil, Fishman, and Kinsella-Shaw (1987) suggest two processes: reevaluating what it means to be a man or woman and integrating new ideas of masculinity and femininity, especially recognizing the limits of gender-role stereotypes (as the BORN FREE program does).

The traditional expectations of society still create barriers for couples who want to engage in role-sharing and equitable decision making and work toward egalitarian relationships. The larger societal issues of equity and gender-role ideology make the movement toward connectedness between equals a slow process (Gilbert and Rachlin, 1987).

Two-Earner Family Dilemmas

Two-earner families face many other dilemmas, many of them interrelated. These include basic child care, child rearing, and parenting; attitudes toward achievement and career; task sharing, time management, and division of labor; impact of changing roles on men's careers; marital satisfaction; available social supports; resource management; power and decision making; and stress and conflict management. These issues will be discussed briefly here.

Child Care, Child Rearing, and Parenting

Whether to have children, how many to have, and when to have them are important issues for many couples. Because women physically bear the babies, they are likely to experience more discontinuity in their careers and to include family goals in their career planning. As pointed out earlier, according to Betz and Fitzgerald (1987), the greatest barrier to women's career development is the attitude in society that women cannot have both career and family. Some choose to stay home with their small children because they want to be the primary influence on their growth and development. Some have no choice in the matter. Others seek other alternatives to try to balance work and family.

Finding adequate and affordable child care that is agreeable to both partners is difficult. My husband and I were fortunate to find a grandmotherly type who for thirteen years assisted us with child-care and household work. Our relationship wasn't exactly equal because my husband took responsibility for most of the lawn mowing, window changing, and gardening—partly because I had a permanent back injury from an auto accident but partly because I had much more evening work than he did. We were committed to role-sharing but didn't expect that that meant we would do everything equally. More important, like most parents, we were deeply concerned about having a quality home life for our children, not always easy to do. I experienced a fair amount of guilt about this issue, since mothers of small children did not work outside the home in my generation or my parents' generation.

Another parenting issue not always acknowledged is the impact of children's attitudes on their parents. Children bring home stereotypes about gender roles and careers that affect their expectations of their parents' roles. I recall clearly how both my daughter and my son told me that I was different from other mothers—and not always in a positive way. As our children grew older, they picked up some equal-gender messages from us, began to notice bias in the writing and pictures of textbooks, and asked a lot of questions about what men and women do. We tried to model role-sharing so that they would understand that women and men can do many things and need not be locked into rigid roles. When they were old enough, we brought them into the household task process.

A troublesome issue for me was that I was seldom home when my children came home from school (although our caretaker was always there). When our son was about ten, I asked him if that bothered him. He said it did, so I asked him why—after all, he always ran right outside to play after having a glass of milk and a snack. He replied, "When you're here, I can come in the front door; when you're not, I have to come in the side door." His response assuaged at least a little of my guilt because that did not seem too compelling a reason.

Attitudes Toward Achievement

Achievement is an issue in two-earner families, both in the home and in the workplace. I suggested in Chapter Four that both men and women need to achieve and to have relationships. Yet the structures and stereotypes of society keep them from becoming fully functioning persons in both sectors. Barriers keep them both from achieving self-sufficiency and connectedness and career professionals need to be aware of the barriers.

For women and men to achieve satisfaction in work and family, career counselors will have to help them examine internal and external barriers. We might raise such questions as, How do men define success? How do women define success? How do men and women obtain their expectations about their life roles, achievements, accomplishments, and activities? What satisfactions do women and men get from family? What satisfactions do they get from work and from parenting? How salient are family and work to both? Whose career is most important at different life stages? What are the satisfactions for each inside and outside the home? How do women manage family relationships and personal life? How do men manage work life and family involvement? How can men's motivations, attitudes, and expectations change to be congruent with current realities of family and work? How can work and home tasks be equitably divided to avoid overload as both partners try to be supermom or superdad?

Task Sharing

Especially in Western cultures, the issue of division of labor is well documented. In 1987 when I was in Finland, where more than 90 percent of the women are in paid work, the major complaint at a conference on women was that men did not carry their part of the family work. (See Haavio-Mannila, 1989, for her description of the role-imbalance situation in Finland.)

As the number of dual-career families continues to increase, many families are developing creative solutions to division of labor problems. For example, tasks are rotated through all family members on a monthly or weekly basis; family members choose tasks most compatible with their needs, with some weighting system in place to assure fairness; points are assigned to tasks according to task desirability, time required to complete it, and the like. Some friends with two professional careers developed a rather sophisticated point system when their children were teenagers. As the family members rotated through tasks, less desirable tasks were worth more points, and family members could choose those they preferred to do (or not to do) as long as the total weekly points were roughly equal. The system seemed to work extremely well for them. The children, now both married and employed, have learned from their parents an egalitarian attitude about family roles.

Impact on Men's Careers

Both women and men may experience slow progress in their careers if they are in dual-career families with children. A newspaper article recently reported that men in two-career families earn less than their peers in single-provider families ("Two Studies of Married Dads," 1994). The exact reasons for this are not yet clear.

Is it because their values change, their dedication to work lessens, their employers are biased, or for other reasons? Perhaps men are now being penalized in the same way that women have been traditionally for not giving 100 percent loyalty to their work.

One study of the role of men in dual-career couples identified three types of men: role-sharing men who were truly equitable in dividing child care and household responsibilities; traditional men, who regarded household responsibilities and child care as women's work; and participant men, who shared child care but thought that household responsibilities belonged to women. Note that traditional men were going to school at the time of marriage, giving priority to the husband's career. Men engaged in role-sharing believed their wives had higher career aspirations than they did. Traditional men had considerably higher salaries than their wives and few thought their children influenced their careers but 40 percent of role-sharing men thought that parenting had affected their careers. Although role-sharing and participant men experienced more stress, they had positive feelings about their lifestyle (Gilbert, 1987).

In families where the wife has a higher education and earns a relatively high income, the spouse is likely to share more of the household tasks. Baruch, Biener, and Barnett (1987) found that men are more involved with families when their wives have nontraditional attitudes toward sex roles and when the marital relationship is of high quality.

The final word is not out on the role of men in families. As the workplace continues to change in the 1990s and many men lose their jobs, it is entirely possible that they will be able to spend more time with family and learn the rewards of enacting the father role. There is also the (remote) possibility that work structures will change to be more responsive to the needs of family and of both partners.

Role Conflicts

There are many ways in which role conflicts occur in two-earner families. Basic family needs, such as procreation, parenting, child-rearing, and household tasks, may conflict with career demands, work schedules, achievement, and traditional notions of success. Other factors that may affect the amount of conflict include economic status, occupational levels and aspirations, educational level of the partners, gender-role orientation and ideology, size of the family and age of the children, and workplace responsiveness. According to a number of recent studies, women and men may perceive these issues very differently.

Greenhaus (1989) described what he called "time-based conflict" and "strain-based conflict" in two-career families. He also added "behavior-based conflict," when behavior in one role is incompatible with that of another.

Greenhaus differentiated between work stressors that led to work-family conflict and family stressors that led to the same. He found that women and men had similar levels of strain or stress-based conflict. A basic question is how dual-career couples can restructure work to meet family needs and restructure family to meet work needs (Brett and Yogev, 1988).

Marital Satisfaction

Marital satisfaction is an important issue in dual-career families and most other family types. Higher levels of marital satisfaction in women are associated with the wife's being more highly educated and the household's having a relatively high total income. Sekaran (1986) identified five factors that are good predictors of life satisfaction: number of multiple role stressors, enabling processes, integration of family and work roles, self-esteem, and hired help. Studies have found that marital strength is associated with the partners' satisfaction with intimacy and congruent perceptions of how marital and work systems coordinate. If partners have an all-consuming attitude toward career or one partner is a workaholic, marital satisfaction may be lowered.

Marital satisfaction may also be affected by the number of household and child-care chores the partners share. Many issues revolve around child-rearing and child-care practices (who takes the child to the doctor or dentist? who goes to games, plays, or recitals?) and perceptions of fairness by both parents. All tasks need not be divided equally but a mutually acceptable scheme must be worked out for getting the family work done that involves the children in the process as they get older. Certainly, there is no one right way to work out the new roles in work and family.

Diane Henze (1984) identified equity as an important aspect of marital satisfaction but pointed out that it is not just a matter of dividing things equally. Rather, it was what she called "perceived fairness." Stoltz-Loike (1992) introduces the idea of five kinds of equity that are important in dual-career families: family equity, couple equity, career equity, home equity, and gender equity. She suggests that family equity and career equity are different for each couple and that kinds of equity can have a positive impact on men's careers.

Social Supports

Another issue is how both partners resolve conflicts at home and at work and the kinds of supports they have, especially from their partner. According to a study by Lois Hoffman (1989), the old "blame the working mother" attitude has somewhat diminished. She found that the issue of the woman's employment in conflict resolution depended on both parents' attitudes, the number of hours the woman was employed, the social supports available, and the child's gender. While daughters left alone to do household chores might resent mother's employment, generally children of employed mothers did not feel deprived (Hoffman and Nye, 1974). Adult daughters of employed mothers were more independent, saw their mother as role models, and named their mother as the person they would most like to emulate (Betz and Fitzgerald, 1987). Daughters of these women also saw adult women in general as more competent and had a more egalitarian view of adult sex roles (Sorensen and Mortimer, 1988).

Power

How two-earner couples make decisions is an important issue. In my traditional family of origin, my father felt he had the right to make all the decisions because he was the breadwinner. There is some indication in the literature that women are more interested in power with or power within than power over someone else (Madsen, 1984). In *Real Power* (1984), Janet Hagberg offers a useful concept for examining power and identifying the levels or stages of power.

How power is gained, used, and lost is an important issue in family relationships. The balance of power often tilts in favor of the spouse who brings more valued resources to the union, for example, greater income. Women may increase their power if they work outside the home. In this way, they can seek more egalitarian role arrangements. Obtaining power or losing it may have an important effect on both partners.

Helping clients assess power dynamics and helping them learn problem solving, conflict resolution, and negotiation skills is an important task for the ILP counselor. Stoltz-Loike (1992) offers an important framework and techniques for developing communication and negotiation skills for dual-career couples.

Synchronism and Asynchronism

The concepts of synchronism and asynchronism have been described by Sekaran and Hall (1989) who use them to analyze degrees of conflict between career and family stages. They define *asynchronism* as "a condition under which the person's or the couple's experience is off-schedule in relation to some sort of 'timetable' of development" (p. 164). They are referring to society's timetable or norms for marriage, family, career, career milestones, and the like. The authors discuss synchronism (lack of conflict) and asynchronism (existence of conflict) in dual-career couples in relation to family stages. The family stages themselves include prelaunching, young married, childless couple, young parenthood, mature parenthood, and empty nest. They stress the need for reconceptualizations of sequential patterns of career and simultaneous concepts of career (toward balance) and say that later career development and advancement opportunities should be provided for both women and men. Essentially, they say that one way to balance two careers, relationship, and family is to do so over time.

The lack of synchrony between marriage decisions and occupational decisions also needs to be examined because we generally do not choose our partners and occupations at the same time. What happens when one partner changes—the wife goes back to school or the husband loses his job, for example—and the family patterns are upset?

Asynchronism has become a problem of particular import today as midlife couples face such issues as a husband getting ready for retirement, or being forced to retire by corporate downsizing, while a wife has just completed professional training and is getting established in her career. Such issues have been confronted by a number of my adult female doctoral students whose career plans are out of sync with those of their husbands. It is an issue in my own situation as well because my husband is ready to retire (not totally by choice) and I am not. Even though he has taken great responsibility for household tasks, I still seem to have overload while he seems free to engage in whatever leisure activity he chooses. We are not just sure when we will get in sync, and it does cause some tension.

Importance of Career and Family

Another issue is the importance of career and family to both partners. Whose career is more important and how important is family to both partners? Conflicts can arise when there is a departure from traditional roles, and one of the partners is not ready for it. For example, what happens if a wife who has been at home with children wants to go back to work or school? How important are the individual goals of each in their jobs? What kind of family lifestyle do they want? What kind of role expectations did they have when they entered the marriage? How do the family roles affect the career progression of the partners? How are their work roles affecting the amount of time and energy they have for children, intimacy, leisure, friends, self? The answers to these questions have to do with priorities and may affect all others.

Coping with Stress

Career professionals need to help dual-earner couples understand and cope with stress and other issues they may encounter. More emphasis needs to be put on what makes dual-earner couples work, especially in a society that is still based on dominant/subordinate rather than egalitarian roles. How do we teach men to be more self-disclosing and less emotionally restricted? How do we teach women to shed their guilt about moving beyond traditional roles to multiple roles? How do such factors as timing of the births of the children, adult education, relocation, promotions (and demotions), and stage of career and family affect the individuals and the family?

The dual-earner family pattern requires much flexibility and adaptability. To limit conflict, working partners may decide to limit their involvement at work to meet the needs of their family better, or vice versa. Sometimes a man or woman decides to try to balance roles better and not focus so much on work. Some women choose to step away from employment to be home with their children, especially when they are preschool age. Power issues may also come into play.

If current trends continue, most working couples will likely be making life choices in a societal context that accepts dual-earner and dual-career patterns but does little to change the traditional gender-role system. ILP professionals need to be prepared. Career counselors need to learn more family counseling competencies, family counselors need to learn more career counseling competencies, and human resource professionals need to learn more of both. Perhaps eventually the preparation for these professions will be integrated!

David Olson (1992) developed the Coping and Stress Profile, which can be used with individuals or organizations to determine major stressors in one's life or in one's workplace. The instrument is unique in integrating several aspects of life that he called *personal coping resources,* including self-esteem, mastery, spiritual belief, exercise, nutrition, and social support, and *relationship coping resources,* such as problem-solving skills, communication skills, closeness, and flexibility. The profile provides an indication of major stressors in life and helps identify other ways of coping. It yields an unusual amount of information about four areas of life: personal closeness, work closeness, couple closeness, and family closeness. Because it integrates various parts of one's life, the Olson profile is very congruent with an Integrative Life Planning approach to helping working families.

Work-Family Issues in Organizations

There is abundant literature on career development in organizations that helps career professionals think about the impact of the workplace on family and on individuals. Most of the theories of careers in organizations are, however, somewhat linear, focusing on the individual in the work organization and seldom on the individual's "other" life. Organizational career development theorists suggest that organizations cannot decide careers for individuals but, increasingly, individuals must take responsibility for developing their own careers in organizations (Hall, 1996; Kummerow, 1991; Schein, 1990).

Many issues continue for women and men in work organizations. Swiss and Walker (1993) cite the continuing glass ceiling for women who want to move to the top in organizations; it is especially apparent when it becomes known that they are pregnant or plan to have a family. Kanter (1977a) vividly describes how women and minorities experience work organizations, especially when they feel isolated. In her "Tale of O" (video and printed guide), she explains the psychological impact of being an "O" (different—either female or minority) in a world of "Xs" (usually white men).

Lotte Bailyn, MIT business professor, has developed a new approach to addressing work-family issues: looking at work through a work-family lens. Her innovative strategy, derived through case studies of corporations such as Xerox, diagnoses specific workplace stresses and conflicts and ways to change them. Her report will be out in fall 1997 (Cummins, 1996).

Mommy and Daddy Tracks

Douglas T. Hall (1990) presents a useful and practical framework for women and men to gain support from their work organization to achieve balance in their lives. Largely in response to Felice Schwartz's (1989) controversial article suggesting that corporations should have more flexible employment arrangements for women who want to combine career and family (erroneously named the Mommy Track), Hall asks if there is a Daddy Track, pointing out that increasingly there are men who are concerned about juggling family and career. He suggests that the Daddy Track is invisible because men do not talk about balance for they want to be seen as "dedicated careerists" (p. 8). He repeats the oft-cited fact that, although some organizations do offer paternity leaves, few men take advantage of them. Thus men are putting time into family-care responsibilities while trying to stay on the fast track.

Achieving Work-Family Balance

Taking a proactive stance, Hall (1990) suggests a whole continuum of activities for organizations to carry out in order to achieve balance between work and family that involve what he calls "less rigid forms of flexibility":

1. Create more flexible work arrangements through restructuring.
2. Recognize that many fast-track women make the same kinds of private career accommodations that men do (but also face problems in the way they are perceived by senior male colleagues).
3. Understand that a woman who wants to opt for a formal type of corporate flexibility may consider varying forms of "time out" from a career (though this may have career costs).
4. Make greater use of home-based work, especially appropriate in technical fields.
5. Do not view a person's work-family choice as a one-time career decision because family and career orientations change over time. There need to be multiple tracks and multiple entrances and exits.

Hall (1990) also recommends steps that organizations can take to resolve the problems of work-family balance.

1. Set policies and values for the organizational change process.
2. Conduct organizationwide diagnosis and create a task force for work-family needs and resources.
3. Implement changes to help employees cope with work-home strain and legitimize boundaries between work and home, that is, regard evenings and weekends as family time and do not consider those who stay late as superachievers but rather as poor time managers.

The main point here is that incisive action should be taken based on identified needs in such areas as policies, benefits, work restructuring, management training, career paths, work-home boundaries, and dependent care. The emphasis is strongly on management and leadership to reevaluate assumptions and values and to be partners in bringing about change.

These are just a few of the issues involved in and proposals offered for resolving work-family balance from an organizational perspective.

Interventions for Life Planning

A number of interventions have been suggested to help couples understand the connection between family and work. Let us look more directly at interventions career development and counseling specialists can use.

The Individual Career Perspective

In examining the individual career, it is important to consider each partner's age, stage of career, career salience, family salience, preferred lifestyle, flexibility or rigidity of work demands, and life goals and values. For example, if partners marry when they are just out of high school, the kind of further education each wants and the sacrifices that need to be made to achieve it are important issues. In the past, many women obtained jobs to put a husband through school only to find that by the time he finished, their relationship had soured and ended. In contrast, if individuals marry in their thirties and have attained higher levels of education, both may have completed at least one phase of their formal education, be established in a preferred lifestyle, be at the same stage in their desire to have or not have children, and be at similar career stages.

The importance of career to each person in a relationship is another consideration. Some individuals have greater career orientation and motivation than others; this needs to be taken into account in life planning. How much time and energy will be taken up by each person's career? What will the consequences be if the wife's career is higher status or higher income than the husband's? The literature indicates that this is a problem only if the husband defines gender roles narrowly (Hiller and Philliber, 1983).

The importance of family to the individual also needs to be taken into account. How important are family and children to each partner and what kind of sacrifices is each willing to make for the children's sake? This is where issues of quality time with children, family time together, and time together as partners enter the picture. Studies have shown that spousal support is important to women's carrying out multiple roles (Baruch, Barnett, and Rivers, 1983; Scarr, Phillips, and McCartney, 1989). Bird, Bird, and Scruggs (1984) found that husbands who held nontraditional views of gender roles were more likely to take over tasks formerly designated as women's in the family.

Probably the most important considerations are the life goals and values of each person. It is important that a couple agrees on what each wants to achieve in life, the need to contribute to society, a desirable or achievable standard of living, goals for children, time for spiritual growth, time with friends, time for leisure—all the things that contribute to a whole life. Of course, in mentioning these I assume that the couple in question has a choice and is not just at the survival level of existence.

The Work and Family Perspective

It is clear that for both women and men to achieve dignity, balance, and fulfillment through a wider range of roles in more humane work and family settings, societal norms need to change more than they have so far. If children learn about these new patterns of work and family when they are in the early school years and continue to do so as they progress into higher education, perhaps there will be fewer divorces. Many women who work outside the home today place a high priority both on family and motherhood. Increasing numbers of men also indicate a high priority for family and some for the father role as well, as Gilbert (1988) and others have demonstrated. However, we need to understand better how different types of families influence their children's development through their child-rearing practices, values, and daily living patterns.

Interventions That Work

"Perceived fairness"—the notion that roles are not identical or equal but are perceived by partners in two-earner families to be fair—may be helpful in working out mutually satisfying relationships. Factors causing partners to change in Henze's (1984) study were the wife's increased work responsibilities; changes in societal attitudes and media; assertiveness courses; and marriage counseling.

The Values Analysis instrument was developed to help families explore the impact of public policies and help them consider both internal and external aspects of work-family dilemmas. Such a tool is helpful because economic and social factors create barriers for two-parent families and single-parent families as well (Walker, Rozee-Koker, and Wallston, 1987). The traditional values analyzed by the authors are family autonomy, minimal government intervention, separation of work and home, and sex-typed division of labor—four areas dissonant with contemporary working families. We need a social policy that does what Kanter (1977b) called for almost twenty years ago: find ways to help work accommodate to family rather than always family to work. Changes and social supports are necessary to help all types of families function more effectively.

Spousal Support

Spousal support (especially from the husband) has been identified as a key factor in making two-earner families work. It involves taking pride in a spouse's abilities and achievements, listening empathetically, providing emotional support, and having nurturing qualities. Strategies that can help partners cope include cognitive restructuring, increased role behavior (taking on additional tasks), and structural and personal role redefinition. These can be accomplished through such techniques as marital enrichment, stress management, and value clarification, which offer valuable ways to improve marital relationships and mental health (Gilbert and Rachlin, 1987). Unfortunately, these are treatment rather than prevention strategies; they do not deal with the larger issues including the need for changes in societal attitudes, socialization patterns, child-rearing practices, and workplace policies.

Changing Men's Attitudes

Effecting changes in men's attitudes and affective skills is another kind of intervention needed to facilitate work-family linkages. The workplace is traditionally the setting where male achievement needs are primarily met. But as their position in the workplace continues to change, some men are angry as they see others taking jobs that they perceive to be theirs. They find that in midlife they are losing what they once thought were lifetime jobs.

The slowly growing men's movement is helping increasing numbers of men find greater fulfillment through development of the relationship and nurturing side of their personalities. As Dwight Moore (1984) pointed out, we rarely teach men the value or skills of emotional expressiveness. Through his study, Moore demonstrated that men can learn to express emotions in more effective ways. Part of the task is to help them recognize that there are benefits for them as well as for women in egalitarian family patterns.

Although the changes in the workforce are causing considerable pain for some men (at least initially), others find that they feel liberated from the expectations of being the sole provider, having one job for life, and seeing work as the center of life. The old equation of "work equals self-esteem" may be replaced as men gain the opportunity for more holistic and balanced lives through greater involvement in nurturing, shared roles, and family time.

Work-Family Role Models

It could be argued that we have a few more role models in the United States today of men and women who are successfully negotiating the work-family connection. For example, the newspaper comic strip *Sally Forth* is about an employed young mother, Sally, her working husband, Ted, and their daughter, Hilary, and the amusing and not-so-amusing problems that occur for this working family. One headline reads, "Can Sally Forth find happiness as a working woman, wife, and mother?" (However, I don't recall a comparable question being asked of husband Ted.)

Career counselors probably can identify real-life role models trying to work out new roles and relationships as well. The more famous power figures come to mind, including Ted Turner and Jane Fonda, Bill Clinton and Hillary Rodham Clinton, Bob and Elizabeth Dole, and Jimmy and Roslyn Carter. But both Elizabeth Dole and Hillary Rodham Clinton quit their careers to support their husbands' political careers. The top leaders still send the message that it is the wife's job to play second fiddle to her husband. Remember the silly 1992 campaign ploy to portray Hillary Clinton as a cookie baker? Or how the public denigrated her when she was given a major role in attempting health care reform? A great opportunity to have a new type of working family in the White House—a president with a professional wife and equal partner—was missed. In 1995 Hillary Clinton was devoting her energies to the important issues of children and families. However, these are issues traditionally regarded as the First Lady's domain.

Perhaps it is better to look to more ordinary people. How about that young couple, Jean and Jim, who have creatively developed new family rules and egalitarian ways of treating each other and thus model the kinds of behavior they hope their children will learn? Or Betty and Bill, who have a traditional family. Betty has never worked outside of the home but regards herself as administrator of the home—the most important job she could have—and believes she has an equal relationship with her husband. Or how about Jennifer, the woman once denigrated for being a single mother, who raised four children alone, supported them through college, and now is a happy grandparent?

Career Development Program Goals

Miller (1994) offers seven goals for career development programs that career counselors and other helpers can use to strengthen the family-work connection:

1. Increase awareness of current trends and demographic information describing changes in the family-career connection.
2. Increase understanding of developmental stages for both individuals' career development and for family development.
3. Identify overlapping family-career developmental stages that create particularly heavy role demands for individual family members.
4. Provide strategies for dealing with or reducing family-career role conflicts that involve accommodation by all family members.
5. Identify barriers to the family-career connection and develop an awareness of individual, family, employer, and community strategies that can reduce these barriers.
6. Identify benefits for both women and men that can result from the successful combination of family-career roles.
7. Develop a family-career plan.

These goals serve admirably as a framework for Integrative Life Planning, especially in relation to family and work. Miller (1994) also offers a number of strategies for career counselors who are working with two-earner families:

- Develop materials on trends in work and family.
- Provide role models of both women and men who have successfully adapted to career and family roles.
- Use activities such as role-playing, case studies, and simulations to help men and women personalize trends and test various role options.
- Provide awareness experiences for parents to understand emerging career and family role options and their feelings about them.
- Offer conjoint family-career counseling for married couples and for couples considering marriage to help them examine gender-role expectations, negotiate roles, and develop cooperative strategies for dealing with role conflict.

If work and family are to connect successfully, and if men and women need to engage in mutual planning and integrative life planning, they must have realistic expectations of each other and their careers and families, a strong commitment to making both work and family *work*, and the will to negotiate and compromise. They also need to seek support to help them deal with stress (including support groups, counseling, and seminars) and to develop patterns for making transitions over the life span (O'Neil, Fishman, and Kinsella-Shaw, 1987).

Stages of Family and Career

Besides being aware of the career stage of each partner, it is important to be aware of the stage through which the family is moving. That is, are they establishing the relationship; having their first child; dealing with school-age children, adolescent children, or adult children; living in an empty nest; grandparenting; caring for aging parents and grandkids? Again, Maslow's (1962) hierarchy of needs can be applied to families as well as to individuals. A family must attend to survival needs (food, shelter, and clothing) before it can worry about self-actualization, lifestyle, or meaningful career choices. A family is also concerned about transporting children (to school events, to the doctor or dentist), arranging work schedules, avoiding or managing marital stress, and changing gender-role attitudes. Career patterns are affected by the stage the family is in.

These are a few of the factors that affect work roles and family roles and make it necessary to think not only about occupational career planning but also about life planning. There is no question that level of income affects the overall standard of living and that some benefits accrue to two-earner families (again, their overall average family income is higher than other family types). But stress and conflict may be the result if new approaches to career planning and family decision making are not used. It is essential that families do mutual planning that takes into account the needs of each partner, the relationship, the children, the workplace, and the community. Integrative Life Planning helps them do this.

Life Planning Perspective

A number of suggestions can be made for changing work-family roles and relationships. Integrative Life Planning offers the following strategies for thinking about life planning:

- Move from planning for job only to planning for life roles and learn how they relate to each other.
- Move from fitting in to the future to creating the future.
- Move from role separation to role flexibility.
- Change the focus from achievement (self-sufficiency) only to achievement and relationships (connectedness) for both women and men.
- Move away from dominant/subordinate relationships toward equal partnerships.
- Move from rational decision making alone to include intuition and spirituality.
- Do not expect stability; rather expect and manage change and transitions in individuals and in both family and work.
- Move from fragmentation to wholeness.

To facilitate work-family integration, we also need to identify new knowledge, attitudes, and skills for both women and men. Career professionals must help women and men to do the following:

- Understand aspects of their own development, gender-role socialization, and stereotypes that may affect their life planning.

- Become familiar with demographic trends and environmental factors that may influence future life planning.
- Clarify their life role values and priorities regarding work and family and develop action plans to implement them.
- Think integratively and creatively about how to achieve shared roles, role flexibility, and role interchangeability.
- Understand and anticipate transitions, dilemmas, and conflict areas they may face at different stages of work and family.
- Become aware of internal and external barriers to new work-family patterns and try to reduce them in themselves, their families, and in their work organizations (as well as in society).
- Become aware of the place of spirituality (purpose, meaning, and hope) in integrating their life plans.

Conclusion

Connecting family and work is a critical task that contains many facets. Different family types, roles and relationships, and individual, work, family, and community issues are involved. Because the family-work connection has been so often overlooked in career development practice, it is time that it took center stage. We can no longer afford to focus only on fitting people into jobs, on the connection between work and learning, work and education, or work and leisure. A crucial task will be for career professionals to help clients, students, and employees understand the relationships between the choices they make about family and work and to help them implement those choices and decisions with maximum benefit to themselves, their families, and their communities.

Connecting family and work has been a missing piece in the career development and planning quilt. Career professionals will need to bring the link between the two into greater consciousness and help their clients and employees make these connections as well. They also will need to recognize the diversity of family patterns in different cultures and, through education, training, and counseling, help bring about constructive changes toward more effective conflict resolution, balance, and partnership.

Chapter Six

Critical Task 4: Valuing Pluralism and Inclusivity

I suspect that for many gay and lesbian individuals, having to come to terms with one's sexual orientation interferes with career development. During adolescence and early adulthood, for example, a gay or lesbian person typically has to focus a lot of psychic energy on figuring out what it means to be gay, how to cope with it, whether to disclose and to whom, how to connect with other gay or lesbian people, and so forth. This process can easily distract one from focusing on a career. If I had not had to wrestle with the realities of homophobia and heterosexism, I think I would have been able to focus on my career development with more energy and at an earlier age.
—Gay Asian American

Another critical task for people in the twenty-first century will be to learn to deal constructively with difference. The globe is increasingly made up of diverse cultures, and the United States itself is a microcosm of cultures that deserve understanding and respect while their members are given access to and opportunity to share the benefits of a democratic society. Integrative Life Planning is a vehicle for understanding diversity. This may be one of the most difficult concepts to incorporate into the thinking about life and career planning.

Valuing Diversity

Effective interpersonal skills always have been important for people on and off the job. Of course, layoffs may occur for many reasons (currently, a likely reason is corporate downsizing). But job loss in general is more likely to occur because of interpersonal problems than because of inability to perform. Learning to value diversity is an essential piece of the Integrative Life Planning quilt. Indeed, human diversity is a sort of quilt in itself, a mosaic or kaleidoscope that changes with one's perceptions. A task of career professionals is to help their clients understand and adapt to this growing diversity as they seek to make successful decisions and choices in their workplace, whether it be in business, government, school or university, or an agency.

Reasons for Valuing Diversity

This chapter has four major objectives: to review the emerging language and concepts of diversity in order to help career professionals gain a better understanding of the meaning and implications; to help career professionals develop a worldview that allows them to function as helpers to culturally diverse people, especially those who have been outside the opportunity structure; to help career professionals understand the gender aspects of multicultural career counseling; and to challenge culturally sensitive career professionals to utilize this knowledge to help diverse clients, students, and workers in educational and organizational settings.

The term *culture* is used broadly here to denote race, gender, class, disability, sexual orientation, age, belief systems, or regionality. Career specialists need some knowledge and understanding of the commonalities and differences among diverse cultural groups, especially as they relate to career planning. They also need to understand the legal, social, political, and economic barriers that hinder people, particularly people of color and women, and the interventions in education and work that can help to reduce the barriers and enhance options.

Traditional Career Development Assumptions

Integrative Life Planning is relevant to culturally different groups for several reasons. First, it challenges traditional assumptions about career and career development. For example, traditional career planning assumes that people have choices—which we know is not true for many minority and low-income groups. Second, career theories assume that people can have control over their lives, that is, what I call "a sense of agency." This too is not true of many who have been victims of personal or institutional bias, racism, or sexism. Third, many people of color have a worldview different from the Eurocentric view, one that emphasizes the group, family, or community rather than the individual. Self-actualization, a goal of traditional career counseling, may not be as important to these people, whose career decisions may be made jointly within the family. Fourth, traditional career counseling may ignore the numerous barriers that ethnic minority members face in seeking educational and occupational opportunity. Finally, as I state throughout the book, traditional approaches to career development focus on occupational choice and ignore the multiple facets of life—the other dimensions of spirituality, gender, and race, and the other life roles within family and community. It has been recognized for some time that both ethnic minorities and women identify with a holistic approach to career, and Integrative Life Planning provides one such approach.

Connection with ILP

Integrative Life Planning incorporates some of these concepts in significant ways. The term *integrative* itself is widely used in multicultural and ethnic counseling literature (Sue and Sue, 1990; Comas-Diaz and Greene, 1994; Arredondo, Psalti, and Cella, 1993; Atkinson, Morten and Sue, 1993; and Bennett, 1993).

To integrate means to renew, to make whole by bringing different parts together. For our purposes in this chapter, we can interpret these parts to signify different cultures. To integrate also means to bring people of different racial groups into free and equal association. It also may be applied to a person, as various traits, feelings, and attitudes may be integrated into one personality. Finally, to integrate may mean to remove legal and social barriers, a mission of the larger society that is applicable to life and career planning when barriers have been ignored and may not have been addressed by career professionals.

It was coincidental that I began writing this chapter on Monday, May 9, 1994, the day that Nelson Mandela was formally elected president of South Africa. That event reminded me again of the real meaning of human dignity and democracy. Winning the fight for freedom after the repression of apartheid was symbolized in the twenty-seven year evolution from Mandela the prisoner to Mandela the president of a new union of white and black. It seemed coincidental, too, that I finished revising this chapter on the Martin Luther King holiday weekend of January 15, 1996.

Although I try to address diversity of all kinds throughout this book, I give greatest attention to race, gender, and ethnicity. This is in no way intended to diminish the importance of other cultural groups; it is merely a recognition of the impossible task of dealing adequately with all culturally different groups in a book of this nature.

A Language of Diversity

To include diversity in our ILP quilt and in our work as career professionals we need to understand several concepts and terms. It is difficult to convey adequately what I mean when I speak of the need to incorporate into our consciousness the critical issues of dignity, difference, and diversity, and how they affect life planning. Many terms are used in the ILP quilt; I describe a few here.

Pluralism generally refers to a state of many cultures, including both domestic and international (immigrant and refugee) cultures, as well as the multiple dimensions of culture, such as ethnicity, gender, disability, sexual orientation, age, and the like. *Multiculturalism* is a term used mostly in educational and counseling settings. Originally the term denoted primarily the four major ethnic minority populations in the United States (African Americans, Asian Americans, American Indians, and Latinos), a "groups approach" to studying cultural difference (also called the *emic* approach), and the universal approach, which emphasizes similarities (called *etic*). More recently, however, the concept of multiculturalism is expanding. *Managing diversity* is the expression used in business and industry to denote attempts to train workers to value difference at all levels. Although a number of terms can express a career professional's cognitive understanding of a diverse clientele, *pluralism* appears to me to be the most appropriate.

Pluralism

An acute awareness of all kinds of differences—racial, ethnic, religious, sexual, and so on—is essential to understanding the people with whom career professionals interact and the environments in which we will work and play in the future. Mario Rivas, a doctoral student, introduced me to the concept of pluralism when he was a guest speaker some years ago in my class on multicultural counseling.

Pluralism has been defined in several ways. According to one dictionary, it is "the quality or condition of being plural, or of existing in more than one part or form; the existence within a nation or society of groups distinctive in ethnic origin, cultural patterns, religion, and the like; a policy of favoring the preservation of such groups within a given nation or society; and the theory that ultimate reality has more than one true explanation." Thus, pluralism seems to reinforce the value of difference, recognize many parts, groups, experiences, and truths, and establish a context for valuing diversity.

In the counseling field pluralism refers to "a society in which members of diverse ethnic, racial, religious and social groups maintain participation in and development of their traditions and special interests while cooperatively working toward the interdependence needed for a nation's unity" (England, 1992).

Pluralism also refers to a means for optimal human development for all, a condition difficult for multicultural societies to achieve (Berry, 1990). Pluralism is a concept of changes that occur when two groups come into continuous contact with each other. Assimilation and acculturation are integral parts of the concept.

Assimilation

Assimilation is the absorption of a minority group into a larger cultural body. The individual faces questions in pluralistic societies that are answered differently depending on the cultural group he or she belongs to. Does the group value maintaining cultural identity and characteristics? Does the group value maintaining relationships with other groups? Depending on how one answers these questions, one may end up in a state of marginalization, separation (that is, keeping a strong ethnic identity), assimilation (that is, losing one's own culture and participating in the larger culture), or integration (that is, maintaining one's culture *and* participating in the larger culture). The latter is considered the most psychologically healthy alternative (Berry, 1990).

Acculturation

As the number of immigrants and refugees in the United States continues to increase dramatically, it is important to understand to what degree these new members of our society wish to become assimilated. *Acculturation* refers to working out relations with those who are different in a community. It also refers to the process of adaptation to a different culture. As people pass through the stages of acculturation, they may change their attitudes, behaviors, and ethnic identity. The ways in which groups deal with what Berry (1990) called "psychological acculturation" depends on such factors as the voluntariness or involuntariness of the contact and the kind of population group in question, including migrants, immigrants, sojourners, or refugees. Individuals—even within a family—vary in the acculturation experiences they have.

Acculturative Stress

Acculturative stress can result in suicide, alcoholism, and drug abuse. Societies that are more open to multiculturalism will exert less stress with less pressure to change, less prejudice, and less discrimination. They will also be more likely to offer social networks and support groups.

An individual's "cognitive control" over the acculturation experience is very important. For example, immigrants or refugees might feel a sense of control when they get off the boat or plane or cross the border to a new land. What is the likelihood of congruity between their aspirations and their attaining those aspirations in the new culture? These concepts are important to mental health and career development and to securing changes in national institutional policies for satisfactory acculturation to take place.

The concept of acculturation provides a useful perspective in that it helps career specialists see relationships between acculturation and pluralism and brings important meanings to the idea of attending to diversity in our work as helpers (Williams and Berry, 1991). It becomes especially useful as we work with career and life planning issues with immigrants and refugees.

My introduction to pluralism, acculturation, and diversity was not academic. Growing up in southern Minnesota as the daughter of a working-class Norwegian immigrant father and Norwegian American mother, I played with children from the Mexican family who lived just down the alley from us and was not aware of any difference. However, my awareness of pluralism grew in junior and senior high when, as editor of the school newspaper, I became friends with the kids in journalism class, most of whom would be going on to college. In contrast, my traditional parents expected me to go to secretarial school "to get a job until I got married." Then one day my principal said, "Sunny, you should go to college" and he arranged for me as class salutatorian to receive the scholarship the valedictorian would not be using—because she did marry right after graduation. Thus, while my neighborhood was a multicultural one, the difference I became most aware of was socioeconomic.

Issues of acculturation and assimilation also surfaced. My parents both spoke Norwegian and we observed some Norwegian traditions at home, but my father was determined to become part of what was then called the Melting Pot. He wanted to be absorbed into American culture; he wanted to become an American citizen. But in this Norwegian Lutheran and Irish Catholic town, I was also surprised at the prejudices that existed between the two religions.

Building Interpersonal Relationships

Developing positive interpersonal relationships has always been an important component of the broad concept of career and life planning. Accepting and valuing the growing pluralism of the workplace is certainly part of the new paradigm for life planning. Although such issues have been addressed at least since the 1960s and 1970s with the passage of such initiatives as the Civil Rights Act, Title IX, affirmative action, and other equal opportunity laws and executive orders, discussions of the issues were likely to be framed in terms of racism, sexism, ageism, and so on.

Although we do not want to avoid the continuing reality of these issues today, the call is for more positive approaches. We call for accepting, valuing, and celebrating diversity. However, there is also a backlash in the 1990s, with some Americans believing that ethnic minorities, women, and other "special groups" have received too much special treatment, especially through affirmative action, and have taken jobs away from those characterized in the press as "angry white men." I believe that as long as we maintain dominant/subordinate worldviews and cultures, these attitudes will continue to present barriers to progress toward an egalitarian society. They will also continue to limit the career development and life planning options of those who are perceived as different from the majority.

Multicultural Counseling

A problem with the term *multicultural* is that because different people define it in different ways, it is difficult to know what is meant by the term. Early definitions emphasized race and ethnicity, and some theorists still prefer to limit the definition to those topics. However, others argue that the concept of multiculturalism, like pluralism, must include all those who are oppressed because of differences. Multicultural counselors face several other issues as well. Gama (1991) makes a case for multiculturalism to be integrated into all psychological systems when she says: "Multiculturalism is a metatheory in the sense that its basic assumptions should underlie all the content areas of psychology whether theoretical or applied. In other words, it is not only generic to counseling but a basic precondition for the correct understanding and explanation of human behavior. All psychology and all counseling must be multicultural" (pp. 3–4).

Multicultural Assessments

An important issue in multicultural counseling is how we assess clients and cultures. There is considerable awareness of the limitations of many standardized tests when administered to multicultural populations. A number of instruments have been developed, however, to measure the competencies and attitudes of counselors in training on several dimensions of diversity. One such instrument is the Multicultural Awareness-Knowledge-Skills Survey (MAKSS), which is useful both in the preassessment of trainers and in evaluating the impact of multicultural training on graduate students (D'Andrea, Daniels, and Heck, 1991). Using a Likert scale format, counseling trainees are asked to express their knowledge of and agreement or disagreement with statements about all kinds of diversity. Numerous other multicultural assessment instruments are described in detail elsewhere (see Ponterotto, Rieger, Barrett, and Sparks, 1994; and Ponterotto, Casas, Suzuki, and Alexander, 1995). Fouad (1993) and others point out the pitfalls of assessment with multicultural clients.

Racial-Cultural Identity Development

It is important for counselors in general and career counselors in particular to understand the concept of racial-cultural identity development (RCID). Various versions of this stage theory have been developed by multicultural theorists to help counselor trainees understand clients better and to assist professionals in perceiving their own cultural identity stage and that of others. In addition to the original work on racial identity development by Cross (1971) and Helms (1984), other authors such as Atkinson, Morten, and Sue (1993) described how individuals move through the stages of viewing themselves, viewing others of the same minority group, viewing others in other minority groups, and viewing those in majority groups.

The stages at which both the client and the counselor find themselves may affect the helping relationship and its outcome. RCID is becoming a large area for exploration in multicultural counseling and it is also of importance in life planning. RCID offers a means to help students or clients become culturally aware of their own biases, values, and assumptions about human behavior and their own worldviews and to help them look at oppression. It is also an excellent assessment tool (Sue and Sue, 1990).

"White Privilege"

Another concept that has been useful in helping white students or clients understand their own whiteness or racial identity and can help career professionals as well is Peggy McIntosh's (1988) paper called "White Privilege and Male Privilege: A Personal Account of Coming to See Correspondences Through Work in Women's Studies." In her powerful and insightful personal statement, McIntosh traces the process by which she came to see that her race gave her unearned advantages relative to the African American women in her building and line of work. She lists forty-six circumstances and conditions of privilege whose benefits she was taught not to recognize. They include (pp. 5–9):

> I can if I wish arrange to be in the company of people of my race most of the time.
>
> I can avoid spending time with people whom I was trained to mistrust and who have learned to mistrust my kind or me.
>
> I can go shopping alone most of the time, pretty well assured that I will not be followed or harassed.
>
> I can turn on the television or open to the front page of the paper and see people of my race widely represented.
>
> I can be sure that my children will be given curricular materials that testify to the existence of their race.
>
> I can arrange to protect my children most of the time from people who might not like them.
>
> I am never asked to speak for all the people of my racial group.
>
> I can remain oblivious of the language and customs of persons of color who constitute the world's majority without feeling in my culture any penalty for such oblivion.

If a traffic cop pulls me over or if the IRS audits my tax return, I can be sure I haven't been singled out because of my race.

I can take a job with an affirmative action employer without having my coworkers on the job suspect that I got it because of my race.

I can choose public accommodation without fearing that people of my race cannot get in or will be mistreated in the places I have chosen.

I can be sure that if I need legal or medical help, my race will not work against me.

These are only twelve examples out of forty-six, but cumulatively they are thought-provoking and reflect unearned advantage and conferred dominance. It is interesting that McIntosh arrived at this understanding of her own white privilege status through the realization of men's unwillingness or inability to acknowledge their privilege. She observes several layers of denial about both male privilege and white privilege and calls for greater awareness of how these advantages affect our daily lives. The question to be asked, McIntosh suggests, is, "Having described white privilege, what will I do to end it?" It can be a powerful workshop, class, or training experience to have white students, clients, or employees write down their own lists and to have students or clients of color write down what they see as "white privilege" and discuss these in dyads or small groups.

While many of these concepts are presented in the context of multicultural counseling, they are also appropriate for those who do multicultural career counseling, because so many of the concepts address important human development aspects that affect career development and life choices—issues of aspirations, bias, discrimination, assessment, and identity, to name a few.

Multicultural Career Counseling

In the broad definition of *career* used in ILP, one may not find many differences between general multicultural counseling and multicultural career counseling. Yet a small body of literature has emerged on the latter. A special section on this topic appeared in a recent issue of the *Career Development Quarterly* (Leong, 1993).

Several articles point out the problems of assessment, especially interest measurement and test bias (Fouad, 1993); the need for different strategies for intervention with different ethnic minority groups; the use of culturally appropriate counseling process (discussed especially with regard to Asian Americans); and the inclusion of both programmatic and individual training interventions.

Career-Relevant Characteristics of Ethnic Minorities

Because of the unique characteristics of ethnic minority cultures, traditional career counseling may be inappropriate. Such characteristics frequently include focusing on family rather than the individual; valuing cooperation over individualism and competitiveness; finding goals of instrumentalism and self-actualization incompatible with family and community goals; perceiving bias in the career counselor; being uncomfortable with techniques such as direct eye contact, confrontation, physical distance, and so on; making assumptions about women's and men's roles; preferring holistic worldviews to fragmented ones; resenting assumptions that all persons within a group are alike; and so forth.

It can be assumed that once we become sensitive to cultural differences—our own and others—we probably will be better career counselors. Knowledge of the contrasting values of Western and Eastern cultures—as in the grid by Kluckhohn and Strodtbeck (1961)—provides a context for both counseling and career counseling.

Exhibit 6.1, an adaptation of the original Kluckhohn and Strodtbeck Value Orientations Model (Carter, 1991), illustrates cultural value differences that are likely to affect how one views oneself, one's role in the world, one's options, and families, organizations, and one's purpose in life. All relate to career development and life planning.

Criticisms of Multicultural Career Counseling

Critics cite the limitations of multicultural career counseling for "visible racial/ethnic group people." This expression, often shortened to VR/EGs, was created to encompass African American, Native American, Latino, and Asian American people and is

Exhibit 6.1. Kluckhohn and Strodtbeck's Value Orientations Model with Alternative Solutions.

Orientation		Alternative	
Human Nature	*Evil:* People are born with evil inclinations. Control of evil behavior is the only hope.	*Mixed:* People are both good and bad at birth.	*Good:* People are basically good.
Person/Nature	*Subjugation-to-Nature:* People have little control over natural forces. Nature guides one's life.	*Harmony-with-Nature:* People are one with Nature. Nature is one's partner in life.	*Mastery-over-Nature:* One is expected to overcome natural forces and use them for one's own purpose.
Time Sense	*Past:* Traditional customs are of central importance.	*Present:* The past and future are of little importance. Here and Now events are most important.	*Future:* The temporal focus is on planning change for events that are to occur.
Activity	*Being:* Emphasis is on activity that is spontaneous self-expression of emotions, desires, and impulses.	*Being-in-Becoming:* Emphasis is on the self-expression aimed at integration of the personality through control.	*Doing:* Emphasis is on action-oriented self-expression, which is measurable by external criteria to the acting person (for example achievement).
Social Relations	*Lineal:* Lines of authority are clearly established and dominate subordinate relationships.	*Collateral:* Individual goals are subordinate to group goals (collective decision making).	*Individualism:* People are autonomous of the group. Individual goals are more important than group goals.

Source: Carter, R. T. "Cultural Values: A Review of Empirical Research and Implications for Counseling." *Journal of Counseling and Development,* 1991, *70* (1), 164-173.

currently believed to be preferable to *minority*. The phrase offers "a culturally relevant perspective for understanding the career paths of visible racial/ethnic group people" (Carter and Cook, 1992, p. 192), but it can be cumbersome if used repeatedly. For a detailed description of preferred terminology, see Atkinson, Morten, and Sue (1993).

Among the reasons that traditional career theories are of limited usefulness with multicultural populations are the following (Carter and Cook, 1992):

- The theories are based on research with white middle-class males.
- The models are based on Euro-American cultural assumptions.
- The theorists and their models ignore the sociopolitical and psychological realities of this group.
- They ignore economic and social circumstances that affect most VR/EG people.
- They ignore the cultural institutions that may serve as "social equalizers" of vocational talents not recognized in the dominant culture.

Need for a Systems Perspective

A systems perspective—viewing the system as an organized whole and each part within the system as interdependent on other elements—is an appropriate way to study these groups. Barbara Okun's (1984) holistic conceptual model of adult career development is a positive example of ways in which individual, family, and career life cycles can be integrated. Because Euro-Americans developed racial and cultural ideologies that determined the roles and functions of VR/EGs, career options of the latter have been subject to social, economic, educational, political, and cultural limits and restrictions. Their career paths are shaped by historical-cultural backgrounds and sociocultural circumstances and often begin with family rather than the individual. In spite of the promises of equal employment opportunities in the wake of the Civil Rights Movement, innumerable psychological, economic, and sociopolitical obstacles persist to limit career opportunities for these groups (Carter and Cook, 1992).

Ethnic minority women are hurt by distorted images of gender roles and negative stereotypes—especially African American and Native American women, who suffer from a "double burden" of racism and sexism—and other forms of gender-related prejudice and discrimination in the work world. Professionals offering career counseling to these groups are urged to examine their own basic assumptions about how the skills, interests, and abilities of members of diverse ethnic backgrounds are expressed, experienced, and valued and to be at all times mindful of within-group differences. Further, the career professional's task is to understand each VR/EG person as a new challenge along with the many variables, systems, and processes that influence his or her career path (Carter and Cook, 1992).

A Sociological Perspective

Hotchkiss and Borow (1996) discuss sociological issues in the career development of ethnic minorities and women. They examine such issues as the new structuralism (the ways in which the structures of the workplace are changing), race and gender effects, motivation for work, and status attainment (the ways in which parental status affects the status of offspring). Youth are especially affected by educational and occupational opportunities or the lack thereof. Minority youth can be assisted with career planning through optimizing chances for completing schooling; strengthening work-related attitudes, information, and skills; and using relevant community resources. The career specialist's role as advocate is stressed.

L. Alvin Leung (1995) calls for a pluralistic perspective in career counseling and urges researchers, scholars, students, teachers, and other helpers to question the validity of current theories, techniques, and strategies used in the profession. He criticizes current models of career counseling as not considering the effects of social and economic barriers on the career behavior of minority individuals, barriers that have limited both actual and perceived alternatives available. He also cites the limitations on the degree of control ethnic minorities have over their lives, in part because many come from a disadvantaged socioeconomic background.

Leung presents a useful model for career intervention that is based on three modes of intervention and two outcome areas. The interventions are individual, group, and systems; the outcomes are career-related and education-related. Noting that most career counseling is one-to-one, he makes a strong plea for systems interventions, in which all participants in a system (such as teachers and counselors or managers and consultants) work collaboratively in the intervention so that it is not just a single-strategy approach.

Multicultural Career Interventions in Organizations

Career planning and coaching or counseling with diverse persons in the workplace is another area of interest. Wigglesworth (1991) emphasizes the importance for career development and human resource professionals to convey respect, personalize knowledge, show empathy, be nonjudgmental, develop role flexibility, demonstrate reciprocal concern, and develop tolerance for ambiguity in this domain. Managers and employees need to know some of the culturally specific characteristics that influence minority persons in the work environment; these include cultural differences in perception, physical distance and space preferences, time orientation, body language, listening and articulation, high- and low-context communication patterns, and conflict resolution styles.

Race Relations and Career Dynamics

Another important issue is how race relations influence career dynamics (Thomas and Alderfer, 1989). Of special importance is the bicultural life structure of racial minorities—especially black Americans as they struggle to adapt to the dominant organizational culture. The link between racial identity and career development is a strong one; relationships between racial minorities and mentors and sponsors are significant. The issue of gender generally has been subordinated to race in the workplace, as in much of social science research.

For several reasons, potential tensions exist in research on minority careers in the workplace: (1) there is an emphasis on professionals and managers rather than blue-collar workers, (2) descriptions of the experiences of various minority groups besides blacks are needed, (3) the special position of minority women is often overlooked, (4) both comparison studies of whites and minorities and within-group studies are needed, (5) research has been done in predominantly white versus minority-dominated systems, and (6) there is a need to study minorities both as subordinates and as superiors (Thomas and Alderfer, 1989). For people who plan to conduct further research on career development in the workplace, these suggestions can serve as a starting point.

Flexibility in the Workplace

In organizational career development and management, several new ideas have emerged to help organizations address both workplace diversity and work-family issues, including assisting organizations to develop new assumptions about change and new strategies for increasing workplace flexibility.

Some suggest that, rather than expecting programs of "managing diversity" and "work and family" to help individuals only, corporations should view them as initiatives that offer a strategic advantage. Hall and Parker (1993) introduce the theory of "workplace flexibility," meaning "attention to the 'whole' of the employee's life (including work-life issues and issues of difference) and investigation into creative ways of enhancing the fit between people and their work roles" (p. 6). They see this as a strategy to enable employees to express both their identities (as women, Latinos, and so on) and their roles (caretakers of children or ill parents, volunteers, and so on) that they have outside the workplace. Hall and Parker have found that more flexibility in the workplace results in lower absenteeism, higher morale, reduced turnover, and improved productivity. Allowing diverse employees to have a voice has resulted in cost cutting as well as the opportunity to capitalize on intelligence and enhance creativity and cooperation among work groups.

According to a survey of four hundred human resource executives, flexibility in the workplace has become widespread in U.S. corporations. Policies include unpaid childbirth leave beyond the normal period (85 percent of companies surveyed offered); part-time work for hourly or nonexempt staff (85 percent offered); flextime (77 percent); unpaid family leave for kincare (75 percent); unpaid parenting leave for men and women (53 percent); flexplace, or the opportunity to work at home or some place outside of the office (29 percent); sabbaticals and career breaks (24 percent); and phased retirement (22 percent) (Hall and Parker, 1993, p. 10).

The survey also revealed that the firms most likely to be flexible have certain common characteristics. They are large (more than ten thousand employees and over $1 billion in sales); they have a high percentage of women workers and employees under age thirty; they are publicly owned and have a high percentage of contingent workers; and they have cutting-edge management philosophies. Three-fourths of survey respondents said the flexible work arrangements were either very positive or positive.

Hall and Parker (1993) suggest that workplace flexibility should be built into the fabric of work organizations and their benefits. Work-life programs and diversity programs should become part of a total system, infused into all organizational functions. This focus would produce more equitable treatment of employees and less concern that some workers (such as women and ethnic minorities) get more benefits than others. Among the major benefits of such a development would be the movement away from the old management philosophy of mechanically fitting human beings into an organizational machine toward a focus on individual differences, the whole person, and the needs not only of diverse cultures but also of diverse family types. It is even likely that the corporation and corporate image would benefit most from this emphasis on flexibility.

Among corporations moving toward this kind of flexibility are Corning of New York and General Electric. Corning's flexibility program includes race and gender awareness training; child-care services and extended family-care leaves; community-oriented projects that are attractive to African Americans; career planning systems for all workers; workplace flexibility tied to management performance ratings; and attention to different employee learning and working styles. Career professionals need to know about these kinds of workplaces because they affect the diverse work and family patterns of today's workers.

Developing Careers Through Valuing Difference

Some organizations are teaching workers to develop their own careers by increasing their self-direction and self-reliance, getting them involved in cooperative problem solving to get the work done, and valuing their differences. "Valuing differences is the work of purposefully focusing on differences in order to help employees learn how to capitalize on differences as a major asset to their personal growth and company productivity" (Walker, 1996, p. 1). In this approach, differences become critical agents of learning, self-discovery, and building productive relationships in the workplace.

This strategy can help individuals explore and chart new career paths. Leaders of these training classes try to create open, safe environments where participants can learn to communicate, be their true selves, learn about differences, develop new mind-sets, and learn "perspective taking," that is, understanding the perspective of the other. They use the technique of storytelling, that is, they learn to share their personal stories with others. In small discussion groups of seven to nine persons they take on four distinct tasks: (1) erasing stereotypes, (2) probing for differences in assumptions of others, (3) raising their own levels of personal empowerment by 'devictimizing,' and (4) proactively building authentic and significant relationships with people they regard as different. People in these groups are willing to be vulnerable, take risks, and reach out to build relationships. They also become aware of dilemmas, change, complexities, and ambiguities.

Other activities used to help employees shift their ways of approaching career development include win-win conflict resolution training, efficacy-type programs, empowerment workshops, mentoring and coaching programs, celebrating differences events, and intercultural communication programs. One of the assumptions underlying these activities is that since workers no longer have the security and stability they used to enjoy, they need to develop new ways to feel safe and learn through relationships. They are seen as a means to help workers find meaning, connection, and community in their lives and work. The relevance of these principles and programs to career professionals and to ILP must be evident.

Valuing Differences at Digital Equipment

A program on valuing differences that seems almost too good to be true has been implemented at Digital Equipment Corporation, a worldwide computer and network provider founded in Massachusetts in 1957. Employees are encouraged not to avoid but to pay attention to their differences, to raise their comfort level with differences, and to capitalize on differences as a major asset to the company. The basic philosophy is "the broader the spectrum of differences in the workplace, the richer the synergy among the employees and the more excellent the organization's performance" (Walker and Hanson, 1992, p. 120).

Digital's program includes a wide range of activities similar to those described in the preceding section. There are awareness and skills training, development-of-leadership groups, support groups, celebrating-differences events and, most important, core group dialogues (core groups are those who have remained with the company after other workers were laid off). The latter are open and candid conversations about topics formerly considered taboo, including race and gender issues. In intensive two-day workshops, employees learn to struggle openly with their prejudices and begin to discuss other topics regarded as taboo in the corporate world, including bonding, intimacy, and love. The goal is to empower everyone through valuing differences.

Digital's goal is to develop strategies for integrating workers from very divergent cultures. The word *diversity* is used to refer to three separate kinds of work: affirmative action and equal employment opportunity, multicultural work, and values and empowerment work. This work may be affected by recent downsizing.

Several fundamental concepts underlie Digital's approach:

- Dialogue is key to personal growth and change.
- To stay in dialogue, people must feel safe.
- There is no substitute for investment of time.
- People are motivated to learn about differences when they see it as an opportunity for personal development.
- The pivotal work is personal empowerment.

In evaluating the program, the corporation reports some specific advantages it has gained:

- A reputation as one of the best places to work
- Empowered managers and leaders who empower others

- Greater innovation
- Higher employee productivity
- A role as an effective global competitor

Although some of the data is anecdotal, the program seems to have had an extremely positive effect in a company that is trying to use networks to replace hierarchies, achieve participative management, include everyone in the organization's thinking and decision making, and increase productivity through synergy, interdependence, and empowered relationships. Career professionals working in a variety of types of organizations can learn from the kinds of strategies for change employed in this business.

Gender Factors in Multicultural Career Counseling

Gender factors can be discussed as part of general multicultural counseling, but for our purposes they will be discussed primarily in relation to career counseling because there is a close connection between the two. Career counselors using the ILP framework also need to be aware of gender factors in multicultural counseling, especially since these factors often have been ignored. There is some controversy over whether the worlds of women and men can be seen as true cultures of their own with specific role definitions, standards, and values. Still, a review of the multicultural counseling literature shows that little attention is given to gender. Furthermore, in texts where culture is identified specifically with race or ethnicity, there is little discussion of gender differences or gender socialization. In fact, where gender is acknowledged, it often has been treated stereotypically, with certain problems identified as typical for women of a particular cultural background, such as alcoholism or suicidal tendencies in black women, submissiveness in Latinas, or silence in Asian women. And although there is a considerable and important body of literature on African American men, the topic is usually approached as one of race rather than gender.

Limitations of Textbook Representation

Several limitations have been identified in the multicultural counseling literature, especially models and texts that present a stereotypical and deficit perspective about ethnic minority women and lead counselors to view such clients in terms of their ethnic group association only. According to Arredondo, Psalti, and Cella (1993), "Such a unidimensional approach ignores the totality of the female experience in terms of how these women think and feel in relation to their life experiences" (p. 6). Cultures are described as giving less freedom to and placing less value on daughters than sons and as expecting women to be submissive to men. The authors point out, however, that such characteristics may change depending on rates of acculturation into the larger society. They state that "there is need to attend to women's individual differences within and across cultural groups; to the interaction of cultural and gender socialization; to forces of sexism, racism, and homophobia and their impact on identity, esteem, and empowerment; and to the portrayals of women in the multicultural counseling literature" (p. 5).

Emerging Literature on Gender and Culture

Although it is important to understand that race is the most salient characteristic for most people of color, gender is certainly central in every culture and career professionals need to be aware of this. Many women of color for years have considered race to be a more important factor than gender and have been especially critical of white feminists. But more recently, just as unique issues related to black males and other ethnically diverse groups are being recognized, issues specific to females also are being examined.

Among theorists who have been addressing gender issues as a factor in culture are Oliva Espin (1985), Lillian Comas-Diaz (1991), Patricia Arredondo (1992), Farah Ibrahim (1991), Elizabeth Gama (1992), and Johnnetta Cole (1986). Comas-Diaz and Greene (1994) powerfully discuss ethnicity and gender in counseling and therapy with women of color. Hansen and Gama (1995) provide a comprehensive analysis of gender factors in multicultural counseling, with historical and sociopolitical arguments and suggestions for counseling, systems interventions, and research.

Myers (1986; Myers and others, 1991) has formulated the Optimal Theory of Identity Development. According to this theory, the view of the individual self moves from a narrow definition to a broad, inclusive one with a holistic worldview. It is possible, for example, for an elderly African American woman to use her African American identity, her female identity, her elderly identity, or any of these combined configurations as opportunities for self-knowledge.

Gender and Ethnicity

It is important to examine the relationship between gender and ethnicity. Focusing specifically on Mexican American and African American women, Davenport and Yurich (1991) discuss the socialization effects of ethnic culture in connection with the self-in-relation theory of gender development. Citing Epstein (1973), they point to the importance of studying both gender and ethnicity, with the two being the "dominant statuses" that determine other statuses (Davenport and Yurich, 1991, p. 70).

Chinese American women also have unique issues to deal with in counseling. The traditional Chinese male-dominated system dictates a "past orientation," including honoring and maintaining tradition and authority. Chinese American women may face cultural or social isolation if they express interest in pursuing nontraditional career areas or changing the balance of family responsibilities. Many traditions, values, and belief systems make it extremely difficult for Chinese American women to achieve equality with men. Yang (1991) refers to the disadvantaged state of Chinese American women as "triple jeopardy," subject as these women are to the cultural impediments of a patriarchal mind-set, problems due to racial and sexual differences, and the stress and strain of loss of cultural identity and living in two cultures. And because Chinese American women are seen as members of a "model minority" that is succeeding without career distractions, professionals may ignore differences among members of this group. Counselors of Chinese American women need to examine the personal and vocational impact of their clients' heritage, including "help-seeking behavior patterns, available support systems, and gender role and work role attitudes" (p. 357).

Multiple Identities

There is little doubt that people who have been oppressed because of their race, religion, or ethnicity will likely specify that identity as most important. However, the important point is that at different times in their lives, because of new awarenesses, new roles, or new experiences, people are likely to emphasize one identity more than another. My own experience provides an example. Through social studies courses in high school I developed a strong sense of social justice and started writing editorials on the issues of the day, such as prejudice. Although I felt social class discrimination, I never was oppressed because of my ethnicity. My identity as a Norwegian American has always been important to me, and its importance was reinforced through a wonderful study-abroad program called SPAN (Student Project for Amity among Nations) I got into in college. Through the program, I was able to trace my Norwegian roots. Gender identity became more important to me in my mid-twenties when I considered going for a Ph.D. For the first time in my awareness, I experienced gender bias in higher education. It is important for career helpers to be aware that different pieces of one's identity may surge in importance or subside depending on age and circumstances.

Definitions and Interventions

Arredondo, Psalti, and Cella (1993) offer a gender-inclusive definition of multicultural counseling that is holistic and encompasses the various dimensions of a person's identity, including cultural membership, historical phenomena, sociopolitical forces, and cultural context: "Multicultural counseling is a process built on self-awareness, knowledge about cultural identity formation, individual dynamics of difference and power, that considers persons as total entities in the context in which they reside and/or have been socialized. Furthermore, multicultural counseling respects that personal culture includes various dimensions of identity including gender, religion, sexual orientation, race and social class" (p. 12). Professional associations have since the 1970s begun to define competencies and set standards for multicultural counseling (Sue, Arredondo, and McDavis, 1992).

Courses on both culture and gender are another type of intervention. For example, a course such as "Asian American Women: Identity Development Issues" integrates issues of racial and cultural identity development with gender identity development (Ibrahim, 1992).

Ibrahim and Kahn (1984) created the Scale to Assess World Views (SAWV), an instrument designed to assess beliefs, values, and assumptions on five variables originally identified in the Kluckhohn and Strodtbeck (1961) value orientations grid. The instrument is useful to help researchers and career and counseling professionals understand the concept of cultural worldviews (see p. 165; see also Ibrahim, 1991).

Tradition and Morality

One last issue that affects women across cultures needs to be mentioned. There is a tendency to assume that all culturally specific customs, values, belief systems, behaviors, and traditions are sacrosanct and that counselors must respect them. Brazilian psychologist Gama (1991) addresses this well when she says: "There are certain behaviors and their associated values, beliefs and attitudes that, although traditional or common among certain cultural groups, are morally wrong. And moral principles are universal and applicable across cultural boundaries. More specifically, I would mention the various forms of abuse that women are subjected to in the Arab world and in many Latino and Asian cultures. Some of the underlying assumptions are that women are inferior, incompetent to make decisions and run their own lives, emotionally unstable, and that their sexuality is evil, etc. Obviously, the effects that such assumptions may have in anyone's perception of self must be devastating" (p. 4).

Gama points out further that in these situations the dominant group abuses other groups and expresses a lack of respect for human freedom and dignity. For example, there is male domination in most Latino cultures (including wife abuse), domestic battering in the United States, restriction of women's freedom in many Arab countries, poor treatment for the Untouchables in India, sale into marriage of young girls in the Hmong culture, and the surgical clitoridectomy practice in some African and Arab cultures.

Because a culture accepts a practice does not guarantee that its assumptions, traditions, or behaviors are right. Counselors must be aware of the underlying ideological assumptions and social-psychological implications of such situations for the client, especially if that client challenges these traditions. And even when

counselors understand how these morally wrong cultural traditions, values, and beliefs are historically constructed, they should
not accept or recommend that clients accept and submit to them
in the name of tradition or cultural uniqueness. However, when
challenging deeply accepted traditions, it is important not to cause
a breakdown in communication with the client (Gama, 1991).
These issues are discussed further in Hansen and Gama (1995).

Empowerment

Much of the counseling literature designed to help counselors assist
their female multicultural clients is found under the topic of *empowerment.* Judith Lewis has created many empowerment workshops for
women, as has Patricia Arredondo. Arredondo's monograph "Promoting the Empowerment of Women Through Counseling Interventions" (1992) describes how some of her women clients define
empowerment for themselves in her workshops.

There is some disagreement in the counseling literature about
the meaning of the word *empowerment,* but a number of researchers
are beginning to conduct research to define it. McWhirter (1994)
provides a definition that can be useful for counseling in general,
for multicultural counseling, and for multicultural career counseling with women and men: "Empowerment is the process by
which people, organizations, or groups who are powerless or mar-
ginalized (a) become aware of the power dynamics at work in their
life context and (b) develop the skills and capacity for gaining
some reasonable control over their lives, (c) which they exercise,
(d) without infringing on the rights of others, and (e) which coin-
cides with actively supporting the empowerment of others in their
community" (p. 12).

No matter how it is defined, the issue of empowerment is
extremely important in counseling women and men of all backgrounds; furthermore, personal and interpersonal relationships
are the core of an individual's empowerment.

Inclusivity

Inclusion means to have or consider as part of a whole. The opposite, as we know, is exclusion—a tendency to exclude all or certain

groups for social or economic reasons. For many years women and many ethnically diverse groups were excluded from such organizations as golf clubs, men's luncheon clubs, service clubs, professional associations, and professional honorary societies. Although these organizations were not all deliberately exclusionary, through tradition or sometimes unaware leadership, certain groups were invisible or minimally represented among them.

Exclusivity

Society excludes people in many ways. Sometimes it does it systematically on the basis of gender, race, class, ethnicity, disability, age, or sexual orientation. Examples come to mind with little difficulty:

- *In leadership.* In education, business, and government women and people of color find barriers, such as glass ceilings and cement floors.
- *In communities.* Individuals are systematically excluded from housing and social organizations on the basis of some perceived difference.
- *In curriculum and knowledge creation.* Especially in schools and colleges, the basics and Eurocentric knowledge are preeminent, and positivist logic and methodology are often considered the only ways of knowing.
- *In technology.* Only small percentages of women and minorities major in or even enter technology-related fields such as physics, engineering, and trades.
- *In economics and the workplace.* The wage gap continues, minorities and women are underrepresented, the feminization of poverty grows, and the gross national product remains the dominant way of measuring human progress.
- *In language.* Inclusivity of half the population is still denied in some influential professional organizations, publications, and parts of the media that refuse to use inclusive language.

These are just a few examples. Yet we know that in societies committed to democratic principles and values, the talents and ideas of all are needed. Universities are now requiring students to take one or more courses in cultural diversity and, as just described, business organizations are developing courses in valuing and managing diversity. However, these developments are fairly recent.

The exclusion phenomenon is described well by the phrase "the presence of absence" (Robertson, 1992). In leadership positions in organizations, the presence of the absence of many racial and ethnic minorities and women is quite visible. Robertson particularly emphasizes the absence of women and minorities in curriculum and in leadership positions in schools.

Some professional associations since the 1970s have developed guidelines for using inclusive language (the American Counseling Association and the American Psychological Association are two that have done so), declaring to their members, editors, and writers that speeches, articles, and books—anything submitted for publication—must recognize the importance of gender-neutral or gender-balanced language. Although there are still businesses and professions today that deny that either language or society is changing, progressive businesses, organizations, government agencies, professions, and religious institutions have adopted such policies and programs (Hansen, 1992).

Organizational Inclusivity

What can professional organizations and career professionals as change agents do to begin the process of moving toward inclusivity? I would like to repeat portions of my response to one organization that asked that question because I believe they may apply to any organization that is beginning to explore diversity issues. The following are some suggestions:

Listen to diverse voices. Assure that the many voices of women and ethnic minorities are heard and responded to in all parts of the system. Members and leaders need to be exposed to the excellent literature being produced by these voices through publications, in conferences and congresses, in organizational libraries, and in our own institutions. Numerous publications are available not just for women and minorities but for career professionals. There needs to be a mutuality, a respect for many voices of women and men of all colors and backgrounds sharing their experience and defining career development and related fields and defining the future.

Seek diversity of membership and leadership. Seek greater diversity both in members and leaders of organizations. It seems important to me that we find ways to create structures and procedures through which diversity—and inclusivity—can become more central themes, including wider participation in conference planning and presentations, publications, and governance.

Expand the agenda. Expand the agenda of topics dealt with in the organization's journal and other publications (including both qualitative and quantitative studies and ways of knowing) and invite diverse authors to write about them. Include topics from which women and minorities frequently are excluded, such global topics as human rights and work, women and men and the environment, the meaning of work across cultures, and men and women defining the future.

Create projects for inclusivity and partnerships. Organizations can develop major diversity or inclusivity projects to focus member and leader attention on diversity within the organization. For example, Hazel Henderson and Bill Halal of the World Future Society are organizing World 2000, a project in which they are trying to write a strategic plan for the planet (they are ambitious!), and have expressly sought gender balance and cultural diversity among the project leadership. Develop work and volunteer projects within organizations to increase understanding of the value of inclusivity, as at Digital Equipment Corporation, discussed earlier in this chapter.

Look at ourselves. If genuine change is to occur, it is most important that we career professionals examine our own attitudes and behaviors and that we look at the unintentional things we do (or neglect to do) that keep our organizations from being inclusive. It helps our own perspective when we are in touch with our own gender and racial issues, our own ethnicity, and our own attitudes about class, age, disability, gender, race, creed, sexual orientation, and regionality.

Racial Inclusivity

Inclusivity with regard to racial and ethnic minorities is of special concern. Psychologist Charles Ridley (1989) defines racism as "any behavior or pattern of behavior that systemically tends to deny access to opportunities or privilege to one social group while perpetuating privilege to members of another group" (p. 60). He suggests that racism is perpetuated by power and that minorities are extremely limited in power.

Ridley describes "adversive racism" as the negative outcomes in mental health services that ethnic minority clients are likely to experience: inaccurate diagnoses; assignment to junior professionals, paraprofessionals, or nonprofessionals rather than senior staff; low-cost, less preferred treatment; disproportionate representation in mental health facilities; a much higher rate of termination; and less favorable impressions of treatment.

Several factors adversely affect counseling for minority clients. There is unintentional racism including "color blindness" (when one assumes erroneously that a minority client is just another client: "I don't see you as being a black person") and "color consciousness," or the assumption that all of a client's problems are caused by his or her minority status.

Almost anyone is capable of behaving in a racist manner. Again, we can find examples in the events of the Los Angeles riots. However, we do not need to look that far for examples. In my own state of Minnesota, for example, we have had repugnant cases of bias against migrant Latino families who have been taunted and rejected as outsiders and Latino children who have been discriminated against in the schools. White and Parham (1990) call attention to "racism among the well intentioned," a way of describing those of us who believe we are egalitarian yet reveal otherwise by our behavior.

Two college experiences with exclusion and discrimination in my own life increased my awareness and sense of social justice. Once I took a bus trip to Louisiana with Violet, an international student friend from India. We were unable to stay at a mutual friend's house because the family considered her skin color too dark. I also felt her pain when she did not know which fountain to use when she saw the "Coloreds Only" sign on the drinking fountains in bus stations. The second experience came through the opportunity to work in the Capitol; the Washington Seminar offered college students the chance to do volunteer work with low-income children in Washington, D.C. Because we were a racially mixed group of students, we were unable to stay in common housing and ended up at the almost entirely black Howard University. I had an unforgettable experience learning what it was like to be a minority, for that is what whites were in that setting.

Age Inclusivity

One group that has not been given much attention in the career and diversity literature is older adults. Stereotypes of what older persons are like are still rampant; a growing body of literature attests to this. Older workers in particular are experiencing discrimination today, and a number of test cases have been won by people over fifty-five who have been unfairly let go because they had been judged unsuitable for retraining or unable to handle fast-paced jobs or to keep up with technology. Jobs of more mature workers have been targeted; these workers have been regarded as "dead wood." Older workers are in a double bind because they are not valued or given an opportunity to retrain, so that after they are let go they are unable to find a job in a new company (Mirvis and Hall, 1994).

A certain amount of cynicism has developed on the part of older workers as they have suffered a lot of unfair bias and discrimination. But there is some evidence that corporations are beginning to recognize that older workers can be capable, reliable, and trainable and that there may be even an economic advantage to the company to keep them, if not employed, at least employable. If corporations develop the kind of flexibility in the workplace discussed earlier in this chapter, all kinds of workers will be affected. They might create career cycles in which older employees have an opportunity to work in all three leaves of the shamrock organization described in Chapter Three. Furthermore, in those companies that strive to be learning organizations, increased opportunity for older adults may develop (Mirvis and Hall, 1994).

If career helpers are to address issues of inclusivity in our organizations and the larger society, we will need to emphasize that *different* is not *deficient*, whatever the nature of the difference. We have begun to make some progress in the United States. Many businesses and corporations are adopting a managing diversity agenda as part of their training and development programs. But there is still much to do. Before we can manage diversity, we need to understand it, value it, and at the highest level celebrate it. I believe constructive changes will come but will require time, energy, values change, and commitment from all of us, including those of us who work in the career counseling and human resource professions.

There is agreement in the multicultural literature that to understand diversity and to help shape these changes, career counselors must start with themselves, their own cultural and ethnic identity, and their own prejudices and biases. As Cross (1971), Helms (1984), and Atkinson, Morten, and Sue (1993), among others, suggest, the most important thing we can do as career counseling professionals may be to look carefully at our racial and cultural identities—no matter what race we are—and refrain from viewing multiculturalism as though it is something that applies only to those who are different. Although Euro-Americans have often been left out of the emerging multicultural counseling theories and models, some leaders in this growing field have included them. We need a vision of inclusivity.

Challenges for Culturally Sensitive Career Professionals

What do we do with all this information about relating pluralism, multiculturalism, and career counseling; valuing diversity; and striving for empowerment and inclusivity?

Obviously, as career professionals we are not going to be able instantly to reduce racism, sexism, or ageism, or free people of prejudice and bias, or intervene in organizations to facilitate the human development of all. The Integrative Life Planning approach acknowledges that attaining such goals takes a lifetime, as does acquiring the skills to accomplish them. They are emotional, complex, and sometimes unattainable; they may be the hardest piece to add to our quilt.

I also recognize that career professionals are not the sole source of change; there are some things that we alone cannot change. The economic system, housing patterns, health care, institutional racism, and power and wealth distribution are societal issues requiring political, legal, social, and policy initiatives over time. But we can work on our own cultural sensitivity and try to create the kinds of family, work, and learning environments we envision for a more inclusive society. So here are eight challenges to get started on.

1.   *Increase your self-awareness.* Become aware of your own unique cultural and ethnic background and your own racial identity and understand how these affect your development and attitudes toward others.

2.   *Learn to value difference.* Develop sensitivity to and understanding of cultures different from your own. Through multicultural counseling training or diversity training, learn to value those differences.

3.   *Increase your knowledge of other cultures.* Seek to increase knowledge about and understanding of the different dimensions of diversity. Learn *from* as well as *about* people from these backgrounds.

4.   *Increase your knowledge of barriers to career development for culturally different people.* Read the abundant literature about the barriers to development, including racial, gender, legal, social, and political barriers, and commit to trying to reduce them in order to assure equality of opportunity in education and occupation.

5.   *Seek opportunities for cultural immersion.* Know that one of the best ways to learn about and understand a culture different from your own is to immerse yourself in it. Immerse yourself in a culture different from yours through study, service, relationships, and work experience in that culture.

6.   *Develop improved intercultural communication skills.* Seek training in intercultural workshops or other vehicles to develop the kind of interpersonal and communication skills that will help you to deal with and value all kinds of difference. Model cultural sensitivity in your attitudes, words, and behaviors.

7.   *Work toward integration.* Integrate cultural sensitivity into your personal and professional life. Use integrative techniques as a career helper to assist diverse clientele to integrate the parts of their lives. Seek connectedness with rather than separation from people who are culturally different from you.

8.   *Work for social change.* Work to eliminate all forms of racism, sexism, classism, and all the other "isms" that prevent social justice and create barriers to the development of human beings. Lead interventions to enhance options for culturally different populations, that is, offer ILP workshops or become a mentor to someone who is culturally different.

Conclusion

Learning to accept and value all kinds of difference and to help establish norms of inclusivity are probably the most challenging of the critical tasks identified in Integrative Life Planning. In all spheres of living, including our workplaces, we will need to welcome opportunities to work with and get to know people who are different in some way from ourselves and to use the occasions to learn both from and about them. As career professionals, we need to examine assumptions and practices, to understand the language and concepts of pluralism and diversity, and to become agents of change to increase access of opportunity for all persons; in short, we must become advocates and not just agents of the status quo.

In our organizations, we need to promote the workplace flexibility that will make work environments more comfortable for all. We need to be aware of people's multiple identities and the intersection of race, gender, and class. And we need to work for a more inclusive society—educational systems, work organizations, agencies, communities—and strive to eliminate stereotypes, bias, and discrimination. The challenges for culturally sensitive counselors and career professionals are to be positive agents for change, to make the promise of democratic societies more available to all. The work that needs doing in this task locally and globally will take not only energy and skill but also a commitment of the heart.

It is appropriate to close this chapter with a quote from Rosa Parks, the African American woman who became a heroine of the civil rights movement because she ignored the rules relegating blacks to the back of the bus and took a seat in the front because she'd had a tiring day. Her act became a catalyst for change, and she perseveres in defense of civil rights today. Parks reflects a central theme of ILP when she says: "There is work to do; that is why I cannot stop or sit still. As long as a child needs help, as long as people are not free, there will be work to do. As long as an elderly person is attacked or in need of support, there is work to do. As long as we have bigotry and crime, we have work to do. . . . We have come so far since the days of segregation, but there is always something to do to make things better. All human beings should have equal opportunities" (1994, p. 72).

Chapter Seven

Critical Task 5: Exploring Spirituality and Life Purpose

The rainbow is a metaphor for my life. I do not know what my future holds, but I know that I love my life and who I have become. I would like my life to continue to grow with purpose. I want to become all that I was destined to become, and I want to enjoy every moment of the becoming. . . . As we disengage from the past and grow and experience new ways of being and becoming, life gives us never-ending opportunities to grow and explore. I want to experience the reality of the rainbow. I want to live in "positive uncertainty," knowing that whatever life may bring, I am a part of the rainbow. I do not want to live my life looking for safety but living all of life's possibilities.
—Adult woman in career development class

The fifth critical task of Integrative Life Planning is to emphasize the spirituality that often has been ignored in career and life planning. Spirituality is central to many people, although it may not always be a conscious center. In addition to the aspects of life planning we have already reviewed—a global context, a search for wholeness, an emphasis on career development for both sexes, the family-work connection and ways to integrate it, the need to respect and value differences in a pluralistic society—we need to include this often neglected dimension.

Spirituality, Religion, and Counseling

Spirituality, an important piece of the ILP quilt, along with the related concepts of meaning and purpose in work, is discussed in this chapter. Just as counselors and career professionals need to understand the place that spirituality plays in their clients' life decisions, they need to understand it in their own lives as well.

This chapter examines several aspects and definitions of spirituality in relation to career planning. The spirituality piece of the quilt is a difficult one to define but it is increasingly important as people seek to deal with change and ambiguity, trauma and crisis, and oppressive barriers in their lives. Spirituality may serve as a source of hope for people who are seeking meaning and purpose.

A considerable body of literature has emerged on spirituality and counseling (Bergin, 1988, 1991). There is some evidence that clients care more about the spiritual and religious aspect of their lives than do their helpers. In a review of literature, Bergin (1991) found that while 90 percent of the American public believed in God in some form, only 43 percent of psychologists did. Similarly, a Gallup poll found that two-thirds of twenty-nine thousand persons surveyed said that religion and spirituality were "the most important" or "very important" aspects of their lives. According to the 1990 *Statistical Abstract of the United States,* 142 million citizens belong to religious bodies that have a membership of fifty thousand or more (Pate and Bondi, 1992). Further, Kelly (1995) found high agreement with the concept that spirituality does not require participation in a religious organization and that mental health professionals, while not expressing their spirituality through traditional religiousness, expressed "high consensual affirmation of values stated in spiritual terms" (p. 6).

We do not have specific figures regarding the beliefs of career professionals. We do know that the traditional models of career planning, usually taking the trait and factor or person-to-environment-match approach, have not paid much attention to spirituality.

In psychological counseling spirituality has been viewed as taboo. As one examines cultural values, as we did in Chapter Six, contrasting views of human beings, relationships, and the environment suggest that cultures that focus on group, family, and community are more likely to emphasize the spiritual aspects of life than those that focus on the individual. As counselors deal with increasingly diverse populations, it is important for them to have an awareness of spiritual and religious beliefs and how they affect life decisions (Pate and Bondi, 1992).

Defining Spirituality

Spirituality has been defined in many ways, in both religious and secular contexts. It is important to distinguish spirituality from religion. *Religion* usually refers to organized religion and an engagement in beliefs and practices through church, temple, synagogue, and so on. In contrast, although *spirituality* may refer to beliefs and a worldview, it does not necessarily imply any organized religion. It merely assumes a higher power outside of oneself. Yates (1983) defines spirituality as "the core of the person—the center from which meaning, self, and life understanding are generated" (p. 60). Boorstein (1980) sees it as "the experience of integration and wholeness, irrespective of religious belief" (p. 124). Kratz (1987) defines it as "the deep integration, wholeness, a sense of the interrelatedness of all of life" (p. 4). The theme of wholeness is conveyed by all three. Although many individuals do express their spirituality through religion, organized religion is not the focus of Integrative Life Planning.

For some, spirituality is a way of life. Thomas Moore (1992) believes that many kinds of spirituality exist. He approaches spirituality as care of the soul. "*Soul* is not a thing but a way of experiencing life and ourselves that has to do with depth, relatedness, value, heart, and personal substance" (p. 5). Spirituality may take various forms as well. There is a spirituality of transcendence—a quest for higher principles—and a spirituality of place—a feeling conveyed by a tree, animal, or stone. Family also conveys spirituality, with its rituals, gatherings, and storytelling. Some see spirituality as harmony with nature and the universe while others find expression of it through rationality or intuition or even higher levels of consciousness. Still others see spirituality mainly as a sense of community and a concern with the ultimate values of meaning and wholeness, as does Redfield (1993) in *The Celestine Prophecy.*

Spirituality and Career

Only in the last decade has spirituality become associated with career. It certainly has not been a common word in public academic institutions with their emphasis on scientific knowledge, objectivity, and empiricism, especially because it cannot be observed or measured. Except for those who work as pastoral counselors or in religious settings, the idea of career counselors dealing with matters of the spirit was usually foreign. The traditional theories of vocational choice and career development tend to stress the rational, cognitive information aspects of career and to avoid issues of meaning and purpose.

It is not clear when the scope began to broaden. Some suggest that it began in the 1950s with the shift from psychology as pathology to psychology as positive human development, especially with the work of Carl Rogers and Abraham Maslow. Practitioners have been writing about spirituality more than have career development theorists. The National Vocational Guidance Association (now the National Career Development Association) has had a special interest group on "work and religious values"—recently rephrased as "work and spiritual values"—since the early 1980s, when the United States seemed to experience a surge of interest in spiritual concerns. Concern about the materialism and self-centeredness of the national character and growing feelings of alienation and isolation led to a search for "new rules" in a "world turned upside down," as Yankelovich (1981) labeled it. A number of writers and practitioners in the career field began discussing the topic more directly in the mid 1980s, variously using the different terms *purpose, meaning,* and *spirituality,* and conducting workshops focused on spirituality's relation to work. In the mid 1990s, as the breakdown of families and communities, crime, domestic violence and other kinds of violence gain increasing public attention, there seems to be a new openness to including spirituality as part of career and life planning.

Let us look first at the relationship between psychology and spirituality.

Spirituality and Psychology

Some psychologists caution us from linking spirituality too closely with psychology. Some feel that the quest for scientific status has kept counselors from addressing spiritual belief issues. Others do not believe the ego-centered focus of psychology is compatible with the spiritual search for the transcendent. Some professionals blame rigid spiritual beliefs for psychological problems. There is also concern that if counselors discussed spirituality, they might impose their particular values on clients (Mack, 1994; Worthington, 1989).

Although spirituality has not been foreign to the field of psychology, counseling and psychology texts have not always emphasized that some of the leading psychological theorists have themelves expressed spirituality, usually in the form of a search for something outside oneself or a search for wholeness. We are aware that conceptions of psychology and spirituality differ from one culture to another; most of those discussed in this chapter are Western rather than Eastern views.

In a study of women and spirituality, Kratz (1987) identified a number of psychologists who have either directly or indirectly dealt with the topic of spirituality. In a detailed analysis of the work of Viktor Frankl, William Gould (1993) discussed the major psychologists and philosophers who had an impact on Frankl and vice versa. Mack (1994) also cites early theorists. These include Carl Jung, whose theory of individuation is that the life process is one of achieving wholeness through a synthesis of conscious and unconscious aspects of the self, and psychiatrist Victor Frankl and psychologist Adrian van Kaam, who were existentialists who looked critically at issues of purpose and meaning, freedom, choice, suffering, and mortality. Mack also mentions contemporary theorists with a focus on spirituality, including Carl Rogers, whose self-actualizing theory is thought to reflect spiritual attainment in calling forth powers of the universe, and Erik Erikson, whose eight life stages from infancy to older adulthood offer opportunity for continual spiritual conversion. Other psychologists, including William James and Rollo May, also clearly speak to the topic of spirituality and meaning.

A few psychological theories encompassing a link with spirituality are relevant to Integrative Life Planning.

Spirituality and Meaning

Psychiatrist Viktor Frankl's (1963) theory of logotherapy grew out of his own experience in Nazi concentration camps. He dealt with the spiritual dimension of human existence through his own search for meaning. He suggested that *logotherapy* (with *logos* connoting not only "meaning" but also "spirit") is a means to help individuals find what is meaningful in their lives. He believed that psychological symptoms stem from lack of meaning and lack of worthwhileness of life. Gould (1993), in a recent analysis of Frankl's impact, suggests that "meaning analysis" can be a resource for rethinking what it means to be more fully human and for discovering meaning in life. Frankl believed that, through the spiritual dimension, a person can find meaning in every circumstance of life. Thus, logotherapy may be especially helpful to those seeking meaning and purpose in their lives.

Spirituality and Self-Actualization

Probably most well known for his hierarchy of human needs and concept of "peak experiences," humanistic psychologist Abraham Maslow also has contributed to the literature on spirituality and meaning. For Maslow, as for Frankl, meaning is tied to values. His theory of the self-actualizing person, although sometimes blamed for the hedonism and materialism of the 1960s and 1970s (Yankelovich, 1981), is a very optimistic and positive view of human nature. It is a holistic model that emphasizes mind, body, and spirit, "a true integration of the person at all levels" (cited in Gould, 1993, p. 132).

Maslow sees spiritual values at the core of our being. He believes that "they propel us to make choices that allow for our full development as human beings and at the same time to come more into harmony with nature" (cited in Kratz, 1987). He believes that self-actualizing people have a greater acceptance of self and others. They are more spontaneous, other-focused, self-detached, egalitarian, and honest in relationships, and they are able to experience pleasure and joy. Peak experiences, though relatively rare, bring people in touch with the spiritual parts of themselves and allow them to perceive the world as a unified and an integrated whole; such experiences also bring people closer to their unique individuality or real self.

Spirituality and Wholeness

A discussion of spirit and meaning would not be complete without a reference to Carl Rogers, who sees human wholeness as a pattern of relationships and urges a phenomenological approach to understanding the self "from the inside." As both a humanist and an existentialist, Rogers tries to establish a holistic sense of being by interweaving beliefs, feelings, perceptions, and values. He emphasizes the subjective processes that lead to self-actualization and to an authentic and congruent self. Although he is not identified with career counseling, Rogers's empathetic view of the whole person, self-acceptance, and ability to change, as well as his emphasis on interpersonal relationships, may be an important piece of a career counselor's repertoire. It is also relevant to ILP.

Spirituality and Personal Values

Another psychologist who contributes to our understanding of spirituality is Gordon Allport. Allport (1961) believes that personal values are the dominating force in life and that all of a person's activity is directed toward the realization of one's values. Allport also wrote about the pursuit of meaning. His six aspects of maturity, which encompass some qualities not unlike Maslow's self-actualized person, include "a sense of self that extends to include all the areas of human existence—family, education, religion, politics, and so forth . . . and the ability to find a meaning or purpose that gives life unity despite tensions, ambiguities, and paradoxes" (cited in Gould, 1993, p. 140). Allport describes an "energized self which welcomes the future rather than being dominated by the past" and realizes that life's conflicts often prevent one from making simple choices (p. 139). He pays special attention to "intentionality," or acting with purpose; the need to mature and grow; and key roles of spiritual and moral values.

Spirituality and Development

Developmental psychologists—in particular, Erik Erikson, Lawrence Kohlberg, and Carol Gilligan—also have contributed to thinking about spirituality, although they are not explicitly identified with this topic. Kohlberg's (1970) structural-developmental stages of development, built on concepts developed by Piaget, and Gilligan's (1982) challenge to them with her "ethic of care" are two examples of these.

Although Kohlberg's (1981) concept of the first five stages of moral reasoning are in the context of natural laws of human social order, the sixth stage appeals to universal ethical principles and seeks answers to such spiritual questions as "Why live?" Although the seventh stage is not always included in descriptions of Kohlberg's work, it is a "cosmic" orientation that integrates universal principles of justice with a view of life's ultimate meaning. According to Kohlberg, its essence is the "sense of being a part of the whole of life" (p. 234).

Gilligan (1977), a student of Kohlberg's, challenged the appropriateness of the six moral stages for women. She sees women's perception of self embedded in relationships with others, driving their concern for others with compassion and care in an ethic of responsible love. Kratz (1987) sees Kohlberg's seventh stage as bringing his and Gilligan's theories closer together, combining abstract principles of justice with the feminine injunction to love responsibly. Although Gilligan did not explicitly discuss the spiritual implications of her theory of women's development, her work gave credibility to the concepts of relationships, caring, and connectedness, and set the stage for an understanding of their different ways of knowing.

Erik Erikson's (1964) eight stages of ego growth and identity crises developed through a psychodynamic framework also relate indirectly to spirituality. His seminal work emphasized the importance of care, the ongoing care for and nurturing of others. In his psychosocial theory, he identifies ego integrity (versus despair) as a central challenge of growing old. He sees a person who has attained integrity as aware of the relativity of all the various modes of living humans employ to find meaning in their lives. For him, integrity occurs around the age of sixty-five and is associated with retirement. It refers to a sense of completeness or wholeness. The developmental process that he terms "generativity" entails gaining a sense of oneness with humankind. It implies a sense of commonality and harmony with others, as well as caring and giving to other people. Clearly, these psychological views relate to the themes of Integrative Life Planning.

Spirituality and Empiricism

Although the American Psychological Association includes the group Psychologists Interested in Religious Issues (PIRI), and the American Counseling Association has a division called the Association of Spiritual, Ethical, and Religious Values and Issues in Counseling (ASERVIC), it has not been easy to mainstream spiritual development into the study of the human being. This is especially so in career development and counseling.

Although some psychologists see science and spirituality as similar in their basic goals, others refuse to accept that there are ways of knowing other than the scientific logical positivist approach. Futurists such as Willis Harman and Howard Rheingold (1984) challenge the existence of an objective and a subjective reality. Although scientists claim objectivity, the futurists maintain that science actually is built on the subjective experience of scientists. Frank (1977) calls both the scientific/humanistic worldview and the transcendental/religious worldview "belief systems," with both serving to order reality and help satisfy human longings for greater understanding and awareness.

As we confront the global, national, and local issues of the twenty-first century, it is likely we will all need to call on our inner resources and on different ways of knowing to find and understand the ultimate meanings and purpose in our life course. It is also likely that researchers and psychologists will need to recognize both qualitative and quantitative ways to seek truth.

Now let us move from theories to real-world issues that relate to the need for emphasis on spirituality in our career development practice.

Spirituality, Values, and Materialism

For many people, values substitute for spirituality as a guiding force in their lives. *Values* are defined as things we prize, cherish, or put value on. Although work values and life values may overlap, life values are not always associated with work. For example, Exhibit 7.1

lists *achievement* as both a life and work value while *authenticity* is a life value alone. Almost every career planning textbook or workbook offers an exercise on work values and life values. Work values tend to reflect qualities valued on the job, while life values come from other parts of one's life.

For many professionals, too, values are the closest they come to spirituality or meaning. In a sense, even this concept is helpful because they can go beyond the narrow examination of interests, aptitudes, and abilities to explore issues that are closer to meaning in life.

From Values Clarification to Values Realization

Three decades ago, Raths, Harmin and Simon (1966) defined *values clarification* as a process in which people identify something they prize and cherish—something chosen freely, from alternatives, and after consideration of alternatives—and then act on it repeatedly and consistently. They stated that values motivate our needs. More recently, Simon and Simon (1996) have conducted workshops on *values realization,* something quite different from values clarification. They state that values help identify our most important needs and provide a meaningful way to explore our spirituality as it relates to life choices. Values give meaning to life and help clarify purpose and mission because they allow us to understand what we most want to develop and hold onto.

Psychologist Martin Katz (1963) suggested many years ago that career decisions are choices among values and value systems. Although values are still a key part of individual career planning, with today's changing work and family patterns, it is necessary to go beyond individual values. Perhaps it is time to put more emphasis on our shared family, community, and planetary values. One limitation of the list of values shown in the exhibit is that they still assume that the individual makes decisions somewhat unilaterally in a vacuum. Let us take a closer look at how some of these values relate to work, family, and community.

Money as a Value in Our Lives

Today, especially in the United States, money has become the day-to-day symbol of most of our life and work values. But although it

Exhibit 7.1. Life Values and Work Values.

Life Values:

Physical health	Pleasure
Emotional well-being	Wisdom
Meaningful work	Self-growth
Affection	Family
Recognition	Authenticity
Security	Social justice
Achievement	Equality
Satisfaction	Societal improvement
Personal growth	Connection to others
Personal freedom	World at peace

Work Values:

Money	Security
Independence/autonomy	Recognition
Leadership	Advancement
Relationships	Personal growth
Achievement	Self-expression
Variety	Sense of duty or mission
Power	Creativity
Service	Social contribution

may seem jarring to discuss money and spirituality in the same breath, the economic self-sufficiency that money brings has to be a part of ILP thinking. In the workplace, the awarding of money is equated with confirmation of personal value and achievement. Because money—how much we have, how much we make, and our earning potential—determines our lifestyle, we need to help our clients examine the part it plays in their lives and how it relates to their other values.

Once, when I was a high school counselor, I asked a male student what his most important value was. Without hesitation, he said, "Money." Although I knew the value of money (mainly because my family had so little of it), I was a bit shocked, perhaps because putting such a blatant value on money did not fit with my social service orientation. I learned some years later that he had acted on his values by becoming a stockbroker, and a very successful one. I do not know what kind of family pattern he chose. But he may not have anticipated the kind of lifestyle depicted in this description of California stockbrokers (Edwards, 1991, p. 114): "As a group, they were the hardest-working, getting to their office before 6:30 A.M. to jump on the New York Stock Exchange, then staying into the night to track the action around the Pacific Rim. Their social lives were barren, their nervous systems shredded, but they toughed it out because getting ahead in their hardball business was measured in how many buckets of blood, sweat, and tears they were willing to shed."

Moving Away from Materialism

Yet it seems clear that values are changing and individuals are making conscious decisions to move away from material values to more existential ones even though for most people the reality of having to earn a living is always there. Edwards (1991) indicates that lifestyles such as the one described in California are as likely to occur in New York and Chicago, where the slogan has traditionally been "ambition above all." One doesn't have to look far to find other examples. In the practice of law, young partner hopefuls are expected to put in seventy- to eighty-hour weeks, with grudging time out to eat or go to the bathroom and virtually no time for social life or family.

One young associate I know works in one of the most prestigious law firms in a midwestern city. Of course, he wants to achieve partner status, and to do so means working from 7:00 A.M. to midnight, even on weekends, leaving no time for a life outside of work. The old American work ethic is alive and well in such firms where "billable hours" reign supreme and where personal and family needs in a changing society are not taken into account. (A 1995 article by Bach indicated that many women are exiting from hard-driving law firms because it is not possible for them to follow that demanding work ethic and still have time for family.) With work patterns like this, it is not surprising that individuals and couples are changing firms and even careers in order to have a lifestyle that allows them to live, that is, to blend life and livelihood, rather than just work. Edwards (1991) suggests that hard-drivers are moving from the fast lane to the middle lane. He reports on "the changing face of ambition," as many have second thoughts about getting to the top of a ladder—a ladder that may no longer even exist in many businesses.

In the same vein, a dialog continues in the media about success, with talk about different kinds of success, work satisfaction, life satisfaction, and "reinventing" or at least redefining success. Stephen Policoff (1985), like Thomas Moore (1992), points out that there are two kinds of success: one comes from making money and one comes from "doing work that satisfies the soul" (p. 34). He identifies a number of people who made career changes to find a different kind of success, many of them to positions that paid less well but increased their sense of meaning.

Matthew Fox (1994) is especially critical of the materialism driving our society. He urges that we not postpone living because of work or because of plans for buying something with the money we make. The primary value in life, he says, is "living life fully"—what I call holistic development. Fox criticizes our "work and spend" mentality in which advertising "stimulates our appetites and makes needs of wants" (p. 34). He is critical of workaholism, which he describes as obsessiveness and an inability to relax, as people work themselves into dishonesty, self-centeredness, isolation, control, perfectionism, and often a broken marriage. In his view, we need to alter employee incentives, improve wages for the lowest paid, encourage gender equality so that work at home is understood as work, preempt spiraling consumption, and establish time as a value in itself. He believes these changes would lead to more available work for the unemployed and underemployed and to more quality time among families.

Amy Saltzman (1991) created the term *downshifting* to describe those who find themselves overburdened and overworked and lacking meaning in life. In her interviews with successful professionals—superwomen and supermen—she discovered many who felt that their striving and seemingly successful lives lacked substance. Although many admitted that their income had far outpaced their needs, they still felt trapped by their lifestyles. "The more successful we were, the more money it seemed we needed just to stay on top of mortgage payments and maintain our expensive offices," recalled a family therapist and writer she cites. "It was hard to see the point of being successful if all it gave us was more work and less time to do the things we really wanted to do"

(Saltzman, 1991, p. 71). It is important for career counselors to help people examine their values and the place of consumerism in their lives.

Work Satisfaction

Other writers decry the lack of "fun" at work. A survey reported by John McClenahen (1991) describes the unhappiness among middle managers and first-line supervisors. More than seven out of ten women (71.4 percent) and six out of ten men (61.9 percent) embrace the sentiment, "A bad day at the beach is better than a good day at work" (p. 20). Overall, 63 percent of people surveyed about whether they were having fun at work said no and 37 percent said yes. Furthermore, more men than women found their jobs to be fun (38 percent versus 29 percent). Primary reasons for unhappiness on the job were the absence of teamwork, a "dog-eat-dog" climate, and initiative-stifling bureaucracies.

Although a third of those surveyed did not offer any recommendations as to what would make their work more enjoyable, those who did make recommendations suggested abolishing titles, working as a team, and offering more individual recognition (significantly, nonmonetary recognition) for their efforts. The survey found that people employed less than a year at their present companies were happiest, while those at the other end of the experience spectrum (sixteen years or more with the same firm) were least happy.

The size of the firm also made a difference. Companies with more than a hundred employees had "more scowlers than smilers." McClenahen pointed out that fun and commitment are created by "organizations that have a clear purpose, organizations that recognize that people at different stages of their careers need different things, organizations that recognize that not everyone is motivated to get to the top, and give people an opportunity to expand their skills" (p. 22). Some observers believe it is organizations like these that are making the 1990s different from the 1980s. (It should be noted that most of those surveyed were of middle-class and professional or managerial workers.)

Money is a special issue for single persons, especially single mothers, so many of whom live in poverty and whose primary need is to survive. It is also particularly problematic for the long-term unemployed, who include many ethnic minorities. Some interesting articles recently raised important questions about money: Have you got enough? Is there enough for everyone? Is money the only security? Can we ensure that everyone has enough to survive? Does pursuing wealth always mean exploiting others? Why do so many relationship problems revolve around money? How much is enough? (Durning, 1991). There is increasing public indignation about the gap between rich and poor in the United States as the public becomes aware of the salaries paid to leading athletes, movie and television stars, corporate executives, and trial and corporate lawyers while also learning about the increasing percentages of homeless and people in poverty.

Reassessing Values

Money even comes to have a different meaning in white-collar families when the main income producer has been fired or laid off. Many formerly comfortable families have been forced to rethink— or perhaps think for the first time—about the meaning of money in their lives as they wonder if they will be able to pay the mortgage, keep their house, make car payments, or send their children to school. With the loss of income, they are forced to take stock of assets and liabilities and, more important, their life goals and values, where they are in relation to them, and how the significant persons in their lives will be affected by the changes they have undergone. Such ruminations sometimes result in a reprioritization of values. Questions such as "What can I do and what do I want to do to make a real difference?" may be replaced by questions like, "What will I need to do to survive?" and "Can I live a life of voluntary simplicity?"

Environmentalist Alan Durning (1991) warns that consumerism and consumerist values are endangering the planet. Durning challenges the level of consumption the earth can support, citing examples from transportation, diet, and raw materials, and suggests that the main determinants of happiness in life are unrelated to consumption. He believes the greatest satisfaction is with family life, especially marriage, which is followed by satisfaction with work, leisure, and friendships. (Of course, if you don't have work, you don't have to worry about being satisfied with it.) In all, one's standard of living is determined by economic needs, values, and earning power.

Social Class and Consumerism

Jonathan Freedman notes that once "above the poverty level, the relationship between income and happiness is remarkably small" (cited in Durning, 1991, p. 48). Durning is especially disenchanted with the proliferation of shopping centers (indeed, some 93 percent of American teenage girls engaged in their favorite pastime, shopping, at such malls in 1987) and government policies that promote high consumption. He believes that too many forces in society nurture acquisitiveness. He eloquently describes a life of "sufficiency" rather than "excess," which he believes "offers a return to what is, culturally speaking, the human home: to the ancient order of family, community, good work, and good life; to a reverence for excellence of skilled handiwork; to a true materialism that does not just care *about* things but cares *for* them; to communities worth spending a lifetime in" (p. 49).

Nora Gallagher (1992) observes that each generation has an attitude toward money that is forged "in the economy of its youth." Social class seems to be a phenomenon that few wish to discuss, even though it may be more important for people than gender or race. Although I grew up during the Depression in a family with minimal income, I never thought of my family as poor. We lived in an apartment and we had enough food and clothing. I knew that my father did not have enough money to pay the medical bills incurred after my mother underwent major surgery at the Mayo Clinic, but he made regular payments. It wasn't until junior high school that I became aware of the existence of the upper class as I learned about those people living on the other side of town—far from where we lived and from the packinghouse where my father worked.

When I began dating, I recall feeling embarrassed when my dates brought me home to the door of our apartment on the alley. I don't think I ever invited anyone in. I believe it was my experience growing up in an apartment and never in a house—not materialism—that has made living in a home of my own so important to me. The opportunity to get a good college education has made it possible for my family to have a lifestyle very different from that in which my husband and I grew up. (I always remind the children about the alley.) Career professionals may make use of their own experiences and personal stories to explore socioeconomic and lifestyle issues with their clients.

Gallagher (1992) makes insightful comments about money and its effect on us. The economy, she says, "is the soup we live in, and when it is going well, it forms a backdrop as invisible as air. When it starts to fail, we notice as quickly as we notice a lack of oxygen" (p. 54). Although monetary fear affects us all, she points out that during the recession of the early 1990s, unlike in 1929, every family felt its own hard time as a personal defeat rather than as a tremor that was part of a general economic earthquake. She observes that layoffs are particularly pernicious because they single out certain people, "as if it were a question of someone being excluded from a lifeboat" (p. 54).

Lifestyle

Because in many families it is taboo to talk about money, many of us do not understand how our parents and grandparents felt about money. Yet it is a huge driving force in our lives that determines where we live, how often we move, what food goes on the table, and what expectations we have. It underlies the family's emotional life, informing, affecting, and shaping it (Gallagher, 1992).

An important statistic is that the median family income in the United States in the 1990s is almost exactly the same as it was in the early 1970s. Economic shifts have produced conflicting expectations from generation to generation. Although the belief that each generation will do better than the one before it is ingrained, as the economy declines, increasing numbers of adult children remain dependent on their parents, with some returning to the formerly empty nest and causing family conflicts. Since information about money is mixed up with "emotional baggage," fear, envy, shame, and guilt may make talking about money difficult.

Indeed, as the gap between the affluent minority and the desperately poor continues to widen, the middle class may disappear altogether (Ehrenreich, 1992). Already, being middle-class in the

1990s does not mean the same thing it meant in previous decades. Ehrenreich emphasizes today's inequitable situation in which nine out of ten Americans pay higher taxes than they did before the Reagan era, while the top 10 percent actually pay less. Middle-class used to mean owning your home, being able to put your children through college, and affording a family summer vacation. It no longer assures any of those things.

Alternatives

Some groups are experimenting with simpler living styles. The New Road Map Foundation in Seattle is trying to teach people to get off the consumer track. Ralph Nader (1992) suggests that action for social change must rest on a new economic base. He suggests that "service credits," "care shares," or "time dollars"—essentially bartering systems or exchange of services at the grassroots level—should represent a new kind of money. In Norway and several other countries, barter has become fairly common (you fix my teeth and I'll fix your plumbing).

In *Money and the Meaning of Life,* Needleman (1991) describes the connection between the pursuit of money and the wasting of time. While people strain to set aside time for things they feel to be humanly important (being with loved ones, studying, enjoying nature, engaging in creative activity), more and more they find it to be a losing battle. Yet what is at stake in the loss of time is the loss of our being, our human presence, in the midst of life. His message is that if you stop buying things, you will need to spend less time earning money; if you borrow, share, buy used goods, volunteer, and accept charity—and work on community and neighborliness— you will gain more time in your life. He says that with time comes being, and money, ultimately, must be grounded in being.

Such profound thoughts are important as career professionals think about individuals and families, self-sufficiency and connectedness, and community and spirituality, all within the framework of ILP.

Guides Toward Spirituality

Mogil, Slepian, and Woodrow (1992) offer additional insight when they assert that money now provides our security because many of the basic institutions that traditionally provided security—extended families, neighborhoods, religious organizations—have broken down. In the United States especially, which has few safety nets—that is, no national health insurance, limited unemployment insurance, a low minimum wage, a regressive tax system, few means to stop plant shutdowns and relocations, a challenged social security system, and inadequate pension systems—it is no wonder that people feel insecure.

Kulin (1991) offers an appropriate message to career professionals who wish to help clients explore the meaning of money and spirituality in their lives: "Money was once a means whereby balance could be maintained or restored within a community. We need to find that function for it again. But only by finding a center of balance and order in ourselves can we establish a new harmony, both inner and outer. The experience of true fulfillment and richness is found within; the outer world may then be helped back to health by this new inner order" (p. 53).

Spirituality and Work

A number of contemporary writers from a variety of disciplines are beginning to address the changing nature of work, although few link work with spirituality. Few of the current career development textbooks deal with the subject of spirituality, although some address the question of purpose and meaning. Although perspectives in career psychology and in industrial/organizational psychology are changing, most of these books are written from a traditional point of view. For example, in addressing the changing nature of work, authors in Ann Howard's (1995) substantial volume overwhelmingly address changes in the context of employment, technology, human resources and personnel selection, and performance appraisal.

Others do attempt to analyze connections between certain parts of life, such as work and family or family and organizations (Zedeck, 1992). Some career development texts (such as Brown, Brooks, and Associates, 1996, and McDaniels and Gysbers, 1992) are beginning to address work-family issues and the connection between life roles, including work and leisure, but these often do not directly deal with issues of spirituality.

Hall and Mirvis (1995) bring an organizational management perspective to the meaning of relationships and spirituality in the workplace. Focusing on lifelong learning, workplace flexibility, and self-development, they note that interesting and challenging work is not the end-all of self-development and that time with family and other personal development issues (including the spiritual) may be important. They state, "If we can set aside the idea that 'self-actualization' is the pinnacle of human motivation, we make room to consider whether community, transpersonal connectedness, and even spirituality are the transcendent aims of human development" (p. 355).

Reinvention of Work

Theologian Matthew Fox (1994) offers a definition of spirituality and work in his comprehensive discussion of the reinvention of work: "Life and livelihood ought not to be separated but to flow from the same source, which is the spirit, for both life and livelihood are about Spirit. Spirit means life, and both life and livelihood are about living in depth, living with meaning, purpose, joy, and a sense of contributing to the greater community" (p. 1). Fox brings a perspective to the work issue that is quite different from that of most career professionals yet his view is relevant to those involved as career helpers looking toward the twenty-first century.

As McClenahen (1991) reports, few find satisfaction in work or balance in their personal and professional lives. Like Moore, Fox urges us to overcome feelings of insecurity, isolation, and alienation by engaging in "soul work," which combines intellect, heart, and health and helps us have life experiences that celebrate the whole person. He proposes a spirituality rooted in the interconnectedness of all things.

Spirituality of work is based in a view that we must try to avoid *bad work* (for example, activities that encourage drug use, crime, prostitution, battering) and seek *good work* (activities that advocate human rights, reduce violence, preserve the environment, and so on), which actually contributes to "turning the cosmic wheel." Many human beings are either unemployed, underemployed, or workaholics. All are suffering in some way. A recent study reports that an estimated 870 million people around the world are unemployed, and that one-third of the world's population does not have choices about work (Reichling, 1995).

The old Newtonian paradigm that viewed both the universe and our bodies and minds as machines no longer fits. According to Fox (1994), work is "a role we play in the unfolding drama of the universe and our good work of making the cosmic wheel go round" (p. 6). Because work is at the center of many lives, unemployment leaves many people devastated. What is needed is healthy work, which, when completed, is let go of. We should go on to find work that needs doing. It is interesting to note that, coming from a very different context, that of management consulting, William Bridges (1993) also talks of finding work that needs doing instead of mourning the loss of work previously available.

We need to do both inner work and outer work—to move away from what I described as people competing for their piece of the occupational pie—to think about global opportunities rather than national boundaries. Fox would like to see work become more relational, as it was before the Industrial Revolution. He suggests that spirituality may be found in all our relations, and work is involved in all our relationships. There is so much new work that needs doing, but we need to work on ourselves (that is, inner work), on the planet (outer work), and bring both together. He is very conscious of what work does to the worker, especially when it is negative. He calls for inclusion of women and recognition of nurturing as important work to be carried out by women and men alike. Once we start paying attention to the inner needs of our species, he suggests, we will find there is no shortage of work.

Work also need to be done on the inner needs of our communities (Fox, 1994). What we need is a strong emphasis on work to prevent environmental degradation—we must go from machine to green, as it is said. *Cosmology* refers to the whole in a world that has been segmented. Indeed, there is great interdependence among professions, cultures, genders, and roles. As many have said, meaning in the universe emerges from a sense of connectedness.

For work to be reinvented, human beings and disciplines must change. For example, the field of education can be reinvented; rather than preparing youth just for jobs it can prepare youth for the work of the world. According to Gregory Bateson, unlike past work, future work will be emotionally friendly and interdependent, take a planetary worldview, not attempt to control the environment but rather be in harmony with it, and go beyond technology (cited in Fox, 1994).

Issues being raised by crises in work around the world are spiritual issues; in order for the planet to flourish, new demands will be put on and new visions will be required of workers. People need to reconnect their daily lives to the great work of the universe. We need to create new vocations, new callings, and new roles. Fox's (1994) "spirituality of work" questionnaire can be useful to career professionals in their work with clients.

When one attempts to connect work and spirituality one elicits many provocative ideas, inspiring both arguments and visions. Career professionals are likely not only to learn from this kind of analysis but to be stimulated to think about creative strategies for integrating spirituality into career planning.

Spirituality and Purpose

This section briefly describes the work of a number of authors writing about career and life planning who have begun to address issues of spirit, purpose, and meaning. Each takes a slightly different perspective. There is no comprehensive body of literature on this topic from a career development perspective. The integrative approach, as with the psychological theories previously discussed, draws on other fields of knowledge as well.

Mission, Religion, and Job Search

Richard Nelson Bolles, author of *What Color Is Your Parachute?* (1970), a comprehensive manual for job hunters and career changers, has incorporated spirituality into his writings, job search workshops, and newsletters. Speaking from a religious perspective, he describes how his Christian orientation affects life work. He discusses "mission" in life and "vocation," the older meaning of which is a calling, such as the ministry. In 1983 he wrote in great detail about "the spiritual life and your life/work" from a Christian perspective, and in 1987 he discussed how to find your mission in life, also from a Christian perspective. There can be no question that *Parachute,* which has been published annually since its first edition in 1970, has helped thousands of job-seekers and career changers.

Purpose and Wholeness

A popular holistic career planning book is *The Inventurers*. The book describes *inventurers* as those who take charge, create their own challenges, look at themselves, consider new options, venture inward, and explore. According to authors Janet Hagberg and Richard Leider (1988), "Inventurers are people who choose to take a fresh look in the mirror to renew and perhaps recycle their lifestyles and careers" (p. 4). The authors' unique contribution is a fairly extensive discussion of body, mind, and spirit, the meaning of spirituality, balance, and purpose, and pursuing one's dreams and goals. They offer a "lifestyle summary" that is an interesting way for would-be inventurers to synthesize their life story into a meaningful whole.

The Power of Purpose

It is also informative to analyze spirituality within the framework of purpose. Leider (1985) was motivated to write his book by the story of Terry Fox, a young Canadian who lost a leg to cancer at age eighteen and died two years later while running across Canada on one leg to raise money for the Canadian Cancer Society. Leider had met Fox when the author and his family were camping in Canada. Leider was clearly inspired by the young man, who succeeded in raising $23 million for cancer research.

According to Leider, purpose includes five major ingredients: (1) it provides meaning for our lives; (2) it serves as a principle around which to organize our lives; (3) it rallies our strengths around that which deeply satisfies us; (4) it clarifies our interests and our work; and (5) it often comes in unexpected forms and packages. *The Power of Purpose* clarifies "the birth of purpose" and offers numerous exercises—or "reflections"—to help individuals clarify their own purpose in life. One such reflection is The Purpose Profile, a twenty-item self-assessment on the extent to which one is living one's life with a sense of purpose.

A more recent volume on career and life renewal is *Repacking Your Bags: Lighten Your Load for the Rest of Your Life* (Leider and Shapiro, 1995). Designed for people in midlife, it also emphasizes a lifestyle rich in purpose. Marcia Sinetar, too, talks of a life with purpose in *Do What You Love, the Money Will Follow* (1987).

Meaning-Making

Career also has been defined as a path or process that has as its central task to make meaning. According to Carlsen (1988) career is "a guiding image or a concept of a personal path, a personal significance, a personal continuity and meaning in the order of things" (p. 186). Marital "meaning-making" is described as stories of "partners in process."

Many discuss the importance of helping clients make sense of their lives, especially when they are in crisis. As a psychotherapist, Carlsen has made the connection between meaning-making and career and provides case studies of clients who have been helped through the process of seeing meaning in what they have done or what has happened to them. For example, she tells the story of a client who contemplated suicide when, after the time and expense of training to be a lawyer, he discovered that law was not his mission. He sought counseling, survived, and eventually found a field that could bring more meaning to his life.

A course on the search for meaning at Duke University taught jointly by a pastor, an economist, and a psychiatrist who were on their own search for meaning has resulted in an extremely relevant book on that topic, *The Search for Meaning* (Naylor, Willimon, and Naylor, 1994). In their personal search they asked many provocative questions about such topics as meaninglessness, separation, having, being, and doing, meaning in the workplace, and community. They suggest that everyone develop a personal philosophy that includes four interdependent elements: (1) a sense of meaning, (2) a statement of values, (3) a statement of ethics, and (4) a statement of social responsibility. They also define a search for meaning process, which includes seven steps:

- Review the most meaningful events in your *life history*.
- Come to terms with the *meaninglessness* in your own life.
- Confront your *separation* from yourself, others, and the ground of your being.
- Contemplate the consequences of a life devoted to *having*.
- Seek meaning through *being*—through your creations, love relationships, sense of community, and pain and suffering.
- Formulate a *personal philosophy* that addresses meaning, values, ethical principles, and social responsibility.

- Formulate a *personal strategy,* including an external environmental forecast, a situation assessment, objectives, goals, and strategies.

Naylor and colleagues' (1994) chapter on meaning in the workplace highlights the importance of management philosophy but also the importance of democracy in the workplace. It provides examples of a number of companies with enlightened human resource and employee benefits policies. For example, the policy at Ben & Jerry's, the ice-cream company, was that no senior executive earned more than seven times the compensation of the lowest-paid worker.

Stories with a Sense of Vocation

A number of writers see career as a mission or vocation. Larry Cochran (1990) studied the career and life development of twenty persons who had a clear mission in life from early youth to old age. Out of these narratives, he constructed a story line with four phases that reveals the pattern for those with a sense of vocation: the sense of vocation begins, it is cultivated, it is enacted in a life's work, and it ends. Designed to help readers who wish to know how to make life meaningful, the book examines lives "that were radiant with meaning, or at least with one kind of meaning" (p. vii). For persons who have a sense of vocation, he states, life is shaped in a way that lights up existence.

Cochran suggests that vocation has been neglected in the field of counseling for several reasons:

1. A vocation is often equated with a job, which Cochran characterizes as "misleading concreteness."
2. In the normative viewpoint of research, vocation is reduced to an abstract and impoverished concept that doesn't fit into theories.
3. Career psychologists have been initiated almost exclusively into a positivistic worldview that is inappropriate for studying individuals and their sense of vocation.
4. The preponderance of theory and research is geared toward current practice and social arrangements, in this case, vocational guidance, which is too narrow.

Career as Story

There is considerable interest today in the use of career stories in career counseling. For many years, I have asked students in my career development classes to write their own "Integrated Career Development paper," an assignment that proves extremely meaningful.

According to Cochran, there are two striking characteristics in the life stories of people with a sense of vocation: repetition and rhythm. He compares the flow of life and phases of life in work to the seasons: summer—incompletion, fall—positioning, winter—positing, and spring—completion. The twenty people he studied are well known (John Stuart Mill, Lincoln Steffens, Yehudi Menuhin, Booker T. Washington, Margaret Mead, Conrad Hilton, Christopher Milne, and Gregory Bateson are among them). Cochran makes suggestions about what others—parents, counselors, clergy, friends—might do to help women or men live their story.

The concept of career as story is gaining momentum in the field of career development (Jepsen, 1992). Although it focuses on a person whose whole life is centered on one mission (which is perhaps less common today with so many people moving from occupation to occupation), the story or narrative concept is important for career specialists who seek to help clients understand the meaning of vocation and story in life. In fact, Mark Savickas (1995) predicts that in twenty years, career counselors will not use the Strong Interest Inventory to help clients compare their interests with successful people in fields of interest but rather will compare them with stories and autobiographies of role models whose narratives form the base for comparison.

"Follow Your Bliss"

Mythologist Joseph Campbell has contributed immeasurably to the dialogue about spirituality and place in the universe. Although he could not and should not be limited to the narrow confines of career psychology, he brought a worldview and psychological interpretation to myths that transcend cultural boundaries. He refused to be put in the "boxes" in which we tend to categorize people and derived his wisdom from anthropology, art, biology, philosophy, history, art, and religion (Campbell and Moyers, 1988). Described by Bill Moyers as a teacher, scholar, and lifelong learner, as well as one who lived an authentic life, Campbell saw the common spirituality across cultures as "the world's dreams . . . which deal with great human problems" (p. 15).

Perhaps of greatest influence on career counseling practitioners is Campbell's advice to "follow your bliss." During one of the Moyer-Campbell interviews, Campbell says: "I feel that if one follows what I call one's bliss—the thing that really gets you deep in the gut and that you feel is your life—doors open. They *do!* . . . Put aside the passing moment that says you *should* live this way. Be informed and go where your body and soul want you to go" (Campbell and Moyers, 1988, p. 120).

I have enormous admiration for Joseph Campbell and found his book to be elevating and liberating. For some people bliss may mean watching a sunrise or a sunset, although some of my students wisely caution that many people who do not have the means for economic survival can't really live on bliss. Yet seen as symbolic language that puts the emphasis not on destination but on life's journey, his message has meaning for many.

Spirituality and Integrative Life Planning

Throughout this discussion, a recurring theme is that of spirituality, community, and connectedness against the backdrop of money and materialism. The increasing importance of this theme in people's lives is evident in the number of people suggesting that community can be achieved through meaning and purpose. Although I have not focused on specific strategies, a number of ideas for helping clients, students, and employees have been suggested along with frameworks for approaching these issues.

Career professionals are likely to approach the issues of spirituality and religious beliefs in different ways, but it is important that they have some understanding of several things: their own spiritual and religious beliefs, the spiritual beliefs and religiousness of the people with whom they work, and how these two dimensions fit together and affect a person's values, sense of purpose, and life choices. A spiritual framework can be especially helpful to women who are breaking out of narrowly defined roles and finding new ways of being and doing. These women may also identify with the values of connection and community.

A number of activities can facilitate exploration of spirituality and life purpose; the Resource at the back of this book offers several. Also helpful are several of the books discussed in this chapter. For example, Richard Leider's *Power of Purpose* (1985) can help readers examine purpose as a part of their identity. For adults in midlife, the more recent *Repacking Your Bags* (Leider and Shapiro, 1995) offers many suggestions on creating a life with purpose. Finally, Naylor, Willimon, and Naylor's *Search for Meaning* (1994) can be recommended to clients to help them on their way to beginning the personal search.

Conclusion

This chapter presents many ideas about purpose, meaning, materialism, and spirituality—complex topics that form an important piece of the ILP quilt. Spirituality is discussed in connection with many aspects of life, work, and human development. The movement away from money and materialism toward a life filled with purpose suggests lofty goals for career professionals and their clients. New ways suggested for reinventing and revisioning work fit well with the Integrative Life Planning critical task and goal of finding work that needs doing. Also important is the emerging strategy for career counseling of approaching the career as story. Though long neglected in career development and counseling, exploring spirituality is a task that speaks to people across cultures, though they may express their spirituality in different ways. It is a piece of the ILP quilt that links with the universal search for meaning.

These ideas should provide considerable food for thought for people who help others making life choices and decisions. Through the stimulus of the theorists and psychologists, career practitioners, and other social observers that we examined who talk about the spiritual dimension in life, counseling professionals can help stimulate their own clients' thinking about ultimate meanings and purpose and highlight these issues in their practice.

Chapter Eight

Critical Task 6: Managing Personal Transitions and Organizational Change

> *The transition process was both painful and*
> *rewarding. Although difficult, this period was one of*
> *tremendous growth and intense learning for me. In*
> *particular, I became very inwardly focused and*
> *learned a lot about myself. I started individual*
> *therapy, working with an excellent counselor who*
> *helped me move through my grief and clarify my*
> *personal and professional identity, goals, aspirations,*
> *and values. As a result, I took the initial steps on a*
> *path eventually leading to a career that lasted more*
> *than fifteen years.*
> —Latino male graduate student

We now approach the sixth critical task of Integrative Life Planning: focusing on transitions and change. As we bring our ILP quilt closer to completion, we begin to realize that, in one way or another, all the critical tasks described in this book involve personal or organizational changes or both; in this way they are all related. Although all the tasks of ILP are important, this last is perhaps the most salient because it affects people in context, the context of the wanted and unwanted changes in their lives and families and work organizations. I offer some pieces of my personal quilt once again in this chapter, including my own family experience with job loss.

This chapter explores several aspects of transitions and change. I examine *personal transitions* as they relate to voluntary and involuntary changes in the different parts our lives, including models of transition that have been used to help negotiate change, expected and unexpected; a case study of a job loss, which is discussed in the context of one of the models; and decision-making concepts and strategies as related to transition-making. I also examine *organizational change,* by which I mean the major changes and trends that have characterized organizational development over the last two decades, including shifting organizational structures, work patterns, values, and leadership patterns and the emerging integrative career patterns. Finally, I examine *global social change.*

Personal Transitions

The term *transition* denotes a variety of changes people make in a lifetime—forming and dissolving marriages or partnerships, having children, changing careers, retiring, being widowed, making a geographical move, losing a job, being promoted, and so on. It is important that career professionals have some familiarity with transition models if they are to be of most help to their clients.

Transition Models

Most transition models in the career and counseling literature address the change and transition process for individuals. Although they take into account related factors, such as the effect of retirement on one's partner or spouse or the effect of a love relationship on one's work, most are directed toward an individual making a transition.

Bridges's Endings and Beginnings

William Bridges (1980) describes the lifelong nature of transitions and the phases of the transition process. Although most think of transitions as beginnings, he describes stages within them: (1) an ending, that is, when we work through the loss of leaving a place, experience, or relationship; (2) a middle, when we begin to make sense of what has happened; and (3) a beginning, when we begin to prepare for a new opportunity or opportunities.

Brammer's Life Transitions

Lawrence Brammer (1991)—drawing from Bridges (1980), Schlossberg (1981), and Hopson (1981)—defines transitions as both the ordinary changes (such as marriage, divorce, illness, unemployment, job shifts, graduation, and promotion) and the extraordinary changes (death, accidents, disasters) that occur continually through people's lives. He characterizes these short, sharp changes as "life transitions," *transition* meaning "a journey through," usually to something unknown, often requiring the courage to take risks and the ability to cope with fear.

A unique aspect of Brammer's approach is his concept of levels of response to change. According to Brammer the levels are adaptation (when one adjusts to the change), renewal (when one sets goals), transformation (when one experiences rebirth), and transcendence (when one experiences the meaning of the change). Figure 8.1 presents the levels in graphic form.

Brammer suggests that the easiest levels of response are at the bottom of the figure and the most difficult toward the top. We may adjust to the situation when the consequences are not important to us or when we know it would be prudent and futile to resist. Coping is a more active approach to adaptation, involving such skills as developing a positive view of change, building support, changing negative thoughts, solving problems, and appraising potential danger. The renewal level is a deliberate process of directing change in a creative personal direction. It involves taking risks, setting new goals, and planning new directions. Transformation represents a basic shift in the way one views a problem or situation. It involves seeing unplanned life events as valued opportunities to learn about oneself, the world, and the process of change rather than as tragedies. At the transcendence level, one experiences the ultimate meanings of life. Brammer views transcendence as a culmination of the search for meaning—an awareness not only of the meaning of a particular transition but of one's whole life. It doesn't happen often, he cautions, so treasure it when it does.

Figure 8.1. Brammer's Levels of Responding to Change.

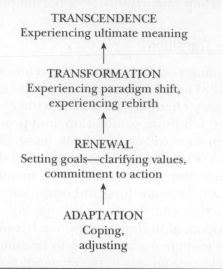

TRANSCENDENCE
Experiencing ultimate meaning

↑

TRANSFORMATION
Experiencing paradigm shift,
experiencing rebirth

↑

RENEWAL
Setting goals—clarifying values,
commitment to action

↑

ADAPTATION
Coping,
adjusting

Source: Adapted from L. M. Brammer, *How to Cope with Life Transitions: The Challenge of Personal Change.* New York: Hemisphere, 1991, p. 8. Reproduced with permission. All rights reserved.

There is a clear relationship between this model and Integrative Life Planning.

Pilder's Outplacement Model

On a more concrete level, Bill Pilder (1985), a former priest, founded an innovative outplacement firm—called Mainstream Access—to help five thousand workers laid off from Bethlehem Steel in Pennsylvania find new identities when the plant closed. Basing his theory on the work of Carl Jung, who believed that change was not only possible but necessary, Pilder helped the workers look inward during this time of widespread job loss and to dream of different ways of doing things. His focus was not on learning new technologies but rather on releasing entrepreneurial energies through a new kind of "cultural therapy" that would guide the workers through inner change and job transition. Despite an atmosphere of hostility and despair, Pilder succeeded in helping them find meaningful work through this approach—much as he himself had done when he left the priesthood.

With the sponsorship of Bethlehem Steel and the U.S. Department of Labor, Pilder developed this program for these blue-collar workers, which was intended in part to get them to break free from the mentality that they would be cared for by an authoritarian corporation or a union. They were encouraged to trust themselves and create security for themselves. Pilder used the Myers-Briggs Type Indicator to help them understand their usual patterns in dealing with the world and then encouraged them to free their inner vision, first by getting in touch with their creative energies and later by learning specific skills.

Almost 30 percent of the unemployed workers expressed interest in starting their own businesses. As a result of the program, one steelworker opened an art supply shop. Another opened a riding stable. Some in the computer division developed new software ideas. One developed a service for fire departments to teach them how to deal with hazardous chemicals.

Although he did not ignore the fact that plant closings like the one at Bethlehem Steel affect people at all socioeconomic levels, Pilder helped the workers to grow and change and view both themselves and their work quite differently. This was a remarkable story of helping people view transitions in new ways and it occurred long before the current downsizing epidemic began.

Kanchier's "Questers"

Another practical model for career professionals is that of psychologist Carole Kanchier (1987), who developed an approach to midlife career change that involves what she calls *questers.* Questers are job seekers or job changers who have dared to take risks, take charge of their careers, and therefore know that they don't have to stay in the same job or lifestyle. Characteristics she ascribes to these people are purposeful, autonomous, intimate, androgynous, achieving, and growing. Although most of Kanchier's tools—such as quizzes and questionnaires—report on such things as job burnout, job satisfaction, and identification as a quester, her basic goal is to help people understand themselves better and evaluate their lives periodically. This kind of process can be helpful to people voluntarily making a transition and who "dare to change."

Schlossberg's Adaptation to Transition

Nancy Schlossberg set forth a useful framework for all kinds of transitions that she described in the scholarly *Counseling Adults in Transition* (Schlossberg, 1984; also Schlossberg, Waters, and Goodman, 1995); in a more mass-market self-help style in *Overwhelmed: Coping with Life's Ups and Downs* (Schlossberg, 1991); and most recently in *Going to Plan B* (Schlossberg and Robinson, 1996), which deals with alternatives and non-events. Because Schlossberg's (1981) model appears to be the most inclusive model and because it is the one that has most influenced my thinking in Integrative Life Planning, it will be described in more detail here.

As I suggested earlier, I prefer the term *life transition* to denote the variety of changes we are likely to make in a lifetime—the developmental decisions that society expects us to make based on a kind of "social clock" that sets norms for life events (such as getting married, having children, making a geographical move, dealing with "the empty nest," and retirement), and the unexpected events that may cause trauma and dramatic change (for example, getting divorced, losing a relationship, losing a child or spouse, being fired, and dealing with the not-so-empty nest).

Schlossberg's framework is designed for individuals but because of its scope it seems uniquely adaptable to Integrative Life Planning and to decision making by either individuals or partners. Career professionals may want to consider this framework in reflecting on their own transitions as well as for possible use with clients, students, and employees.

Schlossberg first suggests that there are four areas to consider in understanding transitions: the triggers of the change, the person whose change or transition it actually is, the consequences of the change, and coping strategies and resources.

Among the triggers of change are *planned events, unplanned events, non-events,* and *chronic events.* A person who decides to change from a field he or she chose at age eighteen is making a planned change. (But in a marriage, a planned change for one spouse may lead to an unplanned change for the other; for example, an executive chooses to take a promotion that requires the geographic relocation of his entire family. Other cases where individuals may be affected by transitions of other people in their lives are the following: a spouse wants to go back to school or make a job change; a son or daughter wants to marry, enter the military, or attend a vocational school; a parent is retiring or going into a nursing home; a friend is moving away; a co-worker is being sexually harassed.)

Unplanned changes mean the individual has little control and may well view the change as a negative one. Such changes include those instigated by random events that occur in people's lives, such as recessions, layoffs, disabling accidents, even wars.

Non-events are those that were hoped for or expected but didn't happen—the child that a couple didn't have, the job that went to someone else, the promotion that was denied, the election that wasn't won (Schlossberg and Robinson, 1996). Although these transitions are more subtle and unconscious, adjustment to a non-event may be just as hurtful and stressful as to unplanned changes. Finally, chronic transitions are triggered by the everyday misery people experience at home or at work, what Schlossberg calls "sleeper" transitions, such as an illness that makes people feel helpless, a chemical dependency that immobilizes, a relationship that becomes abusive, or an ongoing feeling of boredom at work.

In counseling families, especially, it is important for career professionals to think about *whose* transition it really is. As mentioned in the previous paragraphs, in some interpersonal situations the transition of one person deeply affects another or others. Indeed, when one person decides to get a divorce or when one family member loses a job, the whole family is affected. These are what I call "connected transitions" because all significant others play a part in them.

The consequences of transitions can be major or minor. Some may start out as extremely traumatic (such as a separation or job loss) but with the grace of time result in deep positive personal change. Transitions may also affect many or few areas of one's life, including social, work, health, or personal.

Many but not all transitions involve role change. Some are role losses (decremental changes, such as when one is widowed, retires, or loses someone close—as I sadly did at age nine when my only sister died at age five). Other transitions are role gains, such as when one is promoted or becomes a parent. Other factors that determine how disruptive a transition is and how severe its consequences include the following:

- *Positive or negative affect.* For example, when a child leaves home, especially if his or her destination involves risk, parents may experience negative affect.
- *Internal or external sources.* External sources are circumstances outside of one's control—one is fired. Internal sources are voluntary—one seeks job change.
- *Timing.* Is the event on time or not? For example, if a woman is having her first baby between twenty and thirty, she is on time. She is not on time if she is having it closer to age forty (as increasing numbers of women are doing in the 1990s).
- *Gradual or sudden onset.* If the event is anticipated, one has time to prepare—for the loss of a child through a long-term illness, for example. But one does not have time if it is unanticipated—a child is killed in an accident, for example.
- *Permanent, temporary, or uncertain duration.* A transition of uncertain duration occurs, for example, when one learns that one has an illness but doesn't yet know if it's terminal or one is uncertain about getting a new job.

Schlossberg puts a lot of emphasis on coping with or managing transitions because these events result in a change in assumptions about oneself and the world and thus a corresponding change in one's behaviors and relationships. The ways in which our clients cope with a transition depends on many factors, including their individual perception of the particular transition; their individual characteristics; and the balance between their resources and deficits. Again, while Schlossberg envisioned these concepts for individuals, they can be considered by partners in transition as well. Exhibit 8.1 provides a detailed look at Schlossberg's transition model.

To help clients, workers, or students or when training professionals to help others, Schlossberg (1991) developed a simplified model based on her theory. She called it Your Steps in Mastering Change. The three steps are described as approaching change, taking stock, and taking charge.

Exhibit 8.1. Schlossberg's Transition Model.

The Transition Event or nonevent resulting in change	Coping Resources Balance of assets and liabilities			The Transition Process Reactions over time for better or for worse
	Variables characterizing the individual	Variables characterizing the transition	Variables characterizing the environment	

Type
• Anticipated
• Unanticipated
• Nonevent
• Chronic hassle
 	
Context
• Relationship of person to transition
• Setting in which transition occurs
 	
Impact
• Relationships
• Routines
• Assumptions
• Roles
	• Personal and demographic characteristics
	  –Socioeconomic status
	  –Sex role
	  –Age and stage of life
	  –State of health
	• Psychological resources
	  –Ego development
	  –Personality
	  –Outlook
	  –Commitments and values
	• Coping responses
	  –Functions: controlling situation, meaning, or stress
	  –Strategies: information seeking, direct action, inhibition of action, intrapsychic behavior
		• Event or nonevent characteristics
		  –Trigger
		  –Timing
		  –Source
		  –Role change
		  –Duration
		  –Previous experience with a similar transition
		  –Concurrent stress
		• Assessment
			• Social support
			  –Types: intimate family unit, friendship network, institution
			  –Functions: affect, affirmation, aid, feedback
			  –Measurement: convoy
			• Options
			  –Actual
			  –Perceived
			  –Utilized
			  –Created
				Phases of assimilation
				• Pervasiveness
				• Disruptions
				• Integration, for better or for worse
				
				Appraisal
				• Of transition, resources, results
				• Of preoccupation versus life satisfaction

Source: N. K. Schlossberg, *Counseling Adults in Transition*, p. 108. Copyright © 1984. Springer Publishing Company, Inc., New York 10012. Used by permission.

There are several important questions for career counselors to ask to determine the severity of a transition's impact on someone's life: How has the transition changed your roles, relationships, assumptions, and routines? How has it changed your definition of yourself and your ability to plan? Does it come at a particularly difficult time in your life? How much control do you have over the transition? How permanent is the transition? Then assess the Four Ss—situation, self, supports, and strategies. At the taking charge stage, Schlossberg also suggests reviewing the Four Ss, selecting appropriate coping strategies, developing an action plan, reflecting on how a person can profit from the change, and increasing options, understanding, and control. Figure 8.2 summarizes the three-step approach.

Schlossberg (1994) also has developed a useful instrument to help people make transitions. It is called the Transition Coping Guide (TCG). The guide contains forty-five items organized around the Four Ss: situation (how do you see the transition?), self (who are you?), supports (what help do you have from others?), and strategies (how do you cope?). The self-scoring TCG is designed to help clients see how they can maximize their readiness for change, understand why the change may make them uneasy, help them weather the change, and help them improve their personal understanding of it and deal with it more effectively. If a client needs assistance in one of the four areas, the guide suggests that the career specialist begin work in that area. But if the client needs to work on all four areas, it suggests delaying the transition if possible. The TCG offers excellent questions for reflection in all four areas.

A Case Study of a Job Loss

For many men and women today—especially those in midlife—upheaval can have a devastating impact. Such an unexpected upheaval occurred in my own family and it was a piece of my personal life quilt that I would have preferred to do without. Many people facing unexpected job loss deal with consequences that are far more serious than we did; still, emotionally, it was serious enough for us. I will describe our transition experience in the context of Schlossberg's model; I hope that guiding clients through a similar process of analysis can help them in their transition.

Figure 8.2. Schlossberg's Steps to Mastering Change.

Approaching Change

- Identify your transition:
  What it is
  How it has changed your roles, routines, assumptions, relationships
  Where you are in the transition process

Taking Stock

- Assess your potential resources for coping with your transition:
  The four Ss—your situation, self, supports, and strategies

Taking Charge

- Strengthen your coping resources by selecting appropriate coping
  strategies
- Develop an action plan
- Profit from change: increase your options, understanding, and control

Source: Adapted with permission from N. K. Schlossberg, *Overwhelmed: Coping with Life's Ups and Downs,* fig. 6–7. Copyright © 1989, 1994 Jossey-Bass Inc., Publishers. First published by Lexington Books. All rights reserved.

Situation

While our children were completing their college degrees, my husband, Tor, lost his job in technical sales. After twenty-six years of loyal service to his company, of which he was part owner, he was notified abruptly one Friday and received his pink slip the following Monday morning. He was given only two weeks' severance, no pension, no outplacement assistance, and no retirement party. A competing company hired him within a month, but he had worked there for only a year when that company, too, found it necessary to downsize and, under its last-hired, first-fired policy, Tor and other new employees were the first to go. He went on to a year and a half of serious job hunting, but after that he gave up, becoming one of the no-longer-looking and no-longer-counted in the unemployment statistics.

Our transition began in 1990—Tor's first layoff was definitely an unplanned event. It occurred as nationwide reports of downsizing began to hit the media, but that did not help the pain of my husband's sudden unemployment. However, it was after the second job loss and the fruitless search that the truly painful transition began. Although many men like him were having similar experiences and although we were a family of people who rationally understood that job change is okay and that it occurs frequently, Tor's identification with his work and his company made this unanticipated job loss a blow to his self-concept.

Many white men are experiencing the same thing. (Some attribute their sudden loss of careers to affirmative action, which generates a new set of tensions; this was not my husband's response, however.) Our transition experience is no longer uncommon; indeed, it is becoming an extremely frequent one. Organizations around the country are downsizing and paring expenses by cutting off more highly paid professionals. What are the ramifications for the health of family and personal relationships? For us, it changed some of our assumptions about ourselves and the work world and caused us to reassess our resources. It also resulted in some role changes.

Role Reversal

I had my position at the university and was at the office almost every day. In contrast, my spouse had nothing to structure his day around. Professional outplacement help was not available. While he managed to gain a couple of manufacturer's representative contracts through his former company, these required no more than half time. As I told my friends, I was overloaded and he was underloaded. Our family went through some role reversals when he started doing most of the cooking, grocery shopping, errand running, and household chores. (Luckily, he actually liked those tasks.)

Although the job loss was his transition, its effects on the children and me were our transition. For one thing, it meant that the pattern of our lives and roles as a dual-career family changed to essentially a single-earner family. Fortunately, our financial resources (and the fact that our children were nearing college graduation) made it possible for him to semiretire. So after almost two years, Tor quit looking for work and settled down to his part-time contracts, a little volunteer work for our church and a local social service agency, and a lot of time for his favorite sports, including golf in summer and skiing in winter.

Family Impact

In the school year 1993–94, I took a sabbatical from the university. With both of us at home most of the time, I began to feel the full impact of what had happened. Frankly, I found it difficult not having my space alone to do my writing and sabbatical projects. We handled that issue by converting our son's unused bedroom into my office, which became a great haven. Eventually I was able to accept the new pattern—even savored the relief from the dual burden of professional work and housework. During that year I also realized how out of sync we two were in our careers. He was retiring, but I was barely ready to do even preretirement planning. Many couples find themselves in this position today. (See Chapter Five, p. 140, for more on this.)

The transition's impact on our children was different from the impact on me. Our daughter was finishing college in the year of the first shock, about to begin her first regular job as a computer programmer and systems analyst at a publishing firm. Our son was in the third year of a five-year joint liberal arts and engineering program and was concerned that he would not be able to finish it because of Tor's job loss. Fortunately, we had saved enough for the children's college and he was never in any danger.

Self and Roles

In some ways the transition was more difficult for me than for my husband. While Tor was dealing with the loss of his role as a full-time worker—something that still is highly valued as a symbol of success in our society despite the increasing numbers of men and women now working part time—I was dealing with the loss of my role as partner in a dual-career family. That image has been important to me for thirty years. One consequence for me was that I slowed down my pace a bit during that summer, spending more time playing golf with him and friends, for example. That fall, when I went back to the university—where schedules quickly become overloads—we faced another test of our new life pattern.

Supports and Resources

During the sabbatical, I was in the process of writing this book. So I did not yet know what the next consequences of the transition would be. As I finished this book, we had pretty much made the adjustment. However, I was not ready to disengage from my university role, and there was still the problem of my having a strong work ethic and my being unready and unable to change my pattern. In contrast, because Tor was successful in business for many years (and was still handling our business matters) and because he brought his Norwegian family values into our relationship (emphasis on family, balance between family and work), he was able to make a very positive adjustment. He acknowledges nonetheless that he still needs some more meaningful activity to occupy his time. In many ways I felt more anger than he did, partly because of what I perceived as the injustice of this kind of job loss after so many years of service. I had a lot of negative affect, especially when we learned through acquaintances that a company officer had made comments like, "We're keeping the young guys because they've got more mouths to feed" and "He doesn't have to work—his wife has a good income." Further complicating the issue, the action was outside of our control, the timing was not the best, the onset was sudden, and the transition turned out to be of permanent duration.

Coping Strategies

As far as coping with our transition, I find both Schlossberg's and Brammer's views to be helpful. I don't think the word *overwhelmed* would apply to our reaction, but it was certainly a strongly negative one. As far as my husband is concerned, as a very "together" and basically happy person, he did not let the blow keep him down; he found things to do.

My husband adjusted to the transition since he couldn't undo it. He coped by building supports, managing stress, and trying to see the positives in the situation. He did not seriously think about career change or retraining for something new, but he tried to find meaningful activity to structure his day. He is an organizer, so he enjoys getting different groups of friends together and linking those who may have common interests for breakfasts and lunches. He also has several support groups through community and professional organizations.

The unexpected job loss forced us to begin our retirement planning. Generally speaking, however, I don't think this change in our lives has been transformational or transcendent, to use Brammer's terms. However, it has had a powerful impact on our roles, our relationships, our routines, and some of our assumptions about ourselves and the place of work in our lives.

As a postscript to this personal "case study," I wish to point out that we are among the lucky ones. We are perhaps in an enviable situation compared with others who have had the same experience. We were in the later stages of career, our children were young adults and almost through school, our mortgage was paid off, and we had saved for retirement when Tor lost his job. Many others have lost their jobs as early as their forties and fifties and have had more negative financial consequences, with some having to sell their homes, move, change their plans for their children's education, and fundamentally change their lifestyle. The loss has forced some into depression and even suicide. We recognize the advantages of our having been a two-income family for so many years. Financial security, strong self-concepts, and a good relationship carried us through this experience. For families without these, the strains can be greater, their life quilts far more tattered. Yet, without doubt, this has been a major family transition and has increased our empathy for others in such situations.

Women in Transition

Going back to the literature brings us to questions about transitions in women's lives. Another view of personal transitions comes from anthropologist Mary Catherine Bateson's *Composing a Life* (1989), a qualitative study of the lives of five well-educated achieving women—an engineer, a college president, a psychiatrist, a jewelry maker, and herself. One was African American, and the others were white. All were combining career with marriage and family responsibilities and were trying to keep their individuality and be caring partners at the same time. They are multidimensional women.

Bateson believes that women manage change better than men because they have to deal with discontinuities all their lives. They learn how to suffer pain, remain flexible, have multiple lives, and deal with change. Because their lives are no longer dominated by procreation, they have more time to craft their own lives although they still have to balance conflicting demands. "Life is an improvisory art," Bateson (1989) says, with changing settings and opportunities arising out of problems. The lives of the women studied were not characterized as monolithic achievement. Rather, they were characterized as journeys—all of them "migrants in time" (p. 14). The unfolding lives of these women included achievement and caring. They had a consistency about them in spite of their improvisatory nature. They followed husbands, had babies, and made their work fit around marriage, unlike the author's mother, Margaret Mead, who made her marriages fit around her work.

Thus, Bateson depicts achievement through the eyes of these women, whose lives of fluidity and discontinuity are not the exception but common in our era. The women faced changes, midlife crises, and older-adult crises; they were in reassessment and redirection and had patchworks of personal and professional achievement quite different from single-track models of times past. The creative, makeshift lives of these five atypical women— with their multiple identities, commitments, and new beginnings—offer implications for the next generation of men and women.

Bateson (1989) asserts that women have always lived contingent lives. In contrast, men are new to it and vulnerable, just learning how to do it. The pattern that has been identified with women—a pattern of discontinuity and change—may become the pattern of men's lives as well. It is a pattern that does not lend itself as easily to planning. In fact, gaining a sense of agency, of designing one's own life may be more difficult in the future. As the trends continue toward temporary and contingent work, contracts rather than jobs, independent entrepreneurs rather than salaried employees with benefits, that discontinuity is already a reality. Bateson's observations remind me of why I chose to consider both patterns and planning in ILP.

Transitions, Time, and Timing

As noted, the time and timing of a transition is important. While Bridges identifies the endings and beginnings of transitions, Schlossberg sees transitions as adjustment processes over time. Gelatt (1989) describes the importance of both remembering the past and imagining the future. Time—its availability and its use in work, family, learning, and leisure—is an extremely important component of Integrative Life Planning. In two-income families, it is often the man who has more free time than the woman because she has a "double shift" of both family work and on-the-job work. Although this is changing, women generally still bear the heavier work load at home and men have more unscheduled time.

Mark Savickas (1990), who works with both adolescents and adults, describes a "subjective" career and an "objective" career and their relationship to time. Everyone has the latter, but not everyone has the former. In his view subjective career emerges from certain temporal experiences—beliefs and attitudes toward time. There are three parts of time orientation: *time perspective,* or how an individual views and orients self to time and makes the future important; *time differentiation,* or how one sees events within a time period (a differentiated future provides a meaningful context for personal goal-setting and involves being able to name anticipated events); and *time integration* (described later).

Dreams are a part of differentiation. Career counselors must help people, both individuals and couples, create, articulate, and enact their dreams. We might ask clients these questions: What kind of life roles did you envision for yourself when you were in high school? Who were your career influences? Do you remember your first daydreams? Imagine what your life will be like ten years into the future. In one study, college students were asked the latter question. A follow-up study ten years later found that many were doing what they had dreamed of doing. Dreams can help individuals, couples, and families identify goals and shape them into more achievable goals. Doing this may be especially important in times of transition.

The third aspect of time orientation, time integration, refers to the integration of time periods of one's life—past, present, and future. Integration helps people get a sense of connectedness.

This picture of time provides a useful tool for life planning. Integration is putting things together in ways that make sense. Says Savickas (1990), "When life is viewed as an unbroken thread, individuals can become aware of enduring themes and patterns in life, strengthen their sense of identity and choose activities to move into the future—to continue their journey."

Time integration is also important because it provides hope. Clients may dare to hope that goals can be achieved when they are able to see the connectedness of the past, present, and future. But to have hope, they must also have specific plans. Plans bridge the gap between knowledge and purposeful action. States Savickas, "We make plans to reach some inner image of what we imagine our future to be like." As helping professionals interested in life planning, we can use interventions to enhance time integration, such as in ILP, and help clients to see the importance of the future. We can also help to create hope that their goals can be achieved. Time orientation can be useful for all adults, especially those in transition. One caveat, however, is that career professionals need to be aware of cultural contrasts and variations in time orientation.

Decisions and Transitions

People in transition have to make many decisions. The process of decision making is an integral part of the Integrative Life Planning process. How do different approaches to decision making relate to the concepts of transition? Decisions have been defined in many different ways: as choices among values and value systems or as choices among alternatives, for example. When one is making a transition, some decision-making skills are needed. In this section we examine models and strategies of decision making that are relevant to life planning and that career professionals may want to introduce to their clients.

Numerous models of decision making exist in the career development literature. Over time, well-known theorists have contributed a very logical and rational view of the process. The traditional model of decision making fits well with the emphasis on the scientific method that has dominated the behavioral sciences in the twentieth century. Today, with fewer than five years left to go in this century, in a very different, uncertain world, decision making is not quite as straightforward as it once seemed to be. In fact, newer thinking about decision making is that it is intentional and experiential as well as intuitive.

Lillian Dinklage (1967), in a dissertation study of styles of adolescent decision making, describes several decision-making strategies that are utilized by adults as well. These decision-making styles are *the impulsive, the fatalistic, the compliant, the delaying, the agonizing, the planning, the intuitive,* and *the paralytic.* Of all the strategies, Dinklage found that both sexes most frequently used the planning one; this was followed in popularity by the impulsive and the compliant, and then the delaying and the fatalistic, with the remaining styles used much less frequently.

Logical-Rational Models

H. B. Gelatt (1962), formerly a school guidance director and now a career development consultant and speaker in counseling and business, was one of the early theorists whose rational decision-making model has been widely used or adapted in career counseling. According to his model, the decision-making stages are to define objectives, gather data, evaluate information, identify alternatives, determine priorities for alternatives, predict outcomes, and develop an implementation strategy. Although this type of left-brain linear approach seemed appropriate for many years, a number of writers, including Gelatt himself, are questioning whether this approach is appropriate for the twenty-first century.

In developing the ILP model some years ago, I came across Gelatt's new way of thinking about decision making. Although few in the career development field have shifted to new paradigms in their thinking about career, Gelatt offers a new framework that questions his own former views and challenges counseling professionals and career changers to think in very different ways. Although he has not examined the gender factor in decision making, he provides a nonlinear framework that holds promise for integrative life planners.

Gelatt's Positive Uncertainty

In 1989, more than twenty-five years after conceptualizing his first model, Gelatt published a new counseling framework for decision making that he called Positive Uncertainty (or PU, if you use the acronym). Gelatt's framework is intriguing for many reasons. For one, in many ways it is almost the reverse of his 1962 model. It invites people to learn to live with uncertainty and not always expect definite answers and outcomes. His perspective is captured by his parody of the title of David Campbell's (1974) book *If You Don't Know Where You're Going, You'll Probably End Up Somewhere Else*. He changed it to "If you always know where you're going, you may never end up somewhere else." An enthusiast for alliteration, metaphors, and other figures of speech, Gelatt informally refers to career counselors as florists (who give advice and information), farmers (who teach clients how to grow their own plants), and futurists (who help people feel they can do something about their own future). He believes that counselors today need to help people become comfortable with uncertainty and learn to adapt to change.

Gelatt also suggests that the basic technology skill of the future will be *balance,* that is, balance between old basic skills and new basic skills with inclusion of the modern skills of flexibility, imagination, and compassion.

What is Positive Uncertainty? According to Gelatt (1989), modern science shows that in some cases it is not possible to know enough about the present to make a complete prediction about the future. His definition of decision making includes three parts: getting information, arranging and rearranging, and choosing action. Positive Uncertainty suggests using the whole brain, accepting uncertainty, asking for flexibility, and using creativity and intuition. Defining it as a nonsequential, nonsystematic, and nonscientific human process, Gelatt considers it appropriate for the new knowledge methods of the future. PU assumes that facts rapidly become obsolete, that reliability is limited by misinformation, that the content of most information is not objective but rather distorted by the eye of the beholder, and that one's attitude toward the data and their arrangement and rearrangement in an individual's mind is now the most important part of decision making.

Positive Uncertainty suggests two attitudes: (1) accept the past, present, and future as uncertain and be positive about that uncertainty and (2) use four personal factors as a framework for every decision—what you want, what you know, what you believe, and what you do as a framework for its "two-by-four process" of "making decisions when the future isn't what it used to be and we don't know what it will be." The following characterizes creative decision makers under Positive Uncertainty:

1. They are focused and flexible about what they want.
2. They know what they want but aren't sure.
3. They treat goals as hypotheses (that is, they are goal-guided but not goal-governed).
4. They balance achieving goals and discovering them.

Again, PU regards decision making as information processing, that is, arranging and rearranging information into a choice of action. Gelatt recommends the following:

1. Be aware of and wary about what you know.
2. Recognize that knowledge is power and ignorance is bliss.
3. Treat memory as an enemy.
4. Balance using information and imagination.

PU also requires a paradoxical balance. The more you know, the more you realize you don't know. The key is to accept this but not be paralyzed by it. Not knowing for certain opens the opportunity for new knowledge. Gelatt offers guidelines for each stage of the decision-making process:

1. *Information guideline:* Treat your facts with imagination but do not imagine your facts.
2. *Process guideline:* Know what you want and believe, but do not be sure.
3. *Choice guideline:* Be rational unless there is a good reason not to be.

An Intuitive Decision-Making Model for Transitions

Gelatt describes PU as a new balanced decision-making approach that is more holistic, creative, and imaginative than earlier linear ones. He believes it is a process that can be used in many disciplines.

Positive Uncertainty and other approaches combining both reason and intuition seem to hold promise not only for a modern science but for the realities of modern business, education, and counseling and career counseling. Gelatt's book for people who want to try his approach, *Creative Decision Making Using Positive Uncertainty* (1992), offers strategies that career professionals will find helpful to use with clients.

This new framework can help career professionals' clients imagine and invent their own future. Although the main purpose of counseling in the past has been to help people make up their minds, the new purpose is to help them keep their minds open and perhaps even teach them how to change. PU seems uniquely suited to the kinds of complex decisions individuals and families are making today to create more integrated and holistic lives.

Intuition in Organizations

Others besides Gelatt believe that intuition has a role in decision making. Creative and intuitive thinking has been accepted in the business world for a long time. In fact, a number of corporate executives have used intuition to help them make decisions. Westin Agor, the director of the Global Intuition Network (GIN), edited a guide for executives and managers in leading and managing organizations productively (Agor, 1989). GIN was organized in 1986 to sponsor research on intuition. It has created a video called *The Role of Intuition in Decision Making*. It has held international conferences on intuitive decision making in organizations since 1990. Agor has also developed an instrument to measure underlying intuitive ability and to determine whether people are using this ability on the job to guide their decisions.

Organizational Change

Personal changes are sometimes triggered by organizational changes—job loss is one such change. It is therefore important for career professionals to understand the nature of these changes and how they might affect their clients if they are to help their clients see the growing connection between work and personal life and make appropriate decisions.

It is not possible or necessary to review all the important trends characterizing corporate organizations today, so a few that relate directly to ILP will be discussed in this section.

It seems clear that the workplace of the future will be very different from the workplace of today. Organizations have gone through considerable change since the concept of organizational development began at the National Training Laboratory in Bethel, Maine. This organization itself has evolved into the NTL Institute for Applied Behavioral Science while the theory evolved from personal growth to group development to organizational development to human resource development to total resource utilization (Lippitt and Lippitt, 1982). Recently the concepts of human resource management and total quality management have been added, along with those of the learning organization, reinvented and reengineered organizations, horizontal structures, high performance work teams, and new psychological contracts. Some argue that the concept of organizational development is in danger of becoming defunct because it has moved so far away from its original purpose—to focus on organizational processes. A new proposed definition emphasizing process is the following: "Organization development is an organizational process for understanding and improving any and all substantive processes an organization may develop for performing any tasks and pursuing any objective" (Vaill, 1989, p. 261).

Although some organizational trends are cited earlier in this book, a few of those that may affect life planning are highlighted in this section. A number of changes hold promise for new kinds of organizations that create more humane environments for workers.

Shifting Organizational Structures

The main structural changes in organizations relate to *downsizing* or a conscious effort on the part of corporations to reduce their workforce and increase profits. Sometimes it is suggested that the layoffs are caused by new technology, that the technology is now doing what people used to do. Much of the description comes from a management perspective; less comes from the union perspective. Some interpret the dramatic changes in organizational structure as an attempt to eliminate unions. However, the new "horizontal" organization, which has fewer managerial jobs, is affecting workers at all levels, from executives, to managers, to workers.

There is also a new psychological contract between employer and employee. Kenneth DeMeuse and Walter Tornow (1993) describe the difference between the old unwritten contract and the new one. According to the old one: "If I work hard and well and am loyal to the company, I will always have a job and the company will take care of me." There were clear benefits for both parties: the company had an employee who was dependable, hard-working, and loyal, and the employee had job security, a good salary, and fringe benefits. There was a strong bond between employer and employee.

The new psychological contract is one of a shared vision and mutual benefits. Both parties must recognize their interdependence. Information is widely available and decision making more of an employer-employee activity. Power and risks are shared. Yet for this philosophy to work, there must be effective leadership in four areas: *culture, structure, employees,* and *human resource policies.* The *culture* needs to promote continuous learning, simplification, and innovation. The organization's *structure* must be able to respond quickly to changing markets. There must be close relationships between employees, customers, and suppliers. *Employees* need skills that allow them to adapt rapidly to change, for example, they must learn how to learn and exercise judgment. Finally, *human resource policies* need to link business strategies with human resource practices so that employees are empowered to be self-managing. This is the kind of organizational environment in which both employees and employer can face the changes and challenges of tomorrow (DeMeuse and Tornow, 1993).

The corporate change that is most often discussed is that of the learning organization. According to Peter Senge, director of the MIT Center for Organizational Learning, one of the most important implications of this new type of organization is that there must be a commitment to change from many levels of the organization (Senge, 1996). Top management can effect certain kinds of changes, but the need is to work with managers and teams to "develop enhanced learning capabilities such as systems thinking, improving mental models, fostering dialogue, nurturing personal vision, and building shared visions" (p. 45). Doing this requires trust, curiosity, and shared responsibility; in addition, people must learn from each other. Hall and Mirvis (1995) see the new definition of career as lifelong learning. They see it replacing the old definition of the term as people in organizations become more adaptive, self-directed, and responsible for their own careers.

Although this may be one of the organizational changes to have the most positive effect on people's career development, workers need to be prepared in order to succeed in this kind of environment. But if job security and job stability are gone, how can workers develop the relationships, trust, and shared vision that Senge suggests? Who will help them in the process of creating self-directed careers in the projected "dejobbed" organizations? How will learning occur in the shamrock organization with a mixture of core professionals, consultants, and contingent workers?

It would seem that a new role is demanded of human resource personnel. They must care about employees and put priority on their needs and development. This, of course, requires support of top management. A few enlightened organizations, such as United Technologies, are replacing the downsizing strategy with a retraining strategy, along with offering stock options to employees.

Shifting Work Patterns and Human Values

As a result of some of the organizational changes, some human needs seem to be better cared for. Although some human resource development personnel and training programs seem to be moving toward protecting the interests of the organization with a primary emphasis on performance appraisal, others seem genuinely attuned to human needs. Rosabeth Moss Kanter (1977a, 1977b) identified these needs in the 1970s.

One of the most important needs being addressed today is the connection between family and work. (For more on this, see Chapter Five.) Friedman and Galinsky (1992) provide examples of many corporations that are responsive to work and family needs. They stress the importance of a systems approach, rather than an isolated programs emphasis, when addressing these needs.

Parker and Hall (1992) identify some of the characteristics of family-friendly organizations. Organizations need to look at ways in which family and work intersect and be aware of the different types of families today—such as single parents—and take into account the amount of work typically done by women at home.

Also growing as organizational values shift is an awareness of diversity and diversity training. The focus is on valuing all kinds of diversity. Dramatic organizational changes are occurring to make workplaces more humane for women and ethnic minorities. The approach described by Barbara Walker (1996) and Walker and Hanson (1992) is hopeful. It emphasizes "valuing diversity" and provides opportunities for workers to form small work-based groups of people who want to learn about and value differences. Through this approach, they learn about others in a trusting environment supported by management. The changes achieved through this small-group method seem to be more than cosmetic. These change efforts are designed to reduce competition, increase cooperation and collaboration, and develop healthy interpersonal relationships. Career professionals need to be well informed about the organizations that actively promote such activities. They also need to help assure that such valuing diversity initiatives are continued in the new organizational structures (see pages 171 and following).

Shifting Leadership Patterns

Volumes have been written about trends in organizational leadership and the new managerial and worker skills needed in a changing society. One of the most creative and visionary is by Jean Lipman-Blumen, *The Connective Edge: Leading in an Interdependent World* (1996). Based on interviews and historical summaries of the leadership styles of more than five thousand business and government executives and managers around the world, she notes that a new approach in politics, government, business and industry, religion, and education requires movement from competition to collaboration, partnership, and the "connective edge," which she defines as interdependence and diversity. A sociologist and feminist, she also examines leadership from an interdisciplinary perspective. She maps a pattern of leadership for new world leaders and for new world organizations. Her view of leaders, organizations, and change has much to contribute to Integrative Life Planning and to career professionals seeking new paradigms.

The Peter Drucker Foundation offers a remarkable collection of essays by leaders in organizational development and management (Hesselbein, Goldsmith, and Beckhard, 1996). Each presents her or his view of the future of our lives, organizations, businesses, and society. It would be impossible to summarize the views of all of the thirty-six leaders included, but there are some common themes that may be mentioned here.

In the foreword to the book, Drucker himself presents an interesting summary of what effective leaders know and do. They know that a leader must have followers; they are not admired or loved; they are highly visible and set examples; and they regard leadership as a responsibility. Although they may be very diverse in style, personality, and interests, they ask some key questions: What needs to be done? What can and should I do to make a difference? What are the organization's mission and goals and what constitutes performance and results? Concerning their characteristics, they are extremely tolerant of diversity in people; are not afraid of strong associates; and follow the "mirror test"—that is, they make sure the person they see in the mirror is the kind of person they want to be, respect, and believe in.

Here are the thoughts about leader qualities offered by some of the visionaries in the book (Hesselbein, Goldsmith, and Beckhard, 1996):

Peter Senge: Organizations will have multiple types of leaders: local line leaders will worry about the bottom line; executive leaders will be responsible for an operating environment that allows for continual learning; and internal networkers will be the community builders.

Sally Helgesen: Seeing the world as a "web of interconnected parts," there will be "nonpositional leadership" and "nonpositional power."

Gifford Pinchot: Helping people gravitate toward "work that needs to be done," leaders will help create community through shared mission and values, caring for employees, and serving the common good.

Edgar Schein: Leaders are animators of organizations, getting them off the ground; creating organizational culture; sustaining culture; and acting as change agents. Leaders cannot make change happen but can help change evolve through perpetual learning.

John Work: Leadership must be built on socially meaningful visions and change that leads to social betterment in a society of "unending social tasks." This kind of leadership is committed to ethnic sensitivity, workplace vision, new and different employment processes, effective utilization of a diverse workforce, and a connection between the organization and the community.

Rosabeth Moss Kanter: Leaders must be cosmopolitans, integrators, diplomats, cross-fertilizers, and deep thinkers. They must break out of rigid roles and stereotypes, be willing to risk new patterns, and partner with others.

Richard Leider: Leadership consists of YOU, INC. In other words, all change is self-change; with self-change you get emotions. Change requires self-leadership and looking within.

Beverly Kaye and Caela Farren: Leaders can help people develop their careers by being facilitators, appraisers, forecasters, advisers, and enablers.

Some common themes run through many of the essays in the book:

- Many express an almost idealistic fervor about the power of organizations to change—even transform—and believe that good leaders know how to make this happen.
- Several express concerns about community building, the betterment of society, and working for the common good.
- There is a remarkable agreement about the need to move from hierarchical, competitive organizations to cooperative, collaborative ones in which continual learning is central and democratic values are visible.
- Most believe that new kinds of communication, hiring policies, reward systems, and visions are necessary if organizations are to capitalize on all of the diverse human resources available. (It should be pointed out, however, that remarkably few women and ethnic minorities are represented among the authors.)

- The theme of community, community building, building bridges, connecting, and partnering appears in several of the essays.

While many of these ideas are inspiring and congruent with the critical tasks of ILP, one wonders about the extent to which they are or will be accepted and implemented in work organizations. These humanistic expressions seem quite out of sync with the current realities of downsizing and dejobbing of workers who were not financially, psychologically, or emotionally prepared for often abrupt managerial actions.

Changing Leadership of Women and Men

Gender remains an extremely important influence in leadership style. Ragins and Sundstrom (1989) offer a brilliant analysis of gender and power in organizations. In their discussion of the battles for power between women and men, they identify the key processes that affect those relationships in various contexts: gender-role socialization in society, selection and tracking in organizations, perceptions and role expectations in interpersonal relationships, and career aspirations and choices in individuals.

According to Rosener (1990, 1995), women make up 33 percent of corporate middle management positions but only 2 percent of top positions in Fortune 500 companies in the 1990s. Even though the gap has narrowed, there remains a substantial difference in salaries between female and male managers and executives. Rosener also found that men feel more in tune with their surroundings and are more likely than executive women to perceive things as their peers do. In other words, perhaps the top echelons are still reserved for men.

Many women in the corporate workforce have had to put up with a double standard and to work harder to succeed. Mistakes and failures are less acceptable when women make them. Some women report subtle discrimination. "It's not being listened to, not having your ideas implemented, being left out of a meeting, not getting promoted as quickly," according to some. Some companies are reluctant to put women in line positions: they still believe it to be a risky investment to spend money because a woman may leave to have a baby. In fact, only 30 percent of female executives have children, while 95 percent of male executives do (Rosener, 1995).

It is still not clear who makes better organizational leaders, men or women. A number of studies show no differences in women's leadership styles. For example, a study of men and women leaders by Rosener (1990) at the University of California–Irvine found that women were not better able to reduce interpersonal friction and were not more understanding or humanitarian than men. They were no less dominant in leadership situations and no less able to define and attain goals than men. A second wave of women is making its way into top management by drawing on skills and abilities they developed from a shared experience as women. "They are drawing on what is unique to their socialization. They are finding a different way to the top—seeking and finding opportunities in medium-sized, fast-changing and growing organizations and showing they can achieve in a different way" (pp. 119–120). Yet the study also found that women were moving away from the "command and control" methods used by male leaders toward a style described as "interactive leadership." Women were also found to believe they attained their positions as a result of their own efforts, including their charisma, interpersonal skills, hard work, or contacts.

The study found that the women surveyed believed that interactive leadership includes four components:

1. Try to make interactions with individuals positive for everyone.
2. Encourage participation; allow employees to feel powerful and that they are in a win-win situation.
3. Share power and information; hold a series of meetings over time to get input from others.
4. Enhance other people's self-worth and get others excited about their work to energize followers.

Interactive leaders try to develop a group identity. They give praise, refrain from asserting their superiority, do not pull rank, but do hold parties "to celebrate ourselves." Whether exercised by women or men, such strategies hold promise for creating more person-centered, humane work environments.

A convincing case made by Rosener (1995) is that most societies, including the United States, have not learned to utilize women's multiple talents. This is an important loss in terms of untapped economic resources. She suggests that a strong management strategy is to start utilizing the talents of all.

A qualitative study of YWCA leaders provides insight into the leadership development and perceptions of fifty-three women leaders in Minnesota (Hansen and Lichtor, 1987). Mostly white, they ranged in age from thirty-three to seventy-eight (with a mean age of 54.4). They represented a variety of fields (business, education, arts, community, social service) and worked in education and in public and private business organizations. The study found that 92 percent of the women were employed, mostly full time. They valued challenge and creativity most on the job and power and security least. They found gender and occupational stereotypes to be their greatest barrier. They were multidimensional: holding jobs, having families, and doing volunteer work. Two-thirds of the women had experienced a major transition (at the average age of thirty-three), and for 93 percent the change was beneficial. Many reported early support by parents who insisted on education and had confidence in their daughters' ability.

Significantly, 77 percent of these leaders said they had had a mentor, and 88 percent said they themselves had been mentors—advising, encouraging, and providing opportunities and emotional support. They had a strong sense of self, saw themselves as very competent, had a sense of control over what happened to them, and felt hopeful. They saw themselves as risk takers—56 percent rated themselves high on risk taking, 42 percent rated themselves moderate, and 2 percent rated themselves low. In terms of life priorities, 81 percent said that family was most important, 77 percent named occupation or career, 75 percent said friends, and 41 percent said spirituality. Family-career conflict was reported by 74 percent (they had difficulty managing time or finding adequate child care and felt guilty about being away from home), but 93 percent characterized their husbands as very supportive of their career.

These women leaders saw communication skills and vision as the most important characteristics of a leader. They described leaders as people who are able to see the big picture, identify with change, dream, and translate their dream into images so other people can share them. They felt their most important accomplishments were career-related achievement, successful raising of children, and personal growth, in that order. For women in the future they had dreams of equal opportunity, development of full potential without discrimination and stereotyping, and an equal share in decision making. In addition, they believed women will be responsible for bringing about world peace and hoped to see women occupy top leadership positions, including President of the United States. Their advice to employers was to provide equal opportunity, serve as and provide mentors, and offer continuing education. They also should remember that employees have families and help them to be successful in both work and caregiving by offering greater flexibility (Hansen and Lichtor, 1987).

These women's definitions of leadership had a common thread too: "Leadership is the ability to articulate the need for change and the vision of the changed situation, and then to motivate people to move toward the change" and "Leadership is having thoughts, ideas, accomplishments, or positions that are admired and followed by others. A leader is able to stand out from the group, challenge standards or norms, and have a vision" (Hansen and Lichtor, 1987, pp. 54–55).

These studies provide insights into ways in which we approach leadership from both personal and organizational and male and female perspectives. Career counselors need to ponder these concepts as they help clients with their life planning.

Emerging Integrative Career Patterns in Organizations

A humanistic and integrative philosophy of career development is provided in Douglas T. Hall's (1996) edited book that emphasizes a relational approach to career. Building on his earlier definition of the protean career, which suggests that people can change and grow in many ways, Hall's new theory is based on the assumption that life encompasses many changes. Although they write from an organizational perspective, many of the writers in the collection sound like counseling personnel. Rather than presenting typical linear, objective, logical ideas, they offer holistic concepts of connectedness, relationship, diversity, and community, much as ILP does. Hall and his colleagues see a number of issues as part of career that are not always found in typical industrial-organizational psychology or counseling books.

According to these authors, the new career will offer individuals the opportunity to get their identity, satisfaction, and rewards from new kinds of relationships in the workplace. This workplace will emphasize collaboration, learning, meaning, reflection, diversity, and community. Since they can no longer rely on their work for security and stability, workers will become self-directed persons who develop their own careers, gain respect for others, and value difference. They will learn to expect change. Not everyone will feel comfortable with the protean career; some people will not have adequate skills, support, self-esteem, experience, health, or other resources to manage their own career process or make life changes.

The new careerists will have transferable skills. They will constantly learn new skills. They will have to bring new attitudes to work: they will not believe they need to work full-time, they will believe they can create their own careers, and they will believe it is all right to make career transitions. Similarly, in delineating the new emphasis on relationships, Joyce Fletcher (1996) draws on Carol Gilligan (1982), Jean Baker Miller (1976), and Jordan and others (1991) for a relational model of individual growth in the workplace that focuses on interdependence, contextual reasoning, and affective development.

Walker (1996) introduces the concept of "diversity work"—creating systematic strategies to help workers learn about differences and valuing difference as important parts of the protean career. This view of career from an organizational perspective is most congruent with my own view from a career development and counseling perspective. It brings the personal and the organizational, work and family, and the person and the organization into convergence.

Global Social Change

How do personal change and organizational change relate to social change? In 1980, Marilyn Ferguson suggested that out of personal change will come social change. Although I agree—individuals must change in order for significant societal change to occur—I also believe that organizations (especially business and government) can act on their own to bring about significant positive changes in society.

Vision and Social Change

A number of leaders have suggested using vision and visioning to help people imagine a more positive future. In the business sector, futurist and author Joel Barker (1993) describes "the power of vision." He states that the three keys to the future of any organization are *anticipation, innovation,* and *excellence.* Drawing on Marilyn Ferguson (1980), who described a paradigm as a new way of solving old problems, Barker offers this definition of paradigms: "A paradigm is a set of rules and regulations (written or unwritten) that does two things: it establishes or defines boundaries and it tells you how to behave inside boundaries in order to be successful" (p. 32).

Barker also defines a paradigm shift as a change to a new game, a new set of rules. He asks four basic questions: When do new paradigms appear? What kind of person is a paradigm shifter? Who are the early followers of the paradigm shifters and why do they follow them? How does a paradigm shift affect those who go through it? The answers to these questions provide Barker's Paradigm Principles. The most important is watching for the future, that is, anticipating.

And what kind of social change can we anticipate in the future? Barker believes that people who have vision will do something significant in the future. He cites the example of Viktor Frankl (discussed in Chapter Seven), who said that all who survived the Auschwitz concentration camps had this common thread of visioning, of being able to imagine a future. He also offers the example of Eugene Lang, who gave a group of students in elementary school P.S. 121 in Harlem, New York, a dream by personally promising them a college scholarship if they graduated from high school. With a support system of teachers and parents, forty-eight of the fifty-two students in the group graduated from high school and went on to college.

Barker says that this kind of vision works for nations, for children, for adults, and for organizations. The vision in organizations must be initiated by leaders and shared and supported. It must be comprehensive and detailed, positive and inspiring. It should help everyone to grow and to give direction to a "vision community."

Global Social Change Organizations (GSCOs)

Emerging global organizations are also providing expanded visions of social change. A new acronym has been added to the many already in use: GSCOs, for global social change organizations (see Johnson and Cooperrider, 1991). GSCOs focus on people-centered paradigms of service and technologies of empowerment. They engage in an innovative process of transnational cooperation, organizing to bridge traditional barriers to stewardship and sustainable development of the planet. Four such organizations studied by Johnson and Cooperrider are Physicians for Prevention of Nuclear War, The Hunger Project, The Nature Conservancy, and the Institute for Cultural Affairs.

GSCOs act on a Global Integrity Ethic that can lead organizational development professionals to "reclaim the power of their heart in their work as they participate in building a global civic culture" (Johnson and Cooperrider, 1991, p. 224).

Johnson and Cooperrider have the big picture in mind when they describe the characteristics of GSCOs as follows: (1) their primary task is a commitment to serve as an agent of change for a healthier and sustainable world; (2) they are innovative social-organizational arrangements to enable human cooperation across previously constraining boundaries; (3) they seek empowerment, equality, and people-centered forms of social action in accomplishing their mission; and (4) they function across two or more countries without primary loyalty, identification, or reliance.

Here are the five key organizing principles of GSCOs. *Alignment* is the extent to which employees understand, value, and are intrinsically motivated to achieve the mission of the organization. *Attunement* means the organizations are places where individuals respect and trust one another and have a shared vision. *Affirmation* is a principle whereby GSCOs affirm the highest potential for good within each person and demonstrate their capacity for making a difference in the world (and the capacity for members making a difference in the organization) for the highest good. *Authenticity* refers to the way in which people live and enact personal and heartfelt values in response to the compelling vision of the organization, resulting in active rather than alienated responses to global challenges. *Action* is associated with establishing new beginnings; it is defined as enabling action on the part of every organizational participant, the courage to "leave one's hiding place and show who one is" (Johnson and Cooperrider, 1991, p. 253), to begin a story of one's own. The GSCO ethic serves the integrity and interdependence of the planet, ecosystems as well as human systems. GSCOs are interested in fostering cooperation among organizations through linking, connecting, and bridging across cultures.

The main point is this: "OD professionals can and should play a catalytic role in building a global civic culture, to reclaim the power of their heart in their work, and to find new ways to make their lives count and count affirmatively as it relates to the momentous questions of survival and human dignity in our time" (Cooperrider and Thanchankery, 1990, p. 270).

Conclusion

Within the context presented in this chapter, the needs listed in the earlier chapters of this book seem small indeed. This view of transitions and organizational development (OD) provides a message different from that held by many organizations today. Nevertheless, it is one that needs to be heeded. The human being and the planet are at the heart of what our lives are about and changes need to be made to enhance every person's involvement in the stewardship of the planet and other human beings. The message is not unlike that of Matthew Fox (1994), who wrote from a personal and planetary perspective.

For work organizations to accomplish this, they need a more liberated philosophy than we have seen in recent years, a philosophy that goes beyond a focus on restructuring, takeovers, mergers, downsizing, and profits, with little regard for human beings in the workplace. The personal transitions and organizational and global changes discussed in this chapter reflect deep concern about human, organizational, and planetary development. Although they seem quite disparate, promising pieces are emerging that may eventually bring them into synergy in managing creative social change. Career professionals working in a variety of settings (including universities) should be able to help in this process.

Chapter Nine

Integrating Lives, Shaping Society: Implications for Career Professionals

For me, finding my "right livelihood" was a spiritual endeavor that involved becoming more self-aware, clarifying my purpose in the world, and identifying how I might best express myself and provide useful service to others. ILP also led me to reflect on how my ethnicity, culture, and sexual orientation affected my career path. I know that my cultural, personal, professional, and spiritual identities are tightly interwoven.
—Asian American graduate student

This chapter reviews what Integrative Life Planning is about and explains its implications for individuals, career professionals, and society. The concept of ILP is so comprehensive that it is difficult to provide a complete summary, but highlights from each of the critical tasks will be discussed. The chapter concludes with an activity for career professionals to carry out with their clients that may help them bring the pieces of their life quilts together.

Synthesis of the ILP Concept

Integrative Life Planning is a broad new conceptual framework to assist career professionals in helping others make life choices and

251

decisions and gain a big-picture perspective with a view toward the twenty-first century. The framework's metaphorical concept is that of a quilt, in which one puts together and understands the pieces of one's life. ILP is designed to help people become more conscious of the ways in which the various parts of their lives—family, work, learning, and the larger society—are changing in dramatic ways that will have an impact on their life planning in the next millennium.

According to the ILP concept, a number of local and global changes will influence the nature of career development, career counseling, and the work of career professionals in the future. Each decade of this century has produced a different context within which people have had to deal with issues of identity (Who am I?), development (Who do I want to become?), occupational choice (What shall I choose to become?), and the place of work in their lives (Where can I apply my talents?); so too will the next decades present a context that requires new approaches to career planning and career development. Individuals (women and men of all backgrounds), families (of all types), and organizations (whether in business, government, education, or other) will have to engage in self-evaluation and reflection and will need the assistance of well-trained career professionals to help them do so.

The fields of vocational psychology, career development, human resource development, and career counseling also are changing. Often these changes come in response to the societal context. The work of Frank Parsons, who offered a logical, rational vocational guidance framework for occupational choice at the beginning of the century, continues to have powerful impact on the way career counseling is delivered. Yet many professionals have begun to recognize that Parsons's "matching" model of people and occupations is not sufficient for the ways in which society and individuals have changed. The explosion of knowledge about life-span development, adult development, career development, organizational development, and human resource development, along with gender roles and feminism, pluralism and multiculturalism, spirituality, and futurism has changed the ways in which we need to look at ourselves, our institutions, and our professional career practices.

Developmental models and life-span theories of career development have helped us start looking at our lives more broadly to understand our *life roles* rather than just our *occupations* and to see them as a lifetime process, not just a single choice made at one point in time. But most of our theories remain explanations of vocational behavior and, while often connected to assessment instruments, they do not offer theories for practice. Also problematical is that most of our tools for helping, including tests and other formal assessment instruments, are designed to help narrow down choices so people can select an occupation from what is perceived to be a diminishing occupational pie.

New tools for professionals are emerging, although many have not found their way yet into the literature. However, a few new role-based instruments include Nevill and Super's Value Scale (1986b), Crace and Brown's Life Values Inventory (1996), and David Olson's Coping and Stress Profile (1992). Instruments developed to help people examine role priorities, including career salience inventories developed by Nevill and Super (1986a) and Jeffrey Greenhaus (1989), are also based on an expanded concept of career. Only recently have efforts been made to bring major theories and theorists together to explore their commonalities (Savickas and Lent, 1994). A next step is to articulate a theory of career intervention that would originate from practice rather than from abstract principles and concepts (Savickas, 1995).

The events occurring in today's global village also provide a different perspective for life planning in the next century. Although traditional career planning has focused primarily on the self and self-satisfaction, ILP suggests that we need to look at the world through a different lens—one that takes into consideration both local and global needs. The human needs identified in this book—only ten worldwide problems were selected out of an estimated ten thousand global challenges that could be taken on—are large issues within society, work that needs doing. These human needs are felt by individuals, families, work organizations, and communities, and even the earth itself. These tasks are those that need to be done if we are going to make society more just, sustainable, caring, socially concerned, and democratic. The clients of career professionals will need help in seeing the world in new ways, prioritizing the work that needs to be done, and acquiring the knowledge, attitudes, and skills to do it.

Review of ILP Critical Tasks

As this book has explained, six critical tasks form the ILP framework of work that needs to be done. The tasks were chosen because they have been noticeably absent or ignored in most of the career theories that dominated this century. The tasks are to help women and men of all backgrounds develop a global perspective about work and life; engage in holistic life planning, understand the connection between roles and relationships in family and work; increase interpersonal effectiveness through an understanding of one's own uniqueness while valuing diversity among others; see the connection between spirituality, meaning, and purpose in relation to work and life planning; and learn to manage the personal transitions and organizational and societal changes that are already occurring and are likely to become more prominent in the twenty-first century.

Finding Work That Needs Doing

Career professionals need to incorporate a global perspective into career theories and models. This means helping clients find work that needs doing, good work that will improve lives, society, and the planet. Shifts are needed in the way we view the world. Seeing the big picture and understanding the connection between local and global problems and our efforts to solve them can be empowering. For example, domestic battering at home is just as much an evil as ethnic cleansing is on the global scene. Utilizing technology while recognizing both its potential and limitations are also local and global tasks because technology will continue to affect the lifestyles of all human beings. Protecting our local environment is one small part of the global need for environmental preservation. "Think globally, act locally" is the phrase that best sums up this imperative, although in the future we are likely to need both to think and to act locally and globally.

Weaving Holistic Lives

Career professionals need to help their clients acquire a holistic self-view that will allow them to understand their career patterns, their need to plan in both local and global contexts, and the relationships between women and men and between work and other life roles. They will need a larger view of life's possibilities to realize fuller lives as the various parts of their lives (social, intellectual, physical, spiritual, emotional, and career) develop. They will need to set priorities at different life stages. In addition, women and men alike have been limited by pervasive stereotypes perpetuated through the socialization process. Societies, though changing, still communicate different expectations about what men and women can and should do in their lives. Traditionally, men were expected to be the provider and women the nurturer. But this is changing as society changes, and both sexes are developing career patterns that enable them to develop as whole human beings.

Both women and men need to have a worldview that encompasses both self-sufficiency and connectedness and a feeling that they have control over their lives and their futures. They must seek to be economically, socially, and emotionally self-sufficient while recognizing their own spirituality and a sense of community. Ultimately, they must move away from the traditional dominant/ subordinate relationships to egalitarian relationships that are true partnerships between men and women. The rate of movement will vary, of course, across cultures, depending on a variety of factors such as cultural norms, but changes are occurring in both developed and developing countries.

Connecting Family and Work

The ways in which individuals look at themselves, occupations, organizations, and life roles—especially work and family—need to change. The old approaches—knowing yourself, knowing what occupations are out there, and then matching the two—are not sufficient. They are based on the old paradigm and assumptions that lifetime jobs exist and that vocational choice is an individual matter. No longer true! In the future, choices will be made over a life span in concert with one's spouse or partner and family. Career professionals need to understand that the changing needs of individuals and families and the changing structures of the workplace will require an interactive approach to family and work.

Both Freud and Erikson have said that to love and to work are the two main functions in life and in society. These emotions come through family and work organizations. In the United States especially work has been the central focus, primarily identified with men. In contrast, family has been peripheral and primarily identified with women. As a result, family has been considered less important. Fortunately, this is changing. It is important that career professionals help clients understand these changes—how work affects families and how families affect work, and how role conflicts and egalitarian relationships in both areas can develop. Our clients also need to know that some work organizations are doing more than others to meet human needs affecting family and work by offering flextime and flexplace programs, parenting leaves, personal leaves, child-care alternatives, kincare options, and the like. For a long time we have seen programs that link work and education or work and learning; it is now time to develop more programs that link work and family.

Valuing Pluralism

While interpersonal effectiveness always has been an important part of career development, it has become even more important as the demographics of societies shift. All persons, both at home and at work, need to learn to understand, value, and celebrate diversity. The most important task in a pluralistic society—that is, one made up of multiple cultures—is to attain inclusivity. Living in a democratic society, learning to enter the world of "the other" respectfully, will help us to be effective in our work relationships and in other kinds of relationships. We also need to move beyond traditional Eurocentric theories to include those reflecting values of other cultures.

Yet while we learn to value diversity, we also need to recognize our commonalities. Innovative programs developed both in education (for example, the BORN FREE program, which is described in Chapter Two) and in business (for example, valuing-diversity programs offered employees by Digital Equipment Corporation) seem to be helping people gain this kind of understanding. Such programs are helping our society move toward achievement of some of the democratic values ILP espouses. But a number of challenges remain for culturally sensitive career professionals. Gaining enhanced awareness of "the other" and of our own "otherness" will be a lifelong task.

Seeing the Connection Between Spirituality and Purpose

Developing an awareness of our own spirituality and how it relates to work, meaning, values, and purpose is another critical task for career professionals. Spirituality may be defined as our core values, a power outside ourselves, a sense of relatedness to the universe, or "creating a path with a heart." But however it is defined, it has been ignored in traditional rational career decision making. It will take time to learn and reflect on how the spiritual dimension affects our life decisions. It will take time also to evaluate how money, consumerism, and materialism fit into our lives and relate to our values, satisfactions, mission and purpose, and sense of social responsibility and connectedness. Both psychological theorists and career practitioners have addressed this topic and a number of reflective strategies are available for career professionals to help their clients in this process. Some suggest that a "spirituality of relatedness" needs to be reflected upon, with each person evaluating his or her relationship to self, family, community, and social responsibility.

Managing Transitions and Change

The last critical task is to understand the extraordinary changes occurring in society and around the world—personal, organizational, and societal changes. People must even understand the process of change itself. In the next century, people will have to be change agents in their own lives if the expectations of the new workplace and work patterns prove to come true.

Managing change in a way that helps people shape their own lives, facilitate change, and affect the direction of our communities and the larger society will again be lifelong tasks. To expect change, manage change, and live with its ambiguities and uncertainties are all part of our lifelong learning. It is easier to deal with change in an atmosphere of support, shared resources, and cooperation than in one of competition. New models of decision making also are important as many people make transitions in their personal lives and in their work lives. An important new book of essays on career transitions by career development theorists and practitioners offers a glimpse of the thinking of past and present leaders in the field (Feller and Walz, 1996).

Acquiring knowledge about changes occurring in the workplace is also a task of great importance to people and organizations in transition. Shifts in organizational structures, in work values and patterns, in leadership patterns, in relationships between women and men, and in a multicultural workforce are an important part of the learning organization and the learning society. Career professionals and their clients need to know which organizations are flexible and show concern about today's issues.

Career professionals and their clients also need to take into account the outcomes of this personal and organizational change for individuals, families, organizations, and even the larger society. The underlying theme of all six critical tasks is their importance for social change. So we return to the theme of the work that needs doing.

Integrative Life Planning Concepts

What does all this mean for Integrative Life Planning? ILP recognizes the dramatic changes occurring in all facets of life, which require us to have new views of the worlds of self and society. Because of all these changes, we need to shift our thinking from *career planning* to *life planning*. This is a significant change in itself. Career decisions once made in isolation now must be made in context, with consideration for other people affected by the decisions. Also, career planning for occupations now must be planning for life roles and multiple identities; planning for a job alone now must encompass planning for the connection between family and work; career planning that focused on occupational satisfaction now must change to life planning focused on the relational rewards of work; career planning that considered only benefit to self now must become life planning that includes concern for community.

Interactive Tasks

The six critical tasks are interconnected. It may be difficult for career counselors to move beyond the old trait and factor approaches to Integrative Life Planning, although the reaction of professionals in ILP workshops has been extremely positive. They must do so because the critical tasks and interventions identified in these pages are essential to our approaching life career planning in the emerging era. ILP is a systems approach.

The developmental goals of helping people live fuller lives and see their connectedness and spirituality, although long ignored, are central to life planning. Our need to be inclusive and respectful of differences in a multicultural society comes across every day in the media and through our own daily interactions and experiences.

It will take more than a lifetime to understand changing families and work toward more mutually satisfying and positive roles and relationships between women and men in the work and the family sector. Recognizing that we are a small part of the global village can help us begin to see the bigger picture and contribute our talents as change agents to alleviate the universal problems in the global community. Learning to make transitions in our own lives and families and organizations are central tasks as we move into the twenty-first century and help to shape it. Such visions require a different mind-set and paradigm, emphasizing shared leadership, partnerships, community, and connectedness in all parts of our lives.

ILP asks much of career professionals, and there will need to be changes in the preparation of career professionals. Yet ILP is not a how-to model. Rather, it suggests ways in which career professionals can help clients understand their own life roles in work and family and in the global society and navigate personal and organizational changes. Obviously everything cannot be done at once. Career counselors will need to develop a contract with clients to work on one priority or one piece at a time. Integrative Life Planning is like a quilt because it tries to put together the major pieces of people's lives and to help professionals integrate the process into their own work setting.

Connectedness, Wholeness, and Community

Thus, the central goal of Integrative Life Planning is to attain an understanding of connectedness—not only between the tasks themselves but also between all of them and the larger global society.

Internalizing Connectedness

Career professionals need to internalize the concept of connectedness and understand its relationship to wholeness, community, and ILP. Global connectedness undergirds our very existence as nations today, while the issues of inclusivity and partnership relate to our attempts to integrate the various parts of our lives. Because our Western paradigms are individualistic, linear, and rational, we sometimes have looked to Eastern cultures and philosophies to understand this concept more clearly. It is significant that both ethnic minority cultures and women have been calling for more attention to the idea of connection rather than separation. For example, Native American cultures value harmony with nature rather than mastery over nature; they put a higher priority on the circle of life than on the ladder of achievement. Perhaps groups like these feel the need for connection because of their disempowered status in society, which causes them feelings of isolation, disconnection, and powerlessness. Career professionals have much to learn about connectedness from these cultures.

Seeking Wholeness

In the United States we have begun to attend to the various parts of human development beyond the intellectual: the social, physical, spiritual, and emotional. Increased attention is being given to the physical and spiritual as our Western society begins to see the connections between mind, body, and spirit. This more holistic view seems to match the direction society is moving in as we approach the twenty-first century. The dramatic changes in the workplace—including the shift from one-job-for-life to serial careers; the practice of creating jobs rather than just fitting into available slots; the development of contracts and consultancies instead of salaried employment with benefits; the loss of the loyalty factor on the part of both employers and employees; and the change in work ethics—may ultimately have a positive outcome for both women and men because all will have time available for the various roles of their lives, making role integration more possible. The idea of men and women both having balance in work and family and in recreational activities as a part of wholeness has not been given a great deal of attention.

Creating Community

The concept of community is an essential part of Integrative Life Planning. It is the antithesis of violence or exclusivity. I believe that to help ourselves and our clients achieve true community, we have to enlist the talents of all to confront the many problems facing our globe, nations, regions, states, neighborhoods, families. We have to recognize the adverse effects of racism and its effects not only on men and women of color but on all people. We have to recognize how stereotypical gender roles have limited both women and men in all the contexts of their lives. And we have to person-alize and humanize the societal issues. We cannot label teenage pregnancy, rape, battering, sexual harassment, and sexual abuse as "women's issues" but must recognize that they are human issues.

Most important for genuine change to occur in our commu-nities, we need to *look at ourselves*. We must examine our own atti-tudes and behaviors and the unintentional things we do (or neglect to do) that keep us, as individuals and as career profes-sionals, and our organizations from being inclusive. It helps us gain perspective when we are in touch with our own gender and racial issues, our own ethnicity, and our own attitudes about class, age, ethnicity, disability, gender, race, creed, and sexual orientation.

No matter the kind of community in which we help our clients manage and effect change, we can be change agents on several lev-els. We can change our own personal attitudes and behaviors. We can bring about interpersonal change in our relationships with partners, colleagues, students, and employees. We can achieve insti-tutional change through support groups, coalitions, collaborations, and partnerships. I believe firmly with Marilyn Ferguson (1980) that out of personal change will come societal change. However, such change will require all the awareness and commitment as well as the interactive and transformational leadership skills that we can master (Hansen, 1987; Rosener, 1990).

Robert Bellah and colleagues (1985) were early documenters of the need for focus on community in the United States. Peck

(1987), calling for "a revolution of spirit," asks how we can communicate with people of other cultures when we usually do not even know how to communicate with the neighbors next door, much less the neighbors on the other side of the tracks. He calls for individuality as well as wholeness and spiritual healing. He describes community as "a group of individuals who have learned how to communicate honestly with one another, whose relationships go deeper than their masks of composure, and who have developed some significant commitment to rejoice together, delight in the other, and make others' conditions their own" (p. 32).

An important new idea about community in the 1990s is that of *communitarianism*. While acknowledging people's rights as individuals, communitarianism suggests that Americans also have to become aware of their responsibilities to their communities and the nation. It calls for a return to the social contract of democracy. It urges citizens to fight for the institutions of family, school, and neighborhood. It urges more emphasis on responsibilities—an emphasis on *we* rather than *me*. It calls for a community agenda. Some believe that we have given up on old rules and traditions but have put nothing much in their place. To help people learn how to fill the vacuum, a new quarterly newsletter has been created called *The Responsive Community* (Etzioni, 1993).

Columnist Ellen Goodman (1989) offers some poignant thoughts to aid us in this vision. Discussing the San Francisco earthquake of 1989, Goodman points out how disasters often make us more aware of community. She says, "The earthquake has caused those in the San Francisco Bay area to move away from isolation and self-centeredness back to the basics—of survival, cooperation, and a spirit of community." Goodman suggests that such disasters help us examine our priorities. Yet the spirit of community again grows thin as the normalcy of daily life returns; once again people give way to isolation and separation and soon the connections are gone. Of the earthquake, Goodman says, "It was a rumbling, awesome reminder from the Earth that we are all in this together."

Several natural disasters have occurred since the San Francisco earthquake, including devastating fires and more earthquakes in California, floods in the Midwest and Northwest, hurricanes in the East and the South—not to mention all the various calamities that have occurred elsewhere in the world. Such events stimulated the creation of crisis response centers and often brought out the best in the helping professions and the population in general. Unnatural disasters, such as the terrorist bombing of the federal building in Oklahoma City, also brought us together, although in grief and disbelief. In all of these events, the sense of community and connectedness was very strong. Such events bring to the fore as well the spirituality in the individual and in society, the yearning for something larger than oneself, and the need to give back to society. Figure 9.1 provides a graphic synthesis of the many pieces of the quilt of Integrative Life Patterns.

Implications of ILP for Career Professionals

As indicated earlier, this is not a how-to book. Still, it does have implications for career professionals' practice. Whether you are a career counselor, career specialist, adult educator, or human resource specialist, learning about Integrative Life Planning should change what you see and do. This book does not explain exactly how career interventions can be made, but it provides numerous ideas, techniques, and tools that can help clients or employees move from the old Newtonian reductionist framework of vocational planning to ILP's holistic approach. Career counseling approaches will have to change to address the work, family, learning, and community changes, as well as to facilitate the shift individuals and organizations are willing to make to a new paradigm.

For certain cases and clients, the traditional trait and factor methods still may be appropriate. For example, they can help people under pressure get a job to survive or meet immediate needs. For the long-term process of career development, however, the broader approaches of Integrative Life Planning will become far more appropriate for individuals, couples, families, and even organizations.

Several questions arise as we think about implications of ILP for career professionals:

1. How do we help people move from the old to the new paradigm, see the big picture, understand the connection between local and global needs and the changes that the twenty-first century is likely to bring?

Figure 9.1. Integrative Life Patterns.

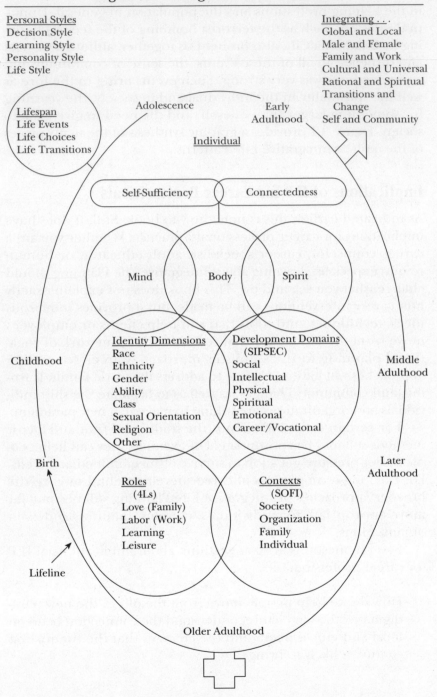

Personal Styles
Decision Style
Learning Style
Personality Style
Life Style

Integrating . . .
Global and Local
Male and Female
Family and Work
Cultural and Universal
Rational and Spiritual
Transitions and
    Change
Self and Community

Lifespan
Life Events
Life Choices
Life Transitions

Adolescence

Early
Adulthood

Individual

Self-Sufficiency   Connectedness

Mind   Body   Spirit

Identity Dimensions
Race
Ethnicity
Gender
Ability
Class
Sexual Orientation
Religion
Other

Development Domains
    (SIPSEC)
Social
Intellectual
Physical
Spiritual
Emotional
Career/Vocational

Childhood

Middle
Adulthood

Roles
    (4Ls)
Love (Family)
Labor (Work)
Learning
Leisure

Contexts
    (SOFI)
Society
Organization
Family
Individual

Birth

Later
Adulthood

Lifeline

Older Adulthood

2. How can individuals achieve greater wholeness when our educational and occupational institutions are still structured on the old Newtonian paradigm, when actual work structures do not keep up with human needs, and when the traditional work ethic—especially in upper management of corporations and institutions—still dominates?

3. How can career professionals help their clients understand the importance of both women's and men's lives and the need for self-sufficiency and connectedness for both? How can both men and women become self-directed agents in their life plans?

4. How can individuals and organizations be helped to understand the link between work and family and to work toward change that will facilitate their connection rather than erect barriers between them?

5. How can career professionals best help clients negotiate in a different world? How can they help them understand their own uniqueness while valuing the differences of "the other" in the workplace and in other areas of their lives?

6. How can clients be helped to become agents for change themselves?

7. How can career professionals help clients learn to integrate the various parts of their lives, set priorities, and put the pieces of their own quilts together in meaningful ways?

Although there is no single answer to these questions, several intervention strategies can be helpful. Strategies commonly used in ILP workshops include awareness activities, career influences, career lifelines, risk-taking exercises, life role identification, mutuality planning, role plays, storytelling (career as story), rebirth fantasies, visualization and imaging, career rainbow, whole-mind learning, and journaling (see "Applying ILP" at the end of the book for more details). More broadly based and integrative assessment tools, some of them informal, include such instruments as Schlossberg's Transition Coping Guidelines (1994), Leider's Purpose Profile (1985), Olson's Coping and Stress Profile (1992), Krumboltz's Career Beliefs Inventory (1993), Moris's Individual Life Planning (1988), Parham's "Rebirth Fantasy" (1996), and Hansen and DeBell's Work-Family Quiz (1988). Most of the formal assessment instruments available are still designed to fit people into jobs. This list, however, is only one of the possibilities for you: you can also create or adapt your own. (Sample strategies are offered in the Resource section at the back of this book.)

Implications for Experiencing Other Cultures

With regard to the critical task of "Valuing Pluralism," career professionals and their clients need to understand what it is like to enter different cultures, learn about them, and how to negotiate them. Juan Moreno, director of the Student Diversity Institute at the University of Minnesota, states that the global village enables us to have "close encounters of the cultural kind with persons quite dissimilar from ourselves" (Moreno, 1996). He offers several powerful suggestions to facilitate entering the realm of the other in a cross-cultural experience, especially when it is for the first time.

- Know yourself before you enter into cultural immersion experiences and learn to know others.
- Enter the realm of the other with humility, recognizing that you can leave at any time. Avoid sweeping generalizations about the culture.
- Enter with the attitude that you are not only teacher but learner as well and that education is reciprocal.
- Temper a tendency to want to do something *for* "these people"; instead, bring a mutual commitment to liberation and transformation with a "we" attitude.
- Identify persons who can be bridge-builders, cultural informers, and interpreters of a different reality, who can help understand the dynamics of internalized oppression.
- Prepare to have all your senses challenged and engage in reflection and journaling.
- Allow all of your ways of knowing (indigenous knowledge, intuition, feelings, wisdom, empathy, and so on) to inform your reality.
- Beware of the tendency to see (or touch, taste, or smell) what you want to see.
- Keep a sense of humor to laugh at yourself, your uninformed behavior, your relative ignorance.

- Be militantly positive about the good points without focusing on the problems.
- Be open-minded, patient, and flexible.
- Keep things simple—simple clothes, open eyes, and an uncluttered mind.
- Stop, look, and listen; be fully present.
- Affiliate with people unlike yourself for extended times rather than seek people who are like yourself.
- Recognize that we are *all* "others" to somebody.
- Reject "unearned privilege" and assert your humanity from a position of equality, dignity, and respect.
- See the world from the perspective of those who are different from yourself; be challenged in your comfort zones, stretched in your mind-set, world view, and realities; and be inspired to be part of personal and societal transformation (pp. 3–9).

Finally, Moreno (1996) urges us "to leave, as much as possible, the sandals of our own cultures at the doorstep." If we leave our fears and prejudices behind, we might find ourselves wearing a new pair of shoes. Moreno states his credo as a new philosophy for crossing boundaries of human differences. His suggestions provide an excellent framework for personal change in "Encountering the Other." They are an essential piece of the ILP quilt.

Implications for the Life Planning Process

The Integrative Life Planning concept has several implications for the planning process. Clearly, an integrative approach requires individuals to use their "right brain" as they look for connections rather than separations. ILP also requires a different set of perceptions about the self and the world. ILP counselors will help clients to move beyond self to make personal decisions with the community in mind. They will help clients see things more holistically.

Clients in schools, business, and agencies may be helped by an introduction to the concept of self-sufficiency and connectedness as described in Chapter Four. Gelatt's (1989) Positive Uncertainty concept may help them deal with the uncertainty and ambiguity of the future. Ideas for assisting employees, clients, or students to self-assess, explore options, engage in dialogue, and develop an integrated picture of themselves and society appear in each chapter of this book.

Implications for Career Practitioners

The following lists some of the things that career professionals can do to assist their clients within the framework of ILP.

1.   They can help students, clients, and workers understand and act on a broader concept of career, work, and life planning with not only satisfaction to self but benefit to society in mind. They can explain that clients can create their own career, as innovative entrepreneurs have always done. Sometimes this may be done through service learning or volunteering (volunteer work can turn into paid work) or by identifying associates who are willing to invest in new ideas.

2.   They can help clients redefine their goals and values and put their lives together. They can help them to have whole careers and be whole persons through loving, learning, laboring, and enjoying leisure; develop their multiple identities; learn to live life more fully; and use their talents for community.

3.   They can help their students, clients, and employees understand that they can redefine work and career to include an emphasis on spirituality, meaning, and purpose and that they can move away from materialism and consumerism toward a global mission of human and natural ecology and societal transformation.

4.   They can help employees see the connectedness of their lives and their work from a variety of dimensions—encompassing the personal and the professional, individual and organizational, local and global, male and female, economic and spiritual.

5.   They can use experiential strategies and activities (and probably fewer tests) to help clients grow and see themselves and the world through a new lens, to understand "inner work and outer work," and to stimulate constructive societal changes.

6.   They can develop new possibilities by identifying and creating integrative instruments or tools to help clients assess the interactive aspects of their lives, roles, and decisions.

7.   They can help students, clients, and workers see the importance of the social and environmental contexts in life planning and

the need for big picture thinking. They can help them understand global needs and how their work can improve both the local and global community.

8.   They can develop or put their clients in touch with training programs to help them improve their interpersonal effectiveness through valuing differences, developing respect for diversity, and embracing inclusivity in their personal lives and work organizations. They can teach the team skills of collaboration, communication, and the commitment to change and for directing one's own career, what Hall (1996) calls the protean career.

9.   They can assist clients to use new styles of leadership involving interactive strategies, team building, flattened organizations, shared group values, learning opportunities, self-directed careers, and flexible organizations.

10.   They can help clients obtain change process skills so that they are better prepared to manage change in their own lives and shape society in ways that will create more humane workplaces, happier families, and more caring communities. They can teach them to engage in a lifelong process of learning, changing, growing, and creating a better quality of life and society for all.

As this list suggests, career and personal counseling are connected in ILP; career interventions are very personal. A recent affirmation of this appeared in the *Career Development Quarterly* when a group of career professionals responded with a resounding "very" to the question "How personal is career counseling?" (Subich, 1993). A number of career development leaders have emphasized the strong connection between the personal and career, including Betz and Corning (1993); Krumboltz (1993); Super (1993); Manuele-Adkins (1992); Brown (1988); Brown, Brooks, and Associates (1996); and Herr (1989), who highlighted the connection between career and mental health.

Implications for Career Research and Knowledge

A concept as comprehensive as ILP does not lend itself easily to quantitative research or the old Minnesota tradition "If it moves, measure it." Qualitative research is also needed in the field of career psychology.

Although academics are more interested than practitioners in epistemology—that is, what we know and how we know it—career professionals are beginning to recognize that there is more than one way of knowing and that scientific empiricism is only one of them. Its assumptions and methods may not apply to needed knowledge in ILP. Practitioners must be aware of knowledge changes; they should not apply old abstract theories and principles to multicultural and female populations. For years leaders in counseling have suggested that theory can derive from practice as easily as practice can derive from theory, but only recently has this concept begun to be taken seriously. Savickas (1996), addressing convergence in career theory, suggests that career counseling is developing a theory from practice and cites such techniques as micropractices, case study analysis, personal narrative, and career as story as enabling the creation of a theory of career intervention.

Career Professionals as Change Agents

There are many personal and organizational change activities that career specialists and human resource development professionals can undertake, several of which were mentioned in earlier chapters. Those working in organizations can implement the principles of planned change, taking into account both the needs of the individual and the organization. Models of work and family balance, organizational management, workplace flexibility, and organizational career development such as those described by Hall (1996) and others can be useful in this process.

Whether one is in counseling, career development, or HRD, the Change Agent as Process Helper Model shown in Figure 9.2 can be useful in helping clients or employees understand and cope with change. It is a model for systems change that I have found useful over the years. It offers anyone working in systems a framework for being a change agent. It suggests six levels of change that "process helpers" such as career professionals must negotiate to be effective in bringing about change. The most important is building relationships and not offering solutions until people recognize the problem. In this way, process helpers help the system in the process of changing itself.

Figure 9.2. Change Agent as Process Helper.

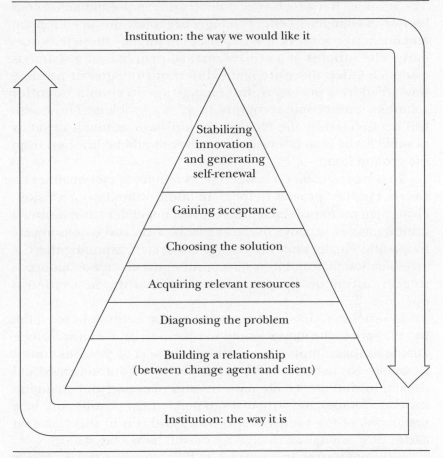

Institution: the way we would like it

Stabilizing
innovation
and generating
self-renewal

Gaining acceptance

Choosing the solution

Acquiring relevant resources

Diagnosing the problem

Building a relationship
(between change agent and client)

Institution: the way it is

Source: R. Havelock, *The Change Agent's Guide to Innovation in Education.*
Englewood Cliffs, N.J.: Educational Technology Publications, 1973. Reprinted
by permission.

If we want to be change agents we need to apply the principles
of change the model depicts. An important starting point is to be
open and honest and have no hidden agendas. Then, working
from the bottom of the pyramid up, the change agent begins
building a relationship with the client, or, in a system, assessing
what that relationship is. The change agent must assess the readiness for change. To effect change, people in a system have to

recognize the problem and share in the process of diagnosing it. The attitude "If it ain't broke, don't fix it" can present an obvious barrier to change. To effect change, organizations need human and financial resources. It is important to identify those resources early. The support of a critical mass of people in the system is essential. Often there are many different strategies or possible ways to address problems. But change agents should not offer solutions until people recognize there is a problem. Those who will be affected by the change should have as much input as possible in the search for solutions; they should be involved from the ground floor.

To gain acceptance, change agents require leader qualities on the part of the "process helper." In addition to having a vision, change agents must be able to persuade, engender trust, muster a critical mass of support, overcome resistance, and communicate frequently. Finally, after the change is effected, assuming there is an evaluation plan and its results positive, the change agent needs to gain institutional support to ensure that the innovation is ongoing.

In order to change our organizations or institutions from the way they are to the way we would like them to be, we must include among us those in power and other members of the community. Resistance has to be dealt with in positive ways. Educating men and women for integrative life patterns and planning and changing societal attitudes and structures to make them possible will be a major task of the twenty-first century and it is in this task that career professionals as change agents will have a big stake.

By its nature, the Integrative Life Planning approach to career development is comprehensive and inclusive. It is a systems approach because it connects many parts of our lives and society. No career development professional or career planner could be expected to absorb all that is within these pages at once. Each career development professional will have to select those tasks that are most important or meaningful at a given time and work on them. Although I have given more attention to some tasks than to others, this does not mean that the others are less important. I hope that career professionals will be able to utilize both the philosophy and practices described in this book in their work with clients, students, and employees. I believe its philosophy represents the direction in which the world is moving and will continue to move.

Learning from Past Experience

The experience of participants in my ILP workshops and classes may be instructive. Since 1986 I have introduced Integrative Life Planning to some four hundred or five hundred career counselors, youth and adult educators, academic advisers, and human resource personnel. I have also developed an independent study course for television around ILP called "Integrative Career Planning." Overall, reaction to ILP has been very positive. Students like the holistic approach, believe it is forward-looking and appropriate for our times, and say it helps them think about their own lives and society and "how we fit into the scheme of things."

Some participants have suggested that the ILP philosophy should be taught in schools, not just to graduate students and professionals. The main criticism is that it is complex and that it takes a long time to understand and use. However, in 1993 I gave an intensive one-week forty-hour workshop that was attended by teachers, school counselors, career counselors, graduate students, academic advisers, and human resource specialists. Afterward, the evaluations were extremely enthusiastic. Students said they were able to take the ILP concept and develop an action plan for use with their particular client populations. Indeed, it was amazing how creative their applications were. Among the interventions participants developed were a program for special education students, one called "Odyssey of the Mind" for a junior high class, a program for low-income women that used the Circle of Life concept (see the following section for more on this), a plan for helping undergraduate advisees, a proposal for changing personnel practices in a business, a program for students in biological sciences, and a program for students in counselor education and in a community college.

Some other interventions developed by professionals with Integrative Life Planning as the conceptual framework bore these titles:

ILP Program in Community Education–One Class at a Time

A Middle School Midsummer Night's Dream: A Life Planning
   Program

Follow Your Bliss: Integrative Life Planning for College Freshmen

ILP for Chemically Dependent Women in Treatment

ILP: A Plan for Curriculum Infusion in a Senior High School

Creating a Regional Career Center Within a Holistic Development
    Framework

A Lifeskills Program for the Differently Abled Using ILP

ILP in a Community College; Developing a School-Based Career
    and Life Management Program for Young Girls and Adoles-
    cents

Life-Course Development Program Plan

Professionals were able to take the concept, or parts of it, and
implement it with their own populations. Said one participant in
my career development class: "I believe that this type of multidimensional model is a very useful tool. It is a model that acknowledges how different we are and how much we have in common.
One gets a picture of the interconnectedness of life. I realize that
in class we got just a crash course. To build skills utilizing this
model would require a longer time and continual dialogue, but
this was beyond the scope of our exposure in class."

Shifting to the New Paradigm

A participant at one of my international ILP workshops once asked
if I thought that the six critical tasks applied to all parts of the
world. I replied that I thought the issues exist in all cultures but
that different cultures are at different places and have different priorities and would consider certain tasks more important than
others.

This difference in emphasis must be taken into account as
career professionals help clients prioritize tasks according to their
personal and societal values. For example, Sweden is often
regarded as the most egalitarian society for men and women. Yet
when I studied the Swedish educational system some years ago,
there was still occupational sex segregation: men were science and
math majors and ended up in jobs in those fields, and women were
the language majors and entered jobs considered "women's work."
Division of household tasks and nurturing may be much more
equal in Scandinavian countries, thanks in part to the economic
safety net, but caring work is still perceived as primarily women's
work. If both women and men have self-sufficiency and connect-

edness, there will be reduced differences between wealth and poverty and greater opportunities for men to nurture. If the theory of self-in-relation becomes prominent in workplaces, as Hall (1996) and his colleagues recommend, the new relational approach to careers will be realized.

Organizational leaders and executives who have dreams for new kinds of organizations will have to "walk the talk" and implement the humane principles they articulate. This requires not blind acceptance of the new psychological contract but a redefined contract in which workers may still be the primary parties responsible for their careers but corporations will move from downsizing to more humane management practices (such as creating family-friendly workplaces, redefining work structures, and reducing the salary gap between workers and top managers by putting human beings before profits and allowing workers a stake in the business, as by giving them stock options). Examples of such changes are beginning to appear as more and more executives publicly admit having second thoughts and social conscience about downsizing as a long-term management strategy.

Racism, sexism, classism, and other forms of bias and discrimination exist in all cultures. For people to learn to value difference will require not only training in valuing diversity but also top-management commitment to diversity through systems approaches, from mission statements to policy to programs, and through resource allocation. Derald Wing Sue's (1995) concept of "multicultural organizational development" should be especially useful in this process.

The paradigm shift needed is one of the new person, the new organization, the new family, and the new community. This is not so much a reinvention of the work organization as an adjustment of the values by which people and systems operate. Finding work that needs to be done must be accompanied by "finding a path with a heart" (Shephard, 1984).

There is a strong democratic bias in my approach to Integrative Life Planning, reflected in the choice of critical tasks and the connections among them. Simply put, I think the resolution of these tasks will move a culture a long way toward achieving democratic values and principles: respect for human dignity; freedom of choice; equal opportunity to develop and use one's talents; the right of all citizens to decent health care, education, housing, and sustenance; and a sense of agency or control over what is happening in people's lives. The authors of *The Quickening of America* (Lappé and DuBois, 1994) make an excellent case for democratic solutions in the workplace and other areas of life.

The new career development paradigm of the twenty-first century will require all of the following:

1. Adopting the concept of "finding work that needs doing" rather than occupational placement, transition to work, tech prep, or other trait- and factor-based approaches for preparing youth and adults for jobs that may not exist when they are ready to enter the labor market. We have the ironic situation in the United States today where parents are losing what they thought would be life-long jobs, yet young people are still being told that there is a "right job" to prepare for and fit into. On the positive side, one of the good things happening to youth and adults is the current increase in service learning, experiential learning, and active learning, some of it in workplaces where people learn the value and satisfaction of volunteering and contributing to community.

2. People making a genuine commitment to consideration of community (and not just job satisfaction) in evaluating why they want to work. This means taking into account the environmental implications of vocational choices as Plant (1995) has suggested and Henderson (1995) and Fox (1994) advocate, and seeking "good work" that will not harm living creatures or the environment.

3. Breaking out of the mind-set that one must choose the "perfect" occupation, prepare for it, and stay in it until one retires. Though we have been discussing the concept of serial careers for years, the idea of continuous learning for employability (instead of retraining) has not yet caught on.

4. Becoming more comfortable with change. Transitions throughout the life span are becoming ever more frequent. If we assume that we will do many things in life because we have multiple talents, we will come to expect transitions and negotiate them better. We will find work that has meaning and contributes to the common good.

5. Continuing the worldwide struggle of women and minorities for equality. Although race and ethnicity have been at the fore-

front, gender has been less so, yet gender is part of every culture, and some people face the triple whammy of discrimination on the basis of gender, race, and class. Systematic interventions in all kinds of workplaces will be essential, as will the need for structural changes in education, health, and housing patterns in order to address this critical task.

6. Being more critical of what we know and how we know it. This has become extremely important in the Information Age and the postmodern era. There has been much public discussion of the positive and negative effects of the "triumph of technology" and the "information explosion" but far less discussion of where knowledge is coming from. We must learn to ask questions about who is creating scientific knowledge, with what methods, using what assumptions, and with what applications to whom. Attention by academics and professionals to new ways of knowing in the career development and human resource fields will be essential, especially as recognition grows that the old quantitative way is not the only way to truth. Recognition that qualitative approaches are valid and often more appropriate ways to understand human behavior is slowly growing, especially with the impetus from women and multicultural populations. This critical task from my own list of challenges may not seem as important in some cultures, but it may be one of the most influential in determining how effectively and rapidly society will be able to change.

Integrative Life Planning and Social Change

The global and local changes discussed in Chapter Three present a very large picture of the context in which individuals, families, and organizations will be functioning into the twenty-first century. I tried to set the stage for thinking about ways in which our decisions, choices, and transitions can be made with the larger community in mind. This would be a paradigm shift in values from the narcissism of the 1970s to the altruism that Yankelovich (1981) describes and the compassion that Theobald (1987) and others anticipate will be the norm in the twenty-first century. Preparation for family life and for work life will take on a new character with the technological, political, economic, and social changes occurring.

But how can a society change? What can individuals or counselors and other helping professionals do to help shape the society in ways more congruent with democratic values and those larger values for which many seem to be yearning? How can we facilitate societal change toward a common vision or "vision community?" There is a vast literature on planned change and organizational change as well as individual change and empowerment. Let us take a look at the relationship between traditions, transitions, and transformations as we think about the changes ahead.

Traditions

The changing roles and patterns of people's lives require new descriptions and definitions and a new integration of work and family at home and in the organization. The new work ethic and work patterns, the women's movement, an emerging men's movement, and new family patterns have given us life patterns that do not fit the traditional model, which has become dysfunctional for both men and women. In real life, "supermoms," single parents, blended families, househusbands, downsized and restructured corporations, learning organizations, flexible workplaces, and high performance work teams are challenging stereotypes about both workplaces and the home. Women and men are living multiple roles and, as the emphasis on pluralism grows, multiple identities. They need help in choosing, preparing for, implementing, and integrating all of them.

There is also a worldwide movement to change the rules, especially to provide literacy, education, health care and reproductive health care for women, as suggested by the 1994 United Nations Conference on World Population and the 1995 International Women's Conference in Beijing. It is still hard for some to accept that the roles and rules by which women and men learn to relate to each other are changing. This fact was brought home to me clearly some years ago when I was coordinator of an international conference in Norway. I told the audience about my disappointment that there were no delegates from developing nations in a group that was discussing changing roles of women and men. A representative from Nigeria stood up and said in response, "Professor Hansen, there were no representatives in the group from my country because there we have rules. We have rules for what men do, and we have rules for what women do, and we follow the rules, so there isn't a problem." (I have learned since from some Nigerian women that that isn't exactly true and that things are changing there, too.)

Tradition is a very important part of our lives. It is a means by which we transmit our stories, our beliefs, our customs from generation to generation. My husband and I are very proud of our Norwegian heritage and have tried to pass on certain aspects of that identity to our children, especially the language and certain holiday traditions. Margaret Mead (1967) said that tradition is what gives structure to our lives, that without it we would face a bleak future. Rollo May (1975), by contrast, spoke positively about the need for "creative courage" to discover new patterns and new symbols on which a new society could be built. Perhaps one of the things we need to do, as we examine traditions in our personal lives, our professions, and our cultures, is to give up the traditions, stereotypes, and concepts that are obsolete, damaging, dysfunctional, and limiting to human development. There are superordinate or universal values—such as respect for human dignity—that transcend culture. Practices affecting girls and women are among them—sexual mutilation, burning, and infanticide are examples— and must be challenged. We need to hold on to the traditions that give us our uniqueness and help liberate the human spirit. We also have to help clients understand the meanings of these traditions.

Transitions

Much of the last chapter was devoted to managing transitions, so I will not dwell on that topic here. However, I wish to emphasize that Schlossberg's comprehensive and integrative model seems especially useful to Integrative Life Planning. Schlossberg (1984) also discusses the concept of "marginality and mattering." People who are in transition—the engineer who has lost his job, the woman going through a divorce, the refugee arriving in a new land—often feel marginal. They feel that they do not matter. Every time people move from one role to another or experience a transition, it is possible that they will get this kind of feeling. Counselors need to help their clients feel that they matter at all stages of their life journey. Opportunity out of crisis is a useful concept to assist those in involuntary transitions, but we also may need to help people grieve their loss before they can move on to the new opportunity or beginnings stage. We also have to help them find ways to take reasonable risks. Counseling people in transition will be an important skill in the future. It will be one of our responsibilities as career professionals to hone those skills.

Transformations

Beyond the traditions and transitions is a more distant and perhaps larger change. To transform is to change the inward or outward form or appearance. Today many leaders in a variety of disciplines are talking about transformation of individuals, of families, of organizations, of society. Marilyn Ferguson (1980) described a conspiracy of people breathing together to bring about constructive change in society. While we help students, families, and employees deal with their real-life transitions, we also need to form a vision of what we want our own personal lives and families, professions, work, organizations, and society to be like.

In the future, both men and women will have more opportunities to develop holistically because people will move from traditional polarized gender roles through androgyny to gender-role transcendence, which is defined as "achievement of a dynamic and flexible orientation to life in which the assigned gender is irrelevant. Individual behavior and emotional choice is based on the full range of possible human characteristics" (Rebecca, Hefner, and Oleshansky, 1976, p. 204). In his transition model, Brammer (1991) described transcendence as the highest level of coping.

Thus, I am suggesting that we need a new vision of what it means to be human, a new vision of the person in Western society and in other cultures. We need to develop more inclusive models of human development that will allow us, both women and men of all backgrounds, to achieve the democratic goals of developing human potential, for the personal and the common good. These goals still seem elusive. For me the transformational model will also include the spiritual, which has been missing from most career development or life planning models of the past. After having been so long on the agentic side of the scale, perhaps this represents an opportunity to move to the communal side with an emphasis on the relational, cooperative, synergistic, integrative approach to making life decisions and solving community and societal problems.

If we are going to expand options for society, our new vision must be one of women and men as equal partners. This means a profound change in our assumptions about who we are and how we relate to each other, for this kind of equality will require us to move away from a society that at its very core is made up of hierarchies of the dominant and the subordinate. We will need to give up the stereotypes and the traditions that exclude large parts of our human family from realizing their full humanity.

Historian Gerda Lerner (1986) offers documentation of the ways in which men's and women's lives and relationships have evolved, starting in Mesopotamia. She makes it clear in her incisive studies that patriarchy is a historical system. History is changing, she observes, because we are now adding the female vision to that of the male. That process is transforming. Furthermore, it is only "when women's vision is equal with men's vision that we perceive the true relations of the whole and the interconnectedness of the parts" (p. 12). Lerner also presents another image: "Men and women live on a stage, on which they act out their assigned roles, equal in importance. The play cannot go on without both kinds of performers. Neither of them 'contributes' more or less to the whole; neither is marginal or dispensable" (p. 11). Counselors, career development specialists, human resource personnel, and other helping professionals are on the stage about which Lerner writes.

If women and men are to be partners in the major roles of life and in the organization, our society will have to give up the system of gender and racial bias that puts less value on women and ethnic minorities. ILP maintains that career professionals (and our clients) can be agents for positive change and, furthermore, that we can choose the level of change with which we feel most effective and comfortable.

We can decide to be change agents in our own personal lives, working on our own cognitions and behaviors with our spouses or partners.

We can decide to be change agents in our interpersonal relations in our workplace, in how we interact with students and clients or employees of all backgrounds, and the messages we communicate about respect for each other—and for diversity—and what is possible for men and women to be and do to "find the work that needs doing."

And we can decide to be change agents in our organizations and institutions, identifying support groups (for one person alone cannot change institutions), clusters of people with similar goals and dreams and visions who believe that organizations and communities can become more humane environments if we break down the barriers that limit the development of any part of the population. To do so, we as career professionals need to know where we are on the continuum of change and where we are in our life journey.

And we need to recognize that the greatest barriers are within ourselves, especially our own fear of change. A story about my son when he was a child of three accentuates the point. My husband and I were playing bridge with some friends one evening when I heard a thump upstairs. I ran up to find that our son had fallen out of his bed. He wasn't hurt, fortunately. "What happened, dear?" I inquired. He replied, "Nothing, Mom, I just stayed too close to where I got in."

That is true with change as well: we remain too close to where we got in—to our old ideas—and are afraid to move over to the new paradigms. But if we are going to help our students, employees, and clients to move, we need to introduce them to the broader concepts, contexts, philosophy, and self and worldviews that Integrative Life Planning represents.

The Circle of Life

I ask career counselors to look at one of the most important activities in Integrative Life Planning, the Circle of Life, which is illustrated in Figure 9.3. (As pointed out earlier, this concept is especially significant in Native American culture.) The Circle of Life is another way of constructing a lifeline—recording significant people, events, and decisions in one's life—and it fits especially

Figure 9.3. The Circle of Life.

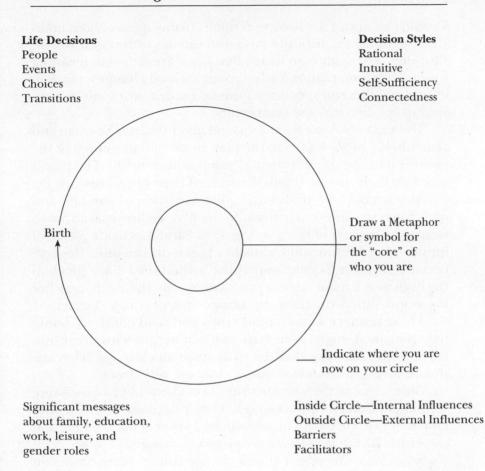

Life Decisions
People
Events
Choices
Transitions

Decision Styles
Rational
Intuitive
Self-Sufficiency
Connectedness

Birth

Draw a Metaphor
or symbol for
the "core" of
who you are

___ Indicate where you are
now on your circle

Significant messages
about family, education,
work, leisure, and
gender roles

Inside Circle—Internal Influences
Outside Circle—External Influences
Barriers
Facilitators

well into ILP. The activity enables career professionals and their clients to look at their own lives holistically and to think through the larger picture.

Look first at the circle. Then think about your own life pattern and how the circle comes together. By doing this, you will be able to see how the pieces fit together and prepare to use the activity with clients and students.

Conclusion

I would like to end the book with some favorite quotes about quilts that exemplify many of the tasks and themes of Integrative Life Planning. The quilt is an image that has a great deal of meaning for me. It is a metaphor for life roles, societal changes, random events, gender roles, connectedness, nature, work and family, spirituality, diversity, and community.

These quotes come from a musical titled *Quilters* (Newman and Damashek, [1982] 1995). In the play, stories about women in the pioneer days are told through a quilt that they made. The play is based on their diaries. It tells the story of their life journeys.

As readers know, traditional quilts are made of patches, and each patch is a different pattern. In the play, eighty-year-old Sarah weaves the patches of the story together. Sarah has made plenty of quilts in her lifetime. She calls her patch on the quilt "legacy" because "I've got to leave something behind me." Each patch of the quilt gets a name: one is the Shadow, one the Birth, another the Storm, others the Butterfly, Losses, and, of course, Legacy.

These pioneer women tend crops and feed children. Some have remained single, some have married but then lost their husbands, some have lost children to death at an early age. They are simple, loving, uneducated women who are very strong.

Gladys, one of the women, reminisces about her late husband. "Mr. Thompson and I worked side by side all these years up until I was sixty-five. He taught me everything I know about building and carpentry. *We was more than married, we was partners.*"

Sarah says, "You can't always change things. Sometimes you don't have control of the way things go. Gale ruins the crops, a fire burns you out. And then you're given so much to work with in a life. And you have to do the best you can with what you got. The material is passed on to you or is all you can afford to buy . . . that's just what's given to you. Your fate. But the way you put the pieces together is your business. You can put them together in any order you like. . . . If you make careful plans, things will come out."

Then they talk about the quilt itself: "The pieces have all the unspoken emotion and devotion of our lives."

At one time quilting was a group activity for many American women. Today that is no longer so. My mother was a quilter. Today some men engage in quilting, including all the men, women, and children who have worked on the AIDS quilt in memory of those who have died of AIDS. Jesse Jackson has talked about the quilt that is the United States. In the Hmong culture, quilts are very special, and the YWCA in the United States recently started a "Hands Quilt."

I think we all remain quilters in our own lives. I think we spend our lives trying to put the patches of the quilt together. We are also quilters in our families. We are quilters in the lives of our children, trying to help them make sense of where they have been, where they are, and where they are going.

We are also quilters in the lives of our students, clients, and employees, helping them to design the various patches—the roles and goals of their lives—and see how their patches fit together. And we are quilters in our organizations and institutions as we work to make them more humane and meaningful places. Finally, to take the metaphor one step further, we are all quilters on this planet, seeking to understand, value, and connect with each other in a sustainable future free from violence. This is the kind of holistic Integrative Life Planning I think we need to be working toward as we try to make our work meaningful and purposeful and to feel that we all matter.

I find it hopeful that there are many people who are perceiving, thinking, acting, and behaving in new ways today, developing new life patterns. Together we may be able to form a new quilt on this planet in which empowered individuals—women and men, whites and people of color, the young and the old—will be able to have happy and fulfilling lives and bring their best talents to bear on "finding work that needs doing" to make the world a better place and to shape their lives and communities for the common good.

Resource

Applying ILP—Strategies for Practice

It has been stated throughout the text that this is not a how-to guide. However, a number of activities have been developed and used in Integrative Life Planning workshops over the last several years. They are presented here as examples of the kinds of activities creative career professionals can do to implement the various critical tasks and themes of ILP with their students, employees, clients, or workshop participants. The text explains the purpose of the strategy, gives directions for its use, and, where appropriate, includes opportunities for personal reflections. One to five activities center around the themes expressed in each chapter.

I hope that these illustrations will stimulate career professionals to develop strategies of their own or to modify or adapt those presented here. The preceding chapters contained activities or presented concepts that can be translated into activities. For example, a life-role activity can be built around Super's Rainbow in Chapter Two or the Four Ls discussed in Chapter Four.

Although these activities are for use in career development groups or life planning workshops, many of them can be adapted for one-on-one situations. In situations involving self-disclosure, participants should always be told to share only what they are comfortable sharing and reminded that they have the option of not participating. This is especially important in multicultural groups. Leaders need to honor ethical codes and limits of training.

Chapter One, Integrative Life Planning: A New Way of Thinking About Career Development
Strategy 1.1. New Paradigm Thinking

Many people are not used to thinking in terms of a paradigm or paradigm shift, yet it has become an important concept in the social and behavioral sciences over the last fifteen years.

Purpose

The activity is intended to help participants think about the meaning of a paradigm shift in the field of career development and how it will affect work, family, personal, and community life. The activity takes about twenty to thirty minutes.

Directions

Read the following two definitions of a paradigm to the group and have group members discuss how they are alike and how they are different and the key characteristics of each. Have them write down three ways in which such shifts from individual career planning to integrative life planning are likely to affect them and their families in the future. Have them discuss their responses with one to three other persons.

> "A paradigm is a pair of different spectacles which can reveal a new view of reality, allowing us to reconceive our situation, reframe old problems and find new pathways for evolutionary change." Hazel Henderson, *Paradigms in Progress*, 1995.

> "A paradigm is a set of rules and regulations (written or unwritten) that does two things: (1) it establishes or defines boundaries; and (2) it tells you how to behave inside the boundaries in order to be successful." Joel Barker, *Paradigms: The Business of Discovering the Future*, 1993.

Have participants think of some of the terms connected with the new paradigm in career development: dejobbing and downsizing, work and family, women and men as partners, local and global change, spirituality and purpose, personal and career, pluralistic societies, holistic development, and the like. Then have them write down two or three aspects of the paradigm shift in career development and the effect that the change might have on them, their family, or their community. Have them share their thoughts and then think about what they learned or discovered from the experience.

Strategy 1.2. Life Planning Influences

Quilters and quilting are used as metaphors throughout this book and in ILP. Ask participants to think about who and what have been their primary influences in relation to work, family, learning, and other life roles.

Purpose

This activity helps participants begin to see the multiple influences in their lives and to think about the consequences of these influences for where they are in life now. It also helps them realize that parts are integrated and that career is more than occupation. The entire activity takes about twenty to thirty minutes.

Directions

Instruct participants to take a three- by five-inch card or four- by four-inch sheet of paper and think of it as a piece of their own life quilt. Ask the group to write on the card according to the following instructions: "Think about the various influences on your life and career. In the upper left corner of the card, write the earliest messages you received from your parents or caretakers about what they expected you to be and do. In the upper right corner, write what kind of life you envisioned for yourself when you finished high school (including education, work, family, and so forth). In the lower left corner, write the name or position of the person or persons who most influenced you or who you wanted most to be like. In the lower right corner, write down what you hope to be doing fifteen years from now—a somewhat realistic fantasy. Then put a symbol in the middle of the piece that expresses the core of who you are, your primary motivator, your center."

Then ask participants to share their pieces, corner by corner, ending with discussion of the symbol. Ask them to share commonalities and differences. A few who wish to do so may share their symbol. Then point out to the group that the card of each member of the workshop—if put together with the cards of the other members of the group—represents a unique quilt of the life patterns of group members. Using colored paper is more effective.

This activity has been used very successfully in many settings with different populations, for example, both college students and adults in midlife.

Chapter Two, Tracing the Interdisciplinary Origins of ILP

Strategy 2.1. Old and New Knowledge

Purpose

This activity can stimulate a more cognitive discussion in a career development class or among counselor educators who teach career development about the changing nature of knowledge and how we know what we know. The activity takes about twenty to thirty minutes.

Directions

Have the workshop or class participants discuss any of the concepts presented (for example, life span and adult development, gender-role theory, the BORN FREE concept, multicultural knowledge). Questions might include the following:

1. How does the new career development literature differ from that which is ordinarily used in thinking about career and life planning?
2. What does integrative research mean? What does the "integrative" concept add to our thinking about career planning? How does it affect how we go about the planning process? What are arguments for an integrative approach? Against?
3. What are the contrasts in the old and new theories of men's and women's development? How do these theories apply to diverse populations?
4. What do you think of the proposition that traditional career theories do not apply to many populations today because they are based on Eurocentric approaches to knowledge?
5. Why has "spirituality" not been a part of career and life planning in the past?

Chapter Three, Critical Task 1: Finding Work That Needs Doing in Changing Global Contexts

Strategy 3.1. Finding Work That Needs Doing

The phrase "Think globally, act locally" has been popular since 1980, when it was the theme of the World Future Society Congress in Toronto, Canada. Focusing on external contexts is an extremely important and sometimes ignored aspect of career and life planning. Of at least 10,233 "global challenges" that have been identified, ten seem especially critical to me. (See Chapter Three, pages 54 and following for entire list.)

Purpose

The purpose of this activity is to help career planners think about the large context of their lives and the global framework that is a part of their planning. The ten critical needs are illustrative of the many cross-cultural issues people face around the globe. It is my hope that career professionals will help their clients identify others that they believe are the most important tasks among the work that needs doing. The next step is to create your own career in which to do it. This is not pie-in-the-sky thinking but a process that has been implemented frequently in the last decade; it is also one of the most critical tasks of the twenty-first century. This activity will take about twenty to thirty minutes.

Directions

After reviewing the ten critical tasks, participants are asked to think about additional work that needs to be done to make society more accountable and responsible and to create a sense of community. Participants should identify needs that they feel are especially important to the twenty-first century. To do this, they must think about the needs that are not being addressed but should get attention from anyone willing to be a change agent. Have participants write down the two or three tasks they believe to represent the most valued work to be done and then discuss in groups of two to four their rationale for selecting those items. After ten minutes of discussion, ask participants to identify careers that would be needed to address their most important work.

Chapter Four, Critical Task 2: Weaving Our Lives into a Meaningful Whole

Strategy 4.1. Holistic Development

Directions

Holistic development has been described differently over time. It may include the six areas of human wellness—social, intellectual, physical, spiritual, emotional, and vocational. Or it may refer to the aspects of salience identified in the Work Importance Study (Super and Sverko, 1995), which examined the degree of importance of five essential life roles: work, study, homemaking, community activity, and leisure activity.

Use the six areas of wellness and the five life roles to help participants draw an activity pie that shows how they spend their time in each of these areas. Look at Super's Life Career Rainbow (see Chapter Two). Choose three roles from among those identified in the rainbow and then imagine what you will be doing in those roles ten to fifteen years from now. (Note that the group should be taken through a relaxation exercise before involving them in a visualization such as this.) Then have participants share their visualizations with two or three other participants and discuss what they learned from the process. This activity takes about thirty minutes.

Strategy 4.2. Self-Sufficiency and Connectedness

The concept of self-sufficiency and connectedness is explained in some detail in Chapter Four, pages 110 and following. After reading this explanation, look at Figure 4.3 (p. 112).

Purpose

This strategy can be used with clients or workshop participants to help them understand these two dimensions in their lives. The activity takes about twenty to thirty minutes.

Directions

Ask participants to think about where they are on a continuum representing the traditional to the contemporary and in the amount of self-sufficiency and connectedness they have in their life. Ask them, How do you define these for yourself and what do you see as the optimum in a balanced perspective for yourself and your significant other?

Then tell them to look at Figure 4.4 (p. 116) and relate it to their own experience. Ask them, To what extent do you have a balance of self-sufficiency and connectedness, and to what extent are these integrated in your own life and in the life of your partner or significant other? What compromises have you had to make along the way?

If you carry out this activity in a group, have participants share their insights with one or two others and discuss how they feel about looking at these two aspects of their lives.

Strategy 4.3. Gender-Role Transcenders

The research of Rebecca, Hefner, and Oleshansky (1976) described three stages of gender-role development through which individuals progress:

Stage I. At this early stage, a child's thinking is global and undifferentiated in conception of behavior, including that related to gender roles.

Stage II. Gender roles are polarized. Children have learned role prescriptions and have a dichotomous view of gender roles as masculine or feminine.

Stage III. Stage III is one of gender-role transcendence. In this highly dynamic stage, individuals move freely from one situation to another, behave adaptively, and choose behaviors from the whole range of human possibilities.

Transcending stereotypes allows and fosters choice of and adaptation to varied lifestyles and occupations. The concept of transcendence differs from the concept of androgyny in that the latter assumes male and female characteristics within each individual. However, sometimes androgyny is considered a stage somewhere between polarization and transcendence. Workshop leaders should read Rebecca, Hefner, and Oleshansky (1976) before conducting this activity.

Purpose

The purpose of this strategy is to help participants understand the importance of gender roles in development and the even greater importance of transcending them. The twenty-minute activity was adapted from the BORN FREE program.

Directions

First, explain the three stages of gender-role development as described in the previous paragraphs. Then have participants enact three role-plays showing how a person with polarized gender-role attitudes, androgynous attitudes, and transcendent attitudes might deal with the same situation. Discussion questions suggested are as follows:

1. What are the advantages or disadvantages of each of the stages?
2. What factors cause an individual to remain at one stage or to move on to another?
3. How do concepts of androgyny fit this model?
4. How does gender-role development relate to life planning and career decisions?
5. What would be the implications for the future if all persons achieved the stage of gender-role transcendence?

Strategy 4.4. Visualizing a Partnership Society

Purpose

This activity is designed to help workshop participants internalize the difference between a dominant/subordinate society and a partnership society. Use the following visualization activity to achieve this goal. The activity was adapted from Eisler and Loye (1990). It takes about thirty to forty minutes.

Directions

Ask members to visualize the year 2020—that is, twenty or so years from now—and what life would be like if men and women of all backgrounds were considered equal partners. Ask the participants to close their eyes. After a relaxation exercise that takes about ten minutes (with appropriate pauses for the imaging to occur), lead them through the following questions:

1. What are the relationships between women and men in the family?
2. In what ways do the child-rearing practices differ from our society's practices?
3. What kinds of differences do you visualize in the elementary school? Junior high or middle school? High school?
4. How is your religious institution different?
5. What differences do you notice in sports and athletics?
6. How do women and men treat each other differently in the workplace?
7. What differences do you see in how men and women engage in leisure and recreational activities?
8. How is this society different for people of ethnic and racial minorities? People with disabilities? People of different social classes? Different religious beliefs? Gays and lesbians? The elderly?
9. What do you see as the cultural norms and values of this equal society?

If you are conducting this activity with an individual, ask her or him to write down a response to the following questions. If you are working with a group, take ten minutes for participants to form dyads and express their feelings about the exercise and the most important visualization they had. Then ask a few participants to share with the group their most important visualizations. This is an extremely important activity because it challenges the patriarchal, dominant/subordinate patterns of today's societies and provides a framework for thinking seriously about social change.

Chapter Five, Critical Task 3: Connecting Family and Work

Strategy 5.1. Role Identification

Since the 1980s, linking roles in work and family has become an increasingly common theme in the career development literature. The following activity is another attempt to help clients understand the link between the two domains and the concept of role integration.

Purpose

This strategy is designed to help clients understand the importance of life roles rather than just jobs.

Directions

Ask participants to take an 8½-by-11-inch piece of paper, draw a line across the middle, and draw five circles on the top half and five circles on the bottom half. In the circles, they should indicate which roles are currently most important to them (numbering them by rank) and which they expect will be most important in ten to fifteen years. Then ask them to examine their circles in light of the following questions:

1. What is the status of these roles within your family system?
2. What are the expectations associated with each role?
3. How important are the roles at different life stages?
4. What happens if the woman's work or career goal becomes more important than the man's?
5. How much of our time, energy, and talents do we give to each role?
6. What is the impact on significant others of the way we carry out our roles?
7. How do these roles affect our relationships with each other? With children (if we have them)?
8. What roles do children play in this configuration?
9. Where do leisure, service, and volunteer roles fit in?
10. How can awareness of role options help us in life planning?
11. Are the roles concurrent and sequential for both partners?
12. Are they flexible or rigid?
13. How are the roles different if we marry at twenty versus thirty or thirty-five? How might they differ in gay or lesbian couples?
14. What happens to roles at the retirement stage of life?

In small groups of three to five people have participants discuss how they labeled their roles and answers to some of the above questions.

Strategy 5.2. Who Is the Provider?

This activity provides a view of the changing roles of women and men in work and family. (See Figure 5.1 [p. 128] in Chapter Five.)

Although work has traditionally been identified with men and family with women, Pleck's figure illustrates how this is changing, as women are rapidly entering the labor force and men are more slowly taking on family and nurturing activities. The new system is of men and women sharing both the provider role and the family role.

Purpose

The purpose of this activity is to help participants better understand the changing roles of women and men and how some couples are moving closer to partnerships. However, these shifts in roles can lead to resistance and role conflict.

Directions

Ask participants to study the figure titled "Who Is the Provider?" Then ask them to give their honest reactions to the changing roles in our society. Ask participants to reflect openly on changing norms and think about the positive implications that might result for families.

Strategy 5.3. Mutual Planning

Although many of the activities in career planning workbooks focus on the individual, just as it is important to stress the interrelatedness of life roles and the intersection of work and family, it is also important for partners or couples to plan together. Gaining an understanding of and commitment to shared values is essential.

Purpose

The purpose of this strategy is to help partners understand the value of planning their careers and life goals together rather than independently. Integrative Life Planning suggests that this is a mutual task and not a separate process for each individual.

Directions

Ask participants to complete the following form. Add spaces where necessary. Afterward, have partners discuss and compare their individual and mutual values and both the barriers and facilitators to reaching accord on them. This activity takes about thirty minutes.

My Personal Values   *Partner's Personal Values*

——————————————   ——————————————
——————————————   ——————————————
——————————————   ——————————————

My Relationship Values   *Partner's Relationship Values*

——————————————   ——————————————
——————————————   ——————————————
——————————————   ——————————————

My Family Values   *Partner's Family Values*

——————————————   ——————————————
——————————————   ——————————————
——————————————   ——————————————

My Work Values   *Partner's Work Values*

——————————————   ——————————————
——————————————   ——————————————
——————————————   ——————————————

My Career Values   *Partner's Career Values*

——————————————   ——————————————
——————————————   ——————————————
——————————————   ——————————————

My Values   *Our Mutual Values*

——————————————   ——————————————
——————————————   ——————————————
——————————————   ——————————————
——————————————   ——————————————
——————————————   ——————————————
——————————————   ——————————————

Chapter Six, Critical Task 4: Valuing Pluralism and Inclusivity

Strategy 6.1. Multiple Identities

The concept that each person has multiple identities is extremely important in multicultural career counseling and human resource development. It needs to be incorporated into valuing diversity groups, such as those suggested by Walker and Hanson (1992). The broad definition presented by Arredondo, Psalti, and Cella (1993) also emphasizes the multiple dimensions of each person's identity. This activity can be especially useful at the beginning of an ILP workshop.

Purpose

This strategy is designed to assist clients, employees, and students to become more aware of their own multiple identities and those of others. It also underlines the idea that different aspects of one's identity may be important at different times of one's life.

Directions

At the beginning of an ILP workshop, ask participants to introduce themselves to the group by sharing the three most important aspects of their identity at the present time. Suggest that they focus on the *dimensions of identity* shown in Figure 4.2 (p. 86) (and not on the life roles or development domains). These dimensions include race, ethnicity, gender, class, religion or beliefs, age, sexual orientation, and physical ability. Some participants might add "being a parent" or "being a son"; if so, point out that although very important, these are roles rather than identity dimensions.

Depending on the size of the group, this activity can be time-consuming. In any case, it is usually time well spent. Ask participants to reflect on the strategy by commenting on what they observed, how they felt, and what they learned from each other and the activity. Allow approximately three minutes per person for this wrap-up, more if time permits.

Strategy 6.2. Rebirth Fantasy

Over the years the use of fantasy has been a popular technique in counseling and in diversity training. It requires people to use mental imagery to put themselves into the life of another who is different from them in some way. This particular activity is adapted from Thomas Parham (1996), who has used it in diversity training workshops with counseling leaders since the early 1990s.

Purpose

This activity can be a powerful one to help people recognize their assumptions, misperceptions, and biases and begin to develop empathy for another group. Participants who allow themselves to get into the fantasy can learn a great deal. Allow thirty minutes.

Directions

Conduct a short relaxation exercise to prepare for the imaging process and then use the following script: "I am going to invite you to be reborn as a person from a different racial or ethnic group in the United States other than your own. Consider African American, Native American, Hispanic or Latino, Asian American, or a person of another ethnicity who may be in your work setting. Take a minute to gather your thoughts and figure out who you want to be. Now, you are a different person. Ask yourself some questions as you image who you are."

After this prologue, lead the group through the following questions:

1. You are a child of this group. What is your childhood like? Where do you live? Who do you play with?
2. You go to elementary school. What is elementary school like for you? How do you get there? Who are your friends? How do you like school? What are your friends like?
3. You are in junior high school or middle school. What do you like about it? Dislike? What do you do during lunch? After school?
4. Now you are in high school. You have a choice of subjects? What subjects do you like? You go to a counselor to get more help for after high school. What kind of help do you get? What do you do in the evening?
5. It is after high school now. What are you doing? Are you in school? Do you have a job? Where do you live? What do you do during your spare time? What do you do on the weekends? How close are you to your family?

6. You have just completed your training. You are in your present job now. How did you get there in the first place? Did you answer an ad? Did you have a mentor? What barriers did you find in getting into the field?
7. What is your opinion of this field you're in? How do you best think that you can deliver services to your population?
8. What is important to you in terms of your functioning in this field? Your values? Why are you in this field? What opportunities do you face? What barriers?
9. What kind of resources do you have both personally and professionally that will impact your success in this field? What kind of life style do you have? Who are your friends? How close is your family?
10. What do you look like as a professional in this field?

Have two or three participants share the person they chose and the images they had in their rebirth. Have all participants examine the assumptions they made about the other ethnic group and how these assumptions impact their beliefs about building diversity in a given field or dealing with diversity in it.

A variation on this activity is to invite participants to be reborn as a person from any oppressed group—for example, people with disabilities, different beliefs, different sexual orientation, and so forth.

Chapter Seven, Critical Task 5: Exploring Spirituality and Life Purpose

Strategy 7.1. Finding Our Core

Although people define spirituality differently, many associate it with "the core of the person—the center from which meaning, self, and life understanding are generated" (Yates, 1983, p. 60) or "the deep integration, wholeness, a sense of the interrelatedness of all of life" (Kratz, 1985, p. 4). Others link spirituality with a connectedness with nature (Fox, 1994).

Purpose
Visualization or imaging is an especially appropriate way to come to terms with one's spirituality. (Although this activity is similar to the Life Planning Influences activity described earlier, it can be used as a separate activity as described here.) Allow twenty-five minutes.

Directions

Have participants think of a symbol that represents the core of who they are, the thing that motivates or drives them. For example, a person who is very achievement oriented might draw a ladder; a person who is nurturing and caring and makes that characteristic the center of his or her life might draw a heart or two hands reaching out. There is no right symbol. Ask participants to draw the symbol on a three- by five-inch card. Then ask them to write in each corner of the card the reasons why it is their core symbol. Participants should discuss their feelings with a partner or with two or three other people in a small group. End the activity by sharing with others in the group and discussing commonalities, differences, and what each learned from the experience.

Strategy 7.2. Search for Purpose

The quest for purpose and meaning is central in the lives of most people, yet it has been pretty well ignored in career planning. However, a number of writers have provided insight into how spirituality relates to people's lives, for example, Leider, (1985); Hagberg and Leider (1988); and Naylor, Willimon, and Naylor (1994). The latter suggest that the search is a very personal one that must take into account personal history, personal philosophy, and a personal strategic plan.

Purpose

This activity is designed to help participants in their own personal search for meaning and purpose and to help them think about how it relates to the rest of their lives. The activity takes about thirty minutes.

Directions

Increasingly people are bringing their work into line with their life mission—to bring the things that really matter back to the center of their lives. Ask participants to explore their own life purpose and meaning by answering the following Ten Questions for Personal Search and reflecting on them (Naylor, Willimon, and Naylor, 1994):

1. Who am I?
2. Where am I going?
3. How can I prevent my life from being a series of accidents?
4. What do I want to be when I grow up?
5. How shall I overcome my separation from others, myself, and the ground of my being?
6. What shall I do to resist the temptation to have?
7. How does one learn to be?
8. Can I find meaningful employment?
9. Is it possible to experience real community?
10. How can I die happy?

The authors suggest that people can help shape their own futures by asking such questions. In my ILP workshops and classes, I ask students to write their career development story, reflecting on past, present, and future in relation to many dimensions of their lives. In shorter workshops, this is not possible. However, helping members reflect on what words they would want to have written on their tombstone or said at their funeral and on their values and life dreams can help put participants in touch with their spirituality. Leider (1985) offers a set of reflections on the issue of mortality that is especially useful.

Strategy 7.3. A Sense of Time

The importance of time and time orientation in career planning has been stressed by a number of authors (Savickas, 1990; Schlossberg, 1991). It is especially important in how it relates to a life journey and how one perceives past, present, and future. Of course, this is culture-related. As pointed out by Kluckhohn and Strodtbeck (1961), Western and Eastern cultures have different perspectives on time.

Purpose
The purpose of this activity is to build a sensitivity to time as it relates to purpose and meaning. How people spend their time gives some indication of their life direction. The activity takes about fifteen minutes.

Directions

Have workshop participants write down important events they expect to happen in the next year, the next five years, and the next ten years. Have them put a checkmark in front of those events over which they have some control. This activity is primarily for individuals to gain some sense of their own perspective and future orientation.

Strategy 7.4. Dreams and Hopes

Dreams are also a part of time differentiation. Individuals, couples, and partners need help in creating and articulating their hopes and dreams. Dreams, like fantasies, often come true. Indeed, one study of first-year college students asked what they thought their lives would be like in ten years: a follow-up study ten years later found that many of them were doing what they had dreamed of doing that first year.

Purpose

Integrative Life Planning workshops help participants envision the past, present, and future and see how they fit together. Integration—including integration of time—helps people get a sense of connectedness, become aware of the enduring patterns and themes in life, strengthen their identity, and gain hope. (The creative thinking of Savickas, 1990, inspired this activity and the next.)

Directions

After a short relaxation exercise, ask participants to identify three dreams they have for the next ten to fifteen years. One should be a dream for their own future; the second should be a dream for the kind of work organization they would like to be a part of; and the third is a vision of what they want their society to be like. Have them assume they are on a cloud overlooking their own life and workplace or on a spaceship hovering over the country. Have them do their visioning from the perspective of the various life roles Super and Sverko (1995) suggest they are likely to have: work, study, homemaking, leisure activity, and community activity.

After they have imaged each, they may want to write down what is happening in each of these roles. Have them meet in groups of four and then discuss the strategy, commenting on what they learned, which of the three dreams was most important to them, how the dreams were related, and so on. You may wish to develop a worksheet for this activity, listing the five roles down the side and each of the dreams along the top.

Chapter Eight, Critical Task 6: Managing Personal Transitions and Organizational Change

Strategy 8.1. Responding to Change

Workshop leaders can draw from any of the personal transition models identified in Chapter Eight. You may wish to ask participants to analyze a major transition in their own lives according to the Schlossberg Transition Model, which is depicted in Exhibit 8.1 (p. 223) and Figure 8.2 (p. 225) and applied in my own Case Study of a Job Loss. Or they can use Brammer's Levels of Responding to Change shown in Figure 8.1 (p. 218) as a basis for thinking about their own transition.

Purpose

The purpose of this activity is to help students, clients, and employees anticipate change in ways that may help them prepare for it. Schlossberg believes that becoming conscious of the transition process and its many components can increase one's ability to cope with the change. Brammer's Levels of Responding to Change (pp. 217–218) is a means to help people cope. The activity takes about twenty minutes.

Directions

Ask participants to review Brammer's response to change model and the text explaining it (see Chapter Eight). Have them identify a major transition they have experienced in their adult life and then examine their coping response as it compares to the five levels in the model. Have participants discuss in small groups of three or four the nature of their transition and the ways in which they coped.

Strategy 8.2. Taking Risks

This is a strategy that has been widely used in ILP workshops and generates a lot of interest and thoughtful response. I usually start by sharing three big risks that I have taken in my own life. (For example, I applied for international study in college even when I was penniless, I confronted my department head about salary discrepancies with male peers when I was one of few women in a basically all-male department, and I had my first baby at a late age.) I usually share at the end of the activity the consequences of these risks.

Purpose

The purpose of this activity is to facilitate thinking about what a risk is and the risks participants have experienced and to gain some insight into the risk-taking process and how it has affected their life planning.

Directions

Use the following worksheet to carry out this activity (Hansen, 1984).

Risk Taking: Connecting Career Decisions and Risk Taking

A risk is an unexpected action you have taken that has had an impact on your career and life planning. Usually people don't take risks unless they are somewhat certain of a positive outcome. However, some people take more risks than others and greater risks than others. Write down an important risk you have taken related to your career development at three different life stages. Describe the risk:

Risk 1:

_____

Risk 2:

_____

Risk 3:

_____

Then ask yourself the following questions about each of the three risks:

How did you know it was a risk?

How big was the risk?

In what way was it a risk for you? For others in your life?

Who or what supported you in taking the risk? Blocked you?

What were the consequences of the risk? Short range? Long range? Positive? Negative?

If you could, would you take the same risk today?

What risk-taking style did you use?

What coping skills did you use?

Of the three risks, which was the greatest risk and why?

When participants have finished answering their own questions, have them choose one of their three risks to discuss in small groups of three or four. After sharing, have them think about the meaning of the exercise for them. What did they learn or discover? What did it tell them about themselves? (thirty to forty-five minutes)

Strategy 8.3. Making Decisions with Positive Uncertainty

Gelatt's (1989) model of Positive Uncertainty is discussed in some detail in Chapter Eight. It fits well with Integrative Life Planning because it is a process that encompasses both reason and intuition. It is more holistic and complex than many of the logical rational linear decision-making models. See pages 234–235.

Purpose
This activity's purpose is to make participants familiar with the model of Positive Uncertainty and think through the kinds of situations in which it might be used. Allow twenty-five minutes.

Directions
Review Gelatt's definition in the text and as follows: "Decision making is the process of arranging and rearranging information into choice or action. Positive uncertainty is a new decision strategy that is basically an attitude of feeling uncertain about the future and feeling positive about the uncertainty. It is a whole brained approach to planning your future. Positive uncertainty involves designing a personal plan for making decisions about the future when you don't know what it will be" (Gelatt, 1989, p. 255).

Often participants struggle with the ambiguity of the future. They may have feelings of hopelessness, fear, and failure. Discuss the ideas Positive Uncertainty embodies and ways in which it may be a helpful approach as we move into the twenty-first century. See also Gelatt's *Creative Decision Making Using Positive Uncertainty* (1992).

Strategy 8.4. Shifting Leadership Styles

The literature on changing leadership styles in organizations is considerable. There is no consensus on distinct leadership styles of men and women, but articles and books such as those of Rosener (1990, 1995) give some indications of similarities and differences between the two. Chapter Eight, which discusses the knowledge, attitudes, and behaviors of leaders, provides an interesting basis for discussion of this topic.

Purpose

This activity is designed to help workshop participants think about new patterns of leadership; it is not intended to provoke debate about whether women or men make better leaders. The activity takes about one hour.

Directions

Have workshop participants reread the description of different behaviors of new leaders in Chapter Eight (p. 241). Ask each member to choose one of the nine types of leadership patterns discussed (including that of Drucker), define exactly what the statement says and means in terms of work organization changes, and suggest implications for workers in these kinds of workplaces. Sum up the discussion.

Chapter Nine: Integrating Lives, Shaping Society: Implications for Career Professionals

Strategy 9.1. Career Professionals as Change Agents

The last chapter in the book puts a great deal of emphasis on career professionals as change agents, although I recognize that they cannot change society alone. Indeed, the problems of society are much greater than can be solved by professionals in any single field. Still, Figure 9.2 presents a model for career professionals who can serve as change agents or "process helpers" to bring about constructive change in institutions. The six-step model depicts how change agents can systematically work to change institutions. The model has worked very well over many years, and there is no reason to believe that it will not continue to work as creative change agents attempt to bring about change in their own institutions. See page 271.

Purpose

The purpose of this activity is to help change agents understand and internalize a model of change process that can be useful in whatever institution in which they are employed. Although this model has been used primarily in educational settings, the same principles can be used in other settings as well. This activity should help provide a complete understanding of the model. The activity takes about thirty minutes.

Directions

Ask participants to think of an organization that they have attempted to change and to assess how this model might have helped them do so. The model suggests that individuals have to understand their own relationship to the organization, be able to diagnose the problem, assess the availability of human and media resources, identify an appropriate solution, and try to ensure that it will gain acceptance in the system and be institutionalized if evaluations confirm its effectiveness.

It should be pointed out that the model was developed with educational institutions in mind. Workshop leaders should help communicate to participants that the purpose of the intervention is to help them become change agents in their own institution. Discussion should follow along these lines.

Strategy 9.2. Inhibitors and Facilitators of Change

Purpose

The purpose of this strategy is to help workers, clients, and employees become aware of the need for change in their system and of the factors that limit their ability to effect change.

Directions

The change agent activity on the worksheet (Exhibit R.1) suggests that a change agent may identify short-range goals and long-range goals and then list examples of personal change, interpersonal change, and institutional change that are challenging. Participants should identify the inhibitors (or barriers) to the changes envisioned as well as their facilitators and then indicate criteria needed for the accomplishment. In small groups of three or four, participants offer suggestions to each other how to reduce the inhibitors and increase the facilitators.

Exhibit R.1. Change Agent Activity Worksheet.

Effecting Positive Changes in My System

Short-range goals for change in my setting (1 or 2):

Long-range goals for change in my setting (1 or 2):

Three levels of possible change	Barriers	Facilitators	Criteria for accomplishment
Personal Change (myself)			
Interpersonal Change (with partner, spouse, students, friends, and so forth)			
Institutional Change (school, college, agency, business, other setting)			

Strategy 9.3. Encountering "the Other"

Entering the world of another can be very difficult if you are not prepared, if the language is different, and if you did not choose to go there. Imagine what it is like for the thousands of immigrants and refugees who have been forced to go to a new place for a variety of reasons and may permanently be leaving their home and family. Think of the grief and loss that they may experience, not only of family and culture, but also if their work credentials from their home country are not recognized.

Purpose

This strategy can help sensitize participants to the multiple aspects of other cultures that they may not have been aware of before. The activity can take twenty to thirty minutes, depending on the size of group.

Directions

Review the list of "close encounters of the cultural kind" that Juan Moreno (1996) identified in Chapter Nine (pp. 266–267). Tell participants to think about each of these in relation to their own experiences and awareness and identify three that they believe would be most challenging to them and in which they need to grow. Discuss in a dyad or groups of three or four. Following smaller discussions, ask participants to share one of the most difficult challenges and explain why it would be difficult.

Strategy 9.4. Connectedness and Community

As we bring this book to a close, it is important to return to the main themes introduced in Chapter One and discussed throughout—the themes of community and connectedness. This strategy is directed at helping participants make their own synthesis of the six critical tasks or themes of ILP—addressing global needs and doing work that needs doing, attaining individual holistic development, connecting family and work, connecting pluralism and inclusivity, understanding spirituality, and recognizing the dramatic social, personal, organizational, and global changes that will affect our lives in the twenty-first century.

Purpose

The purpose of this strategy is to help participants see the connection among the six critical tasks of ILP and to understand how they relate to community.

Directions

Ask participants to think about each of the critical tasks and select one that reflects work that needs doing. How might this task be translated into community action? What will need to be done to gain attention for this need and develop change processes and implementation strategies to effect change? Have participants identify the specific needs of the global village in which they believe they can make a difference (probably representing a life-long task). Helping participants to identify these needs is one of the most important tasks suggested by this book for career professionals.

Strategy 9.5. The Circle of Life

Purpose

This activity already has been described in Chapter Nine. However, the Circle of Life metaphor is the perfect one with which to close this book for it is one that has been used for years by Canadian First Nations people and American Indian communities. Their Circle of Life—also called the Medicine Wheel or Sacred Hoop—represents the directions of the compass, the seasons of the year, and multiple cultures. It is a pluralistic and inclusive concept.

Directions

Ask each participant to complete his or her own Circle of Life based on the framework shown in Figure 9.3 (p. 283) in order to gain a better sense of the holistic and integrative nature of ILP and of the connecting themes of the concept. Allow thirty minutes.

If possible, participants should discuss their own circle with a significant other or partner and explain the meanings of the various parts of it. The act of completing their own circle should put them in touch with the larger circle that is the globe and the global and local needs that exist in it—that is, the work that needs doing.

The Circle of Life is the framework and message of Integrative Life Planning. It should tell them a great deal about their own lives as well as about commitment to community.

References

Aasen, P. "A Causal Model of the Life Planning of Women Leaders." Unpublished doctoral dissertation, Department of Educational Psychology, University of Minnesota, 1990.

Agor, W. (ed.). *Intuition in Organizations: Leading and Managing Productively.* Thousand Oaks, Calif.: Sage, 1989.

Allport, G. W. *Pattern and Growth in Personality.* Austin, Tex.: Holt, Rinehart and Winston, 1961.

American Association of University Women. *Shortchanging Girls, Shortchanging America: A Nationwide Poll to Assess Self-Esteem, Educational Experiences, Interest in Math and Science, and Career Aspirations of Girls and Boys Ages 9–15.* Washington, D.C.: American Association of University Women, 1990.

Andersen, P., and others. "The Excelsior Model." Integrative model of development created at the National Career Development Association Women's Conference, Excelsior Springs, Mo., Oct. 1990.

Arredondo, P. "Promoting the Empowerment of Women Through Counseling Interventions." *Counseling and Human Development,* 1992, *24* (8), 1–12.

Arredondo, P., Psalti, A., and Cella, K. "The Woman Factor in Multicultural Counseling." *Counseling and Human Development,* 1993, *25* (8), 1–8.

Atkinson, D. R., Morten, G., and Sue, D. W. "A Minority Identity Development Model." In D. R. Atkinson, G. Morten, and D. W. Sue (eds.), *Counseling American Minorities: A Cross-Cultural Perspective.* (3rd ed.) Dubuque, Iowa: W. C. Brown, 1989.

Atkinson, D. R., Morten, G., and Sue, D. W. *Counseling American Minorities: A Cross-Cultural Perspective.* (4th ed.) Madison, Wis.: Brown and Benchmark, 1993.

Bach, A. "Nolo Contendere." *New York,* Dec. 11, 1995, pp. 49–55.

Bakan, D. *The Duality of Human Existence: An Essay on Psychology and Religion.* Skokie, Ill.: Rand McNally, 1966.

Barker, J. A. *Paradigms: The Business of Discovering the Future.* New York: HarperCollins, 1993.

Baruch, G. K., Barnett, R. C., and Rivers, C. *Lifeprints: New Patterns of Love and Work for Today's Women.* New York: McGraw-Hill, 1983.

Baruch, G. K., Biener, L., and Barnett, R. C. "Women and Gender in Research on Work and Family Stress." *American Psychologist,* 1987, *42,* 130–136.

Bateson, G. *Steps to an Ecology of the Mind.* New York: Ballantine Books, 1985.

Bateson, M. C. *Composing a Life.* New York: Atlantic Monthly Press, 1989.

Belenky, M. F., Clinchy, B., Goldberger, N., and Tarule, J. M. *Women's Ways of Knowing: The Development of Self, Voice, and Mind.* New York: Basic Books, 1986.

Bellah, R. N., and others. *Habits of the Heart: Individualism and Commitment in American Life.* Berkeley: University of California Press, 1985.

Bem, S. "The Measurement of Psychological Androgyny." *Journal of Consulting and Clinical Psychology,* 1974, *42,* 155–162.

Bennett, M. J. "Towards Ethnorelativism: A Developmental Model of Intercultural Sensitivity." In R. M. Paige (ed.), *Education for the Intercultural Experience.* (2nd ed.) Yarmouth, Me.: Intercultural Press, 1993.

Benson, P. L. *Developmental Assets Among Minneapolis Youth.* Minneapolis, Minn.: Search Institute, 1996.

Benson, P. L., and Roehlkepartain, E. C. "Single-Parent Families." *Search Institute Source,* 1993, *9* (2), 1–3.

Bergin, A. E. "Three Contributions of a Spiritual Perspective to Counseling, Psychotherapy, and Behavior Change." *Counseling and Values,* 1988, *33,* 21–31.

Bergin, A. E. "Values and Religious Issues in Psychotherapy and Mental Health." *American Psychologist,* 1991, *42,* 394–402.

Bernard, J. "The Good-Provider Role: Its Rise and Fall." *American Psychologist,* 1981, *36* (1), 1–12.

Berry, J. W. "Cross Cultural Counseling, Pluralism, and Acculturative Stress." Closing keynote address, National Convention of the American Association for Counseling and Development, Cincinnati, Mar. 19, 1990.

Betz, N. E., and Corning, A. F. "The Inseparability of 'Career' and 'Personal' Counseling." *Career Development Quarterly,* 1993, *42* (2), 137–142.

Betz, N. E., and Fitzgerald, L. F. *The Career Psychology of Women.* Orlando, Fla.: Academic Press, 1987.

Bird, G. W., Bird, G. A., and Scruggs, M. "Determinants of Family Task Sharing: A Study of Husbands and Wives." *Journal of Marriage and the Family,* 1984, *46,* 345–355.

Block, J. H. "Conceptions of Sex Role: Some Cross-Cultural and Longitudinal Perspectives." *American Psychologist,* 1973, *28* (6), 512–526.

Bly, R. *Iron John: A Book About Men.* Reading, Mass.: Addison-Wesley, 1990.

Bolles, R. N. *What Color Is Your Parachute?* Berkeley, Calif.: Ten Speed Press, 1970.

Bolles, R. N. "The Spiritual Life and Your Life/Work." *Newsletter About Life/Work Planning,* 1983, *5–6,* 1–9.

Bolles, R. N. "How to Find Out What Your Mission in Life Is, Part I." *Newsletter About Life/Work Planning,* 1987, *2,* 1–6.

Boorstein, S. *Transpersonal Psychotherapy.* Palo Alto, Calif.: Science and Behavior Books, 1980.

Bower, B. "Teenage Turning Point: Does Adolescence Herald the Twilight of Girls' Self-Esteem?" *Science News,* 1991, *139* (12), 184–186.

Brammer, L. *How to Cope with Life Transitions: The Challenge of Personal Change.* New York: Hemisphere, 1991.

Brett, J. M., and Yogev, S. "Restructuring Work for Family: How Dual-Earner Couples with Children Manage." *Journal of Social Behavior and Personality,* 1988, *3* (4), 159–174.

Bridges, W. *Transitions: Making Sense of Life's Changes.* Reading, Mass.: Addison-Wesley, 1980.

Bridges, W. "Where Have All the Jobs Gone? Career Planning in the Twenty-First Century." Video workshop presented at the University of Minnesota, Dec. 1993.

Bridges, W. "The End of the Job." *Fortune,* Sept. 19, 1994a, pp. 62–67.

Bridges, W. *JobShift: How to Prosper in a Workplace Without Jobs.* Reading, Mass.: Addison-Wesley, 1994b.

Brown, D. "Life Role Development and Counseling." Paper presented at the National Career Development Association Conference, Orlando, Fla., Jan. 1988.

Brown, D., Brooks, L., and Associates. *Career Choice and Development: Applying Contemporary Theories to Practice.* (3rd ed.) San Francisco: Jossey-Bass, 1996.

Brown, D., and Minor, C. W. (eds.). *Working in America: A Status Report on Planning and Problems.* Washington, D.C.: National Career Development Association and National Occupational Information Coordinating Committee, 1989, 1992.

Browning, D., and Taliaferro, J. (eds.). "The 21st Century Family: Who Will We Be? How Will We Live?" *Newsweek,* Winter/Spring 1990 (special issue).

Campbell, D. P. *If You Don't Know Where You're Going, You'll Probably End Up Somewhere Else.* Allen, Tex.: Argus Communications, 1974.

Campbell, J., and Moyers, B. *The Power of Myth* (B. S. Flowers, ed.). New York: Doubleday, 1988.

Capra, F. *The Turning Point: Science, Society, and the Rising Culture.* New York: Simon & Schuster, 1982.

Carlsen, M. B. *Meaning-Making: Therapeutic Processes in Adult Development.* New York: Norton, 1988.

Carlson, R. "Understanding Women: Implications for Personality Theory and Research." *Journal of Social Issues,* 1972, *28* (2), 17–32.

Carter, R. T. "Cultural Values: A Review of Empirical Research and Implications for Counseling." *Journal of Counseling and Development,* 1991, *70* (1), 164–173.

Carter, R. T., and Cook, D. A. "A Culturally Relevant Perspective for Understanding the Career Paths of Visible Racial/Ethnic Group People." In H. D. Lea and Z. B. Leibowitz (eds.), *Adult Career Development: Concepts, Issues, and Practices.* (2nd ed.) (pp. 192–217) Alexandria, Va.: National Career Development Association, 1992.

Charland, W. *Career Shifting: Starting Over in a Changing Economy.* Holbrook, Mass.: Adams, 1993.

Chekola, M. G. "The Concept of Happiness." Unpublished doctoral dissertation, University of Michigan, 1975.

Chetwynd, J., and Hartnett, O. (eds.). *The Sex Role System: Psychological and Sociological Perspectives.* New York: Routledge, 1977.

Chodorow, N. *The Reproduction of Mothering: Psychoanalysis and the Sociology of Gender.* Stanford, Calif.: Stanford University Press, 1978.

Clay, R. "Working Mothers: Happy or Haggard?" *APA Monitor,* Nov. 1995, *11* (26), pp. 1, 37.

Cleveland, H. "The Global Commons." *Futurist,* 1993, *27,* 9–13.

Cochran, L. *The Sense of Vocation: A Study of Career and Life Development.* Albany: State University of New York Press, 1990.

Cochran, L., and Laub, J. *Becoming an Agent: Patterns and Dynamics for Shaping Your Life.* Albany: State University of New York Press, 1994.

Cole, J. B. *All-American Women.* New York: Free Press, 1986.

Coleman, E. "Counseling Adolescent Males." *Personnel and Guidance Journal,* 1981, *60* (4), 215–218.

Comas-Diaz, L. "Feminism and Diversity in Psychology: The Case of Women of Color." *Psychology of Women Quarterly,* 1991, *15,* 597–609.

Comas-Diaz, L., and Greene, B. *Women of Color: Integrating Ethnic and Gender Identities in Psychotherapy.* New York: Guilford Press, 1994.

Commission on the Economic Status of Women. "Women, Work, and Family." (Newsletter No. 161). St. Paul, Minn.: Commission on the Economic Status of Women, 1991.

Cook, E. P. "Androgyny: A Goal for Counseling?" *Journal of Counseling and Development,* 1985, *63* (9), 567–571.

Cook, E. P. "Annual Review: Practice and Research in Career Counseling and Development, 1990." *Career Development Quarterly,* 1991, *40* (2), 99–131.

Cook, E. P. (ed.). *Women, Relationships, and Power: Implications for Counseling.* Alexandria, Va.: American Counseling Association, 1993.

Cooperrider, D. L., and Thanchankery, T. "Building the Global Civic Culture: Making Our Lives Count." In P. Sorenson and others (eds.), *Global OD.* Falls Church, Va.: Stripes, 1990.

Cornish, E. "Responsibility for the Future: Thoughts from Yesterday Guide Us Toward Tomorrow." *Futurist,* 1994, *28,* 60.

Crace, R. K., and Brown, D. *Life Values Inventory.* Minneapolis, Minn.: National Computer Systems, 1996.

Cross, W. E., Jr. "The Negro-to-Black Conversion Experience: Towards a Psychology of Black Liberation." *Black World,* 1971, *20,* 13–27.

Cummins, H. L. "Fixing Workplace May Fix Work-Family Conflicts as Well." *Minneapolis Star Tribune,* July 7, 1996, p. 414.

D'Andrea, M., Daniels, J., and Heck, R. "Evaluating the Impact of Multicultural Counseling Training." *Journal of Counseling and Development,* 1991, *70* (1), 143–150.

Davenport, D. S., and Yurich, J. M. "Multicultural Gender Issues." *Journal of Counseling and Development,* 1991, *70* (1), 64–71.

DeMeuse, K. P., and Tornow, W. W. "Leadership and the Changing Psychological Contract Between Employer and Employee." *Issues and Observations,* 1993, *13* (2), 4–6.

Dinklage, L. B. "Decision Strategies of Adolescents." Unpublished doctoral dissertation, Harvard University, 1967.

Drucker, P. F. *The New Realities: In Government and Politics, in Economics and Business, in Society and World View.* New York: HarperCollins, 1989.

Drucker, P. F. "Foreword." In F. Hesselbein, M. Goldsmith, and R. Beckhard (eds.), *The Leader of the Future.* (pp. xi–xv) San Francisco: Jossey-Bass, 1996.

Dupuy, P. "Women in Intimate Relationships." In E. P. Cook (ed.), *Women, Relationships, and Power.* Alexandria, Va.: American Counseling Association, 1993.

Durning, A. "How Much Is Enough?" *New Age Journal,* July-Aug. 1991, pp. 45–49.

Edwards, O. "The Changing Face of Ambition." *GQ,* June 1991, pp. 114–118.

Ehrenreich, B. "Are You Middle Class?" *Utne Reader,* Sept.-Oct. 1992, pp. 63–66.

Eisler, R. T. *The Chalice and the Blade: Our History, Our Future.* New York: HarperCollins, 1987.

Eisler, R. T., and Loye, D. *The Partnership Way: New Tools for Living and Learning.* San Francisco: Harper San Francisco, 1990.

England, J. "Pluralism and Community." Speech given at the National

Conference of Association for Counselor Education and Supervision, San Antonio, Tex., Sept. 1992.

Epperson, S. E. "Studies Link Subtle Sex Bias in Schools with Women's Behavior in the Workplace." *Wall Street Journal,* Sept. 16, 1988, p. 19.

Epstein, D. F. "Positive Effects of the Multiple Negative: Explaining the Success of the Black Professional Woman." In J. Huber (ed.), *Changing Women in a Changing Society.* Chicago: University of Chicago Press, 1973.

Erikson, E. H. *Insight and Responsibility.* New York: Norton, 1964.

Espin, O. M. "Psychotherapy with Hispanic Women." In P. B. Pedersen (ed.), *Handbook of Cross-Cultural Counseling and Therapy.* Westport, Conn.: Greenwood Press, 1985.

Espin, O. M. "Feminist Approaches." In L. Comas-Diaz and B. Greene (eds.), *Women of Color: Integrating Ethnic and Gender Identities in Psychotherapy.* (pp. 265–286) New York: Guilford Press, 1994.

Estor, M. "Conclusions of the General Rapporteur." In Council of Europe, *Conference on Equality Between Women and Men in a Changing Europe: Proceedings, Poznan, Poland.* Strasbourg, France: Council of Europe Press, 1994.

Etzioni, A. *The Spirit of Community: Rights, Responsibilities, and the Communitarian Agenda.* New York: Crown, 1993.

Farrell, W. *The Liberated Man: Beyond Masculinity—Freeing Men and Their Relationships with Women.* New York: Random House, 1974.

Farrell, W. *Why Men Are the Way They Are: The Male-Female Dynamic.* New York: McGraw-Hill, 1986.

Feller, R., and Walz, G. *Career Transitions in Turbulent Times.* Greensboro, N.C.: ERIC/CASS Counseling and Student Services Clearinghouse, 1996.

Ferguson, M. *The Aquarian Conspiracy: Personal and Social Transformation in the 1980s.* Los Angeles: Tarcher, 1980.

Figler, H. E. "Expressing Career Potentials in Uncertain Times." Keynote speech presented at the Minnesota Career Development Association meeting, Minneapolis, Apr. 1992.

Fletcher, J. K. "Personal Development in the New Organization: A Relational Approach to Developing the Protean Worker." In D. T. Hall (ed.), *Career Is Dead—Long Live Career: A Relational Approach to Careers.* (pp. 105–131) San Francisco: Jossey-Bass, 1996.

Fouad, N. "Cross-Cultural Vocational Assessment." *Career Development Quarterly,* 1993, *42,* 4–10.

Fox, M. *The Reinvention of Work: A New Vision of Livelihood for Our Time.* San Francisco: Harper San Francisco, 1994.

Frank, J. D. "Nature and Functions of Belief Systems: Humanism and Transcendental Religion." *American Psychologist,* 1977, *32* (7), 555–559.

Frankl, V. *Man's Search for Meaning.* Boston: Beacon Press, 1963.

Friedman, D. E., and Galinsky, E. "Work and Family Issues: A Legitimate Business Concern." In S. Zedeck (ed.), *Work, Families, and Organizations.* (pp. 168–207) San Francisco: Jossey-Bass, 1992.

Friedman, L. "Mathematics and the Gender Gap: A Meta-Analysis of Recent Studies on Sex Differences in Mathematical Tasks." *Review of Educational Research,* 1989, *59* (2), 185–213.

Fukuyama, M. A. "Taking a Universal Approach to Multicultural Counseling." *Counselor Education and Supervision,* 1990, *30,* 6–17.

Gallagher, N. "Feeling the Squeeze." *Utne Reader,* Sept.-Oct. 1992, pp. 54–61.

Gama, E.M.P. "Multiculturalism as a Basic Assumption of Psychology." Paper presented at the Minnesota International Counseling Institute, University of Minnesota, Minneapolis, Aug. 1991.

Gama, E.M.P. "Toward Science-Practice Integration: Qualitative Research in Counseling Psychology." *Counseling and Human Development,* 1992, *25* (2), 1–12.

Gelatt, H. B. "Decision Making: A Conceptual Frame of Reference for Counseling." *Journal of Counseling Psychology,* 1962, *9,* 240–245.

Gelatt, H. B. "Positive Uncertainty: A New Decision-Making Framework for Counseling." *Journal of Counseling Psychology,* 1989, *36* (2), 252–256.

Gelatt, H. B. *Creative Decision Making Using Positive Uncertainty.* Los Angeles: Crisp Publications, 1992.

Giddens, A. *Modernity and Self-Identity.* Stanford, Calif.: Stanford University Press, 1991.

Gilbert, L. A. (ed.). "Dual-Career Families in Perspective." *Counseling Psychologist,* 1987, *15* (entire issue 1).

Gilbert, L. A. *Sharing It All: The Rewards and Struggles of Two-Career Families.* New York: Plenum, 1988.

Gilbert, L. A., and Rachlin, V. "Mental Health and Psychological Functioning of Dual-Career Families." *Counseling Psychologist,* 1987, *15* (1), 7–49.

Gilgun, J., Daly, K., and Handel, G. *Qualitative Methods in Family Research.* Thousand Oaks, Calif.: Sage, 1992.

Gilligan, C. "In a Different Voice: Women's Conception of Self and Morality." *Harvard Educational Review,* 1977, *47,* 181–217.

Gilligan, C. *In a Different Voice: Psychological Theory and Women's Development.* Cambridge, Mass.: Harvard University Press, 1982.

Goldberg, H. *The Hazards of Being Male: Surviving the Myth of Masculine Privilege.* New York: New American Library, 1976.

Goldsmith, E. B. *Work and Family: Theory, Research, and Applications.* Thousand Oaks, Calif.: Sage, 1989.

Goman, C. K. *The Loyalty Factor: Building Trust in Today's Workplace.* New York: MasterMedia, 1991.

Goodman, E. "Out of Disaster—Community." *Minneapolis Star Tribune,* Oct. 1989.

Gould, W. B. *Frankl: Life with Meaning.* Pacific Grove, Calif.: Brooks/Cole, 1993.

Greenhaus, J. H. "The Intersection of Work and Family Roles: Individual, Interpersonal, and Organizational Issues." In E. B. Goldsmith (ed.), *Work and Family: Theory, Research, and Applications.* (pp. 23–44) Thousand Oaks, Calif.: Sage, 1989.

Haavio-Mannila, E. "Influence of Work Place Sex Segregation on Family Life." In K. Boh, S. Giovanni, and M. Sussman (eds.), *Cross-Cultural Perspectives on Families, Work, and Change.* Binghamton, N.Y.: Haworth Press, 1989.

Hackett, G., and Betz, N. E. "A Self-Efficacy Approach to the Career Development of Women." *Journal of Vocational Behavior,* 1981, *18* (3), 326–339.

Hagberg, J. *Real Power: The Stages of Personal Power in Organizations.* Minneapolis, Minn.: Winston Press, 1984.

Hagberg, J., and Leider, R. J. *The Inventurers: Excursions in Life and Career Renewal.* (3rd ed.) Reading, Mass.: Addison-Wesley, 1988.

Hage, D., Grant, L., and Impoco, J. "White Collar Wasteland: A Hostile Economy Has Cut Short Careers for Many of America's Best and Brightest." *U.S. News and World Report,* June 28, 1993, pp. 42–52.

Hall, D. T. "Promoting Work/Family Balance: An Organization-Change Approach." *Organizational Dynamics,* 1990, *18* (3), 5–18.

Hall, D. T. (ed.). *Career Is Dead—Long Live Career: A Relational Approach to Careers.* San Francisco: Jossey-Bass, 1996.

Hall, D. T., and Mirvis, P. H. "Careers as Lifelong Learning." In A. Howard (ed.), *The Changing Nature of Work.* San Francisco: Jossey-Bass, 1995.

Hall, D. T., and Parker, V. A. "The Role of Workplace Flexibility in Managing Diversity." *Organizational Dynamics,* 1993, *22* (1), 5–18.

Hall, F. S., and Hall, D. T. *The Two-Career Couple: He Works, She Works, but How Does the Relationship Work?* Reading, Mass.: Addison-Wesley, 1979.

Hamlin, S. "Time Flies—and We Are Having More Fun, According to New Study," *Minneapolis Star Tribune,* Sept. 17, 1995, pp. E1, E7.

Handy, C. "The New Language of Organizing and Its Implications for Leaders." In F. Hesselbein, M. Goldsmith, and R. Beckhard (eds.), *The Leader of the Future.* (pp. 3–9) San Francisco: Jossey-Bass, 1996.

Hansen, L. S. "BORN FREE: A Collaborative Approach to Reducing Sex-Role Stereotyping in Educational Institutions." *Lyceum,* June 1979, pp. 7–11, 21–23.

Hansen, L. S. "Interrelationship of Gender and Career." In N. C. Gysbers and Associates, *Designing Careers: Counseling to Enhance Education, Work, and Leisure.* (pp. 216–247) San Francisco: Jossey-Bass, 1984.

Hansen, L. S. "The Life Career Journey for Men and Women: Traditions, Transitions, Transformations." *Canadian Journal of Guidance and Counselling,* 1987, *3* (2), 36–54.

Hansen, L. S. "Partnerships, Inclusivity, and Connectedness for the Twenty-First Century." Keynote speech presented at the World Future Society Conference, Anaheim, Calif., Aug. 14, 1992.

Hansen, L. S., and Biernat, B. "Dare to Dream: Career Aspirations in Childhood and Adolescence." In J. A. Lewis, B. A. Hayes, and L. G. Bradley (eds.), *Counseling Women over the Life Span.* (pp. 13–54) Denver: Love Publishing, 1992.

Hansen, L. S., and DeBell, C. "Work-Family Quiz: Integrative Life Planning Packet." Unpublished manuscript, 1988.

Hansen, L. S., and Gama, E.M.P. "Gender Issues in Multicultural Counseling." In P. B. Pedersen, J. G. Draguns, W. J. Lonner, and J. E. Trimble (eds.), *Counseling Across Cultures.* (4th ed.) (pp. 73–107) Thousand Oaks, Calif.: Sage, 1995.

Hansen, L. S., and Lichtor, M. B. *Career Patterns of Selected Women Leaders: An Exploratory Study.* Minneapolis, Minn.: YWCA, 1987.

Hansen, L. S., and Rapoza, R. S. *Career Development and Counseling of Women.* Springfield, Ill.: Thomas, 1978.

Hardesty, S., and Jacobs, N. *Success and Betrayal: The Crisis of Women in Corporate America.* New York: Simon & Schuster, 1986.

Hare-Mustin, R. T., and Maracek, J. (eds.). *Making a Difference: Psychology and the Construction of Gender.* New Haven, Conn.: Yale University Press, 1990.

Harman, W. W. *Global Mind Change: The New Age Revolution in the Way We Think.* New York: Warner Books, 1988.

Harman, W. W., and Rheingold, H. *Higher Creativity: Liberating the Unconscious for Breakthrough Insights.* Los Angeles: Tarcher, 1984.

Havelock, R. *The Change Agent's Guide to Innovation in Education.* Englewood Cliffs, N.J.: Educational Technology Publications, 1973.

Helms, J. E. "Toward a Theoretical Explanation of the Effects of Race on

Counseling: A Black and White Model." *Counseling Psychologist,* 1984, *12,* 153–165.

Henderson, H. *Paradigms in Progress: Life Beyond Economics.* San Francisco: Berrett-Koehler, 1995. Reprinted with permission of the publisher. © 1986 by H. Henderson, Berrett-Koehler Publishers, Inc., San Francisco. All rights reserved.

Henderson, H. *Building a Win-Win World.* San Francisco: Berrett-Koehler, 1996.

Henze, D. L. "Equity in Family Work Roles Among Dual Career Couples: The Relationship of Demographic, Socioeconomic, Attitudinal, and Personality Factors." Unpublished doctoral dissertation, Department of Educational Psychology, University of Minnesota, 1984.

Herr, E. L. "Career Development and Mental Health." *Journal of Career Development,* 1989, *16,* 5–18.

Hesselbein, F., Goldsmith, M., and Beckhard, R. (eds.). *The Leader of the Future.* San Francisco: Jossey-Bass, 1996.

Hiller, D. V., and Philliber, W. W. "Relative Occupational Attainments of Spouses and Later Changes in Marriage and Wife's Work Experience." *Journal of Marriage and the Family,* 1983, *45,* 161–170.

Hines, A. "Jobs and Infotech: Work in the Information Society." *Futurist,* 1994, *28,* 9–13.

Hoffman, L. W. "Effects of Maternal Employment in the Two-Parent Family." *American Psychologist,* 1989, *44* (2), 283–292.

Hoffman, L. W., and Nye, F. I. *Working Mothers.* San Francisco: Jossey-Bass, 1974.

Hopson, B. "Response to the Papers by Schlossberg, Brammer, and Abrego." *Counseling Psychologist,* 1981, *9* (2), 36–39.

Hotchkiss, L., and Borow, H. "Sociological Perspective on Work and Career Development." In D. Brown, L. Brooks, and Associates, *Career Choice and Development: Applying Contemporary Theories to Practice.* (3rd ed.) (pp. 281–334) San Francisco: Jossey-Bass, 1996.

Howard, A. (ed.). *The Changing Nature of Work.* San Francisco: Jossey-Bass, 1995.

Ibrahim, F. A. "Contribution of Cultural Worldview to Generic Counseling and Development." *Journal of Counseling and Development,* 1991, *70* (1), 13–19.

Ibrahim, F. A. "Asian-American Women: Identity Development Issues." *Women's Studies Quarterly,* 1992, *1–2,* 41–58.

Ibrahim, F. A., and Kahn, H. *Scale to Assess World Views (SAWV).* Storrs, Conn.: Schroeder Associates, 1984.

International Women's Rights Action Watch. *Newsletter.* Minneapolis: Women, Public Policy, and Development Program, Hubert Humphrey Institute of Public Affairs, University of Minnesota, July 1992.

Ivey, A. E., Ivey, M. B., and Simek-Morgan, L. *Counseling and Psychotherapy: A Multicultural Perspective.* (3rd ed.) Boston: Allyn and Bacon, 1993.

Jepsen, D. A. "Understanding Careers as Stories." Paper presented at the National Convention of the American Association of Counseling and Development, Baltimore, Mar. 1992.

Johnson, P. C., and Cooperrider, D. L. "Finding a Path with Heart: Global Social Change Organizations and Their Challenge for the Field of Organizational Development." *Research in Organizational Change and Development,* 1991, *5,* 223–284.

Johnston, W. B., and Packer, A. E. *Workforce 2000.* Indianapolis, Ind.: Hudson Institute, 1987.

Jordan, J., and others. *Women's Growth in Connection: Writings from the Stone Center.* New York: Guilford Press, 1991.

Kanchier, C. J. *Questers: Dare to Change Your Job and Your Life.* Saratoga, Calif.: R&E Publishers, 1987.

Kanter, R. M. *Men and Women of the Corporation.* New York: Basic Books, 1977a.

Kanter, R. M. *Work and Family in the United States: A Critical Review and Agenda for Research and Policy.* New York: Russell Sage Foundation, 1977b.

Kanungo, R. N., and Misra, K. S. "An Uneasy Look at Work, Nonwork, and Leisure." In M. A. Lee and R. N. Kanungo, *Management of Work and Personal Life.* (pp. 143–165) New York: Praeger, 1984.

Katz, M. R. *Decisions and Values: A Rationale for Secondary School Guidance.* New York: College Entrance Examination Board, 1963.

Keen, S. *Fire in the Belly: On Being a Man.* New York: Bantam Books, 1991.

Keierleber, D., and Hansen, L. S. "A Coming of Age: Addressing the Career Development Needs of Adult Students in a University Setting." In H. D. Lea and Z. B. Leibowitz (eds.), *Adult Career Development: Concepts, Issues, and Practices.* (2nd ed.) (pp. 312–339) Alexandria, Va.: National Career Development Association, 1992.

Kelly, E. W., Jr. *Spirituality and Religion in Counseling and Psychotherapy: Diversity in Theory and Practice.* Alexandria, Va.: American Counseling Association, 1995.

Kidder, R. M. *An Agenda for the 21st Century.* Cambridge, Mass.: MIT Press, 1987.

Kiechel, W. "A Manager's Career in the New Economy." *Fortune,* Apr. 4, 1994, pp. 68–72.

Kimmel, M. S. (ed.). *Changing Men: New Directions in Research on Men and Masculinity.* Thousand Oaks, Calif.: Sage, 1987.

Kluckhohn, F. R., and Strodtbeck, F. L. *Variations in Value Orientations.* New York: HarperCollins, 1961.

Kofodimos, J. R. "To Love or to Work: Must We Choose?" *Issues and Observations,* 1986, *6* (2), 1–7.

Kohlberg, L. "Stages of Moral Development as a Basis for Moral Education." In C. Beck and E. Sullivan (eds.), *Moral Education.* Toronto: University of Toronto, 1970.

Kohlberg, L. *The Philosophy of Moral Development.* San Francisco: Harper San Francisco, 1981.

Kratz, K. "Women's Spiritual Journey." Unpublished master's thesis, Department of Educational Psychology, University of Minnesota, 1987.

Krumboltz, J. D. "Integrating Career and Personal Counseling." *Career Development Quarterly,* 1993, *42* (2), 143–148.

Kuhn, T. S. *The Structure of Scientific Revolutions.* Chicago: University of Chicago Press, 1962.

Kulin, J. "Your Money or Your Life (The Value of Currency, Power, and Success in History)." *Parabola,* 1991, *16* (1), 48–53.

Kummerow, J. M. (ed.). *New Directions in Career Planning and the Workplace: Practical Strategies for Counselors.* Palo Alto, Calif.: Consulting Psychologists Press, 1991.

Kutner, N. G., and Brogan, D. "Sources of Sex Discrimination in Educational Systems: A Conceptual Model." *Psychology of Women Quarterly,* 1976, *1* (1), 50–69.

Lappé, F. M., and DuBois, P. M. *The Quickening of America: Rebuilding Our Nation, Remaking Our Lives.* San Francisco: Jossey-Bass, 1994.

Leider, R. J. *The Power of Purpose.* New York: Ballantine, 1985.

Leider, R. J., and Shapiro, D. *Repacking Your Bags: Lighten Your Load for the Rest of Your Life.* San Francisco: Berrett-Koehler, 1995.

Leong, F. T. (ed.). "A Symposium on Multicultural Career Counseling." *Career Development Quarterly,* 1993, *42* (1), 3–55.

Lerner, G. *The Creation of Patriarchy.* New York: Oxford University Press, 1986.

Leung, L. A. "Career Development and Counseling: A Multicultural Perspective." In J. Ponterotto, J. M. Casas, L. Suzuki, and C. Alexander, *Handbook of Multicultural Counseling.* (pp. 549–566) Thousand Oaks, Calif.: Sage, 1995.

Lewis, B. A. *The Kids' Guide to Social Action.* Minneapolis, Minn.: Free Spirit, 1991.

Lewis, J. A. "Empowerment for Women." Workshops sponsored by the American Association for Counseling and Development, 1991.

Lindberg, P. S. "An Investigation of Female Identity and Self-Esteem." Unpublished doctoral dissertation, Department of Educational Psychology, University of Minnesota, 1989.

Lipman-Blumen, J. *The Connective Edge: Leading in an Interdependent World.* San Francisco: Jossey-Bass, 1996.

Lippitt, G., and Lippitt, R. "Downsizing: How to Manage More with Less." *Management Review,* 1982, *71* (3), 9–14.

Locke, D. C. "A Not So Provincial View of Multicultural Counseling." *Counselor Education and Supervision,* 1990, *30,* 18–25.

Locke, D. C. *Increasing Multicultural Understanding: A Comprehensive Model.* Thousand Oaks, Calif.: Sage, 1992.

Loeffler, T. A. "An Interpretive Qualitative Analysis of Factors Which Influence Women's Career Development in Outdoor Leadership." Unpublished doctoral dissertation, University of Minnesota, 1995.

Mack, M. L. "Understanding Spirituality in Counseling Psychology: Considerations for Research, Training, and Practice." *Counseling and Values,* 1994, *39* (11), 15–31.

Madsen, L. "Power Within vs. Power over." Unpublished doctoral dissertation, Department of Educational Psychology, University of Minnesota, 1984.

Manuele-Adkins, C. "Career Counseling Is Personal Counseling." *Career Development Quarterly,* 1992, *40* (4), 313–323.

Maslow, A. H. *Toward a Psychology of Being.* New York: Van Nostrand Reinhold, 1962.

May, R. *The Courage to Create.* New York: W. W. Norton, 1975.

McClenahen, J. S. "It's No Fun Working Here Anymore." *Industry Week,* Mar. 4, 1991, pp. 20–22.

McDaniels, C. *The Changing Workplace: Career Counseling Strategies for the 1990s and Beyond.* San Francisco: Jossey-Bass, 1989.

McDaniels, C., and Gysbers, N. C. *Counseling for Career Development: Theories, Resources, and Practice.* San Francisco: Jossey-Bass, 1992.

McIntosh, P. "White Privilege and Male Privilege: A Personal Account of Coming to See Correspondences Through Work in Women's Studies." Working Paper Series No. 189. Center for Research on Women, Wellesley College, Wellesley, Mass. 02128-8259. © 1988 P. McIntosh.

McWhirter, E. H. *Counseling for Empowerment.* Alexandria, Va.: American Counseling Association, 1994.

Mead, M. *Male and Female.* New York: Morrow, 1967.

Meadows, D. H. "If the World Were a Village of 1,000 People . . ." In J. D. Hale Sr. (ed.), *The Old Farmer's Almanac.* Dublin, N.H.: Yankee, 1992.

Merriam, S. B., and Clark, M. C. *Lifelines: Patterns of Work, Love, and Learning in Adulthood.* San Francisco: Jossey-Bass, 1991.

Miller, J. B. *Toward a New Psychology of Women.* Boston: Beacon Press, 1976.

Miller, J. V. "The Family-Career Connection: A New Framework for Career Development." Columbus, Ohio: ERIC Clearinghouse on Adult Career and Vocational Educational, the Ohio State University, 1994.

Mirvis, P., and Hall, D. T. "Psychological Success and the Boundaryless Career." *Journal of Organizational Behavior,* 1994, *15,* 365–380.

Mogil, C., Slepian, A., and Woodrow, P. "Do You Need More Money—or More Security?" *Utne Reader,* Sept.-Oct. 1992, pp. 56–57.

Moore, D. "An Investigation of Changes in Affective Expressiveness in Men as a Result of Participation in a Multimodal Psychological Intervention." Unpublished doctoral dissertation, Department of Educational Psychology, University of Minnesota, 1984.

Moore, D., and Leafgren, F. (eds.). *Problem Solving Strategies and Interventions for Men in Conflict.* Alexandria, Va.: American Counseling Association, 1990.

Moore, T. *Care of the Soul.* New York: HarperCollins, 1992.

Moreno, J. "On Entering the World of 'the Other.'" Paper presented at Diversity Dialogues, BORN FREE Center, University of Minnesota, Minneapolis, Feb. 1996.

Moris, A. *Individual Life Planning.* Seattle: Sabah House/Individual Development Center, 1988.

Myers, L. J. "A Therapeutic Model for Transcending Oppression: A Black Feminist Perspective." *Women and Therapy,* 1986, *5* (4), 39–49.

Myers, L. J., and others. "Identity Development and Worldview: Toward an Optimal Conceptualization." *Journal of Counseling and Development,* 1991, *70* (1), 54–63.

Nader, R. "Time Dollars." *Utne Reader,* Sept.-Oct. 1992, pp. 74–76.

Naisbitt, J. *Megatrends: Ten New Directions Transforming Our Lives.* New York: Warner Communications, 1982.

Naisbitt, J., and Aburdene, P. *Megatrends 2000: Ten New Directions for the 1990s.* New York: Avon, 1990.

National Career Development Association. *National Survey of Working America, 1990* (Gallup Survey Report). Alexandria, Va.: National Career Development Association, 1990.

Naylor, T. H., Willimon, W. H., and Naylor, M. R. *The Search for Meaning.* Nashville, Tenn.: Abingdon Press, 1994. © 1994 by Abingdon Press. Reprinted by permission.

Needleman, J. *Money and the Meaning of Life.* New York: Doubleday, 1991.

Nevill, D. D., and Super, D. E. *The Salience Inventory Manual: Theory, Application, and Research.* Palo Alto, Calif.: Consulting Psychologists Press, 1986a.

Nevill, D. D., and Super, D. E. *The Values Scale Manual: Theory, Application, and Research.* Palo Alto, Calif.: Consulting Psychologists Press, 1986b.

Newman, M., and Damashek, B. *Quilters.* In A. Favorini (ed.), *Voicings: Ten Plays from the Documentary Theater.* Hopewell, N.J.: ECCO Press, 1995. (Originally published 1982.)

Noer, D. M. *Healing the Wounds: Overcoming the Trauma of Layoffs and Revitalizing Downsized Organizations.* San Francisco: Jossey-Bass, 1993.

O'Hara, M. "Creating the Twenty-First Century: Institutions and Social Change." Keynote speech given at the World Future Society Conference, Anaheim, Calif., Aug. 14, 1992.

Okun, B. F. *Working with Adults: Individual, Family, and Career Development.* Pacific Grove, Calif.: Brooks/Cole, 1984.

Olson, D. *Coping and Stress Profile.* Minneapolis, Minn.: Innovators, 1992.

O'Neil, J. "Male Sex Role Conflicts, Sexism, and Masculinity: Psychological Implications for Men, Women, and the Counseling Psychologist." *Counseling Psychologist,* 1981, *9* (2), 61–80.

O'Neil, J. M., Fishman, D. M., and Kinsella-Shaw, M. "Dual-Career Couples' Career Transitions and Normative Dilemmas: A Preliminary Assessment Model." *Counseling Psychologist,* 1987, *15* (1), 50–96.

Osherson, S. *Finding Our Fathers: How a Man's Life Is Shaped by His Relationship with His Father.* New York: Fawcett, 1986.

Parham, T. A. "Multicultural Counseling Competencies: Essentials in a World of Change." Workshop sponsored by the Association for Multicultural Counseling and Development, presented at the World Conference of the American Counseling Association, Pittsburgh, Pa., Apr. 19, 1996.

Parker, V. A., and Hall, D. T. "Conclusion: Expanding the Domain of Family and Work Issues." In S. Zedeck (ed.), *Work, Families, and Organizations.* (pp. 432–451) San Francisco: Jossey-Bass, 1992.

Parks, R. *Quiet Strength: The Story of Rosa Parks.* Grand Rapids, Mich.: Zondervan, 1994.

Pate, R. H., and Bondi, A. M. "Religious Beliefs and Practice: An Integral Aspect of Multicultural Counseling." *Counselor Education and Supervision,* 1992, *32,* 1009–1115.

Peck, M. S. "A New American Revolution." *New Age Journal,* May-June 1987, pp. 32–37, 50–52.

Pedersen, P. B. (ed.). "Multiculturalism as a Fourth Force in Counseling." *Journal of Counseling and Development,* 1991, *70* (entire issue 1).

Pilder, B. "Mainstreaming America's Displaced Workers." *Tarrytown Newsletter,* June 1985, pp. 1–3.

Plant, P. "Green Guidance." Presentation at the Sixteenth International Congress of the International Association for Educational-Vocational Guidance, Stockholm, Aug. 10, 1995.

Pleck, J. H. "Two Worlds in One: Work and Family." *Journal of Social History*, 1976, *10* (2), 178–195.

Pleck, J. H. "Men's Power with Women, Other Men, and Society: A Men's Movement Analysis." In D. Hiller and R. Sheets (eds.), *Women and Men: The Consequences of Power.* Cincinnati, Ohio: Office of Women's Studies, University of Cincinnati, 1977a.

Pleck, J. H. "The Work-Family Role System." *Social Problems*, 1977b, *24* (4), 417–427.

Pleck, J. H. *The Myth of Masculinity.* Cambridge, Mass.: MIT Press, 1981.

Policoff, S. P. "Working It Out." *New Age Journal,* May 1985, pp. 34–39, 73.

Pollitt, K. "Are Women Morally Superior to Men?" *Nation,* Dec. 28, 1992, pp. 799–807.

Ponterotto, J. G., Casas, J. M., Suzuki, L. A., and Alexander, C. M. (eds). *Handbook of Multicultural Counseling.* Thousand Oaks, Calif.: Sage, 1995.

Ponterotto, J. G., Rieger, B. P., Barrett, A., and Sparks, R. "Assessing Multicultural Counseling Competence: A Review of Instrumentation." *Journal of Counseling and Development,* 1994, *72* (3), 316–322.

Population Crisis Committee. *Country Rankings of the Status of Gender: Poor, Powerless, and Pregnant.* Population Briefing Paper No. 20. Washington, D.C.: U.S. Government Printing Office, 1988.

Postman, N. *Technopoly: The Surrender of Culture to Technology.* New York: Knopf, 1992.

Ragins, B. R., and Sundstrom, E. "Gender and Power in Organizations: A Longitudinal Perspective." *Psychological Bulletin,* 1989, *105* (1), 51–88.

Rapoport, R., and Rapoport, R. "The Dual Career Family." *Human Relations,* 1969, *22* (2), 3–30.

Raths, L. E., Harmin, M., and Simon, S. B. *Values and Teaching: Working with Values in the Classroom.* Columbus, Ohio: Merrill, 1966.

Raymond, J. "The Visionary Task: Two-Sights-Seeing." *Women's Studies International Forum,* 1985, *8* (1), 85–90.

Rebecca, M., Hefner, R., and Oleshansky, B. "A Model of Sex-Role Transcendence." In D. Ruble, J. H. Frieze, and J. E. Parsons (eds.), "Sex Roles: Persistence and Change." *Journal of Social Issues,* 1976, *32* (3), 197–206.

Redfield, J. *The Celestine Prophecy.* N.Y.: Warner, 1993.

Reichling, J. "Statement to the IAEVG Congress." Paper presented at the International Congress of the Association for Educational-Vocational Guidance, Stockholm, Aug. 10, 1995.

Richardson, M. S. "Occupational and Family Roles: A Neglected Intersection." *Counseling Psychologist,* 1981, *9* (4), 13–23.

Richardson, M. S. "Work in People's Lives: A Location for Counseling

Psychologists." *Journal of Counseling Psychology*, 1993, *40* (4), 425–433.

Ridley, C. R. "Racism in Counseling as an Adversive Behavioral Process." In P. B. Pedersen, J. G. Draguns, W. J. Lonner, and J. E. Trimble (eds.), *Counseling Across Cultures.* (3rd ed.) (pp. 55–77) Honolulu: University of Hawaii Press, 1989.

Rifkin, J. *The End of Work: Technology, Jobs, and Your Future.* New York: Putnam, 1995.

Robertson, H. "Gender and School Restructuring: Thoughts on the Presence of Absence." Paper presented at the Conference on Restructuring Education: Choices and Challenges, International Conference Linking Research and Practice, Ontario Institute for Studies in Education, Toronto, Mar. 1992.

Rosener, J. B. "Ways Women Lead." *Harvard Business Review*, 1990, *68* (6), 119–125.

Rosener, J. B. *America's Competitive Secret: Utilizing Women as a Management Strategy.* New York: Oxford University Press, 1995.

Rothenberg, P. S. *Race, Class, and Gender in the United States: An Integrated Study.* (3rd ed.) New York: St. Martin's Press, 1995.

Sadker, M., and Sadker, D. *Failing at Fairness: How America's Schools Cheat Girls.* New York: Scribner, 1994.

Saltzman, A. "Downshifting: The Search for Ways to Change Your Life and Reinvent Success." *Inc.*, Aug. 1991, pp. 70–71.

Sandler, B. R. *The Campus Climate Revisited: Chilly for Women Faculty, Administrators, and Graduate Students.* Washington, D.C.: Project on the Status and Education of Women, Association of American Colleges, 1986.

Savickas, M. "Career Interventions That Create Hope." Paper presented at the National Conference of the National Career Development Association, Scottsdale, Ariz., Jan. 12, 1990.

Savickas, M. "Linking Career Theory and Practice." Speech presented at the National Career Development Conference, San Francisco, July 6, 1995.

Savickas, M. "A Framework for Linking Career Theory and Practice." In M. Savickas and W. B. Walsh (eds.), *Handbook of Career Counseling Theory and Practice.* Palo Alto, Calif.: Davies-Black, 1996.

Savickas, M., and Lent, R. W. *Convergence in Career Development Theories: Implications for Science and Practice.* Palo Alto, Calif.: Consulting Psychologists Press, 1994.

Scarr, S., Phillips, D., and McCartney, K. "Working Mothers and Their Families." *American Psychologist*, 1989, *44* (11), 1402–1409.

Schein, E. H. *Career Anchors: Discovering Your Real Values.* San Diego, Calif.: University Associates, 1990.

Scher, M. "Counseling Males." *Personnel and Guidance Journal,* Dec. 1981, *60* (4), (special issue).

Schlossberg, N. K. "A Model for Analyzing Human Adaptation to Transition." *Counseling Psychologist,* 1981, *9* (2), 2–18.

Schlossberg, N. K. *Counseling Adults in Transition: Linking Practice with Theory.* New York: Springer, 1984.

Schlossberg, N. K. *Overwhelmed: Coping with Life's Ups and Downs.* San Francisco: New Lexington Press, 1994. (Originally published 1989.)

Schlossberg, N. K. *Transition Coping Guidelines.* Minneapolis, Minn.: Personnel Decisions International, 1994.

Schlossberg, N. K. "Grandparents Raising Grandchildren: An Unexpected Career Transition." Paper presented at 1995 National Conference of National Career Development Association, San Francisco, July 6, 1995.

Schlossberg, N. K., and Robinson, S. P. *Going to Plan B: How You Can Cope, Regroup, and Start Your Life on a New Path.* New York: Simon & Schuster, 1996.

Schlossberg, N. K., Waters, E. B., and Goodman, J. *Counseling Adults in Transition.* New York: Springer, 1995.

Schor, J. B. *The Overworked American.* New York: HarperCollins, 1991.

Schwartz, F. "Management Women and the New Facts of Life." *Harvard Business Review,* 1989, *67* (1), 65–76.

Sekaran, U. *Dual-Career Families: Contemporary Organizational and Counseling Issues.* San Francisco: Jossey-Bass, 1986.

Sekaran, U., and Hall, D. T. "Asynchronism in Dual-Career and Family Linkages." In M. B. Arthur, D. T. Hall, and B. S. Lawrence (eds.), *Handbook of Career Theory.* (pp. 159–180) Cambridge, Mass.: Cambridge University Press, 1989.

Senge, P. "Leading Learning Organizations: The Bold, the Powerful, and the Invisible." In F. Hesselbein, M. Goldsmith, and R. Beckhard (eds.), *The Leader of the Future.* (pp. 41–57) San Francisco: Jossey-Bass, 1996.

Sheehy, G. *New Passages: Mapping Your Life Across Time.* New York: Random House, 1995.

Shephard, H. A. "On the Realization of Human Potential: A Path with a Heart." In M. B. Arthur, L. Bailyn, D. J. Levinson, and H. A. Shephard (eds.), *Working with Careers.* New York: Columbia University School of Business, 1984.

Siegel, B. S. *Peace, Love, and Healing.* New York: HarperCollins, 1989.

Simon, S., and Simon, S. *Simon Workshops in Values Realization.* Hadley, Mass.: Simon and Simon, 1996.

Sinetar, M. *Do What You Love, the Money Will Follow: Discovering Your Right Livelihood.* Mahwah, N.J.: Paulist Press, 1987.

Skovholt, T. M. "Counseling and Psychotherapy Interventions with Men." *Counseling and Human Development,* 1993, *25* (6), 1–16.

Skovholt, T. M., and Morgan, J. I. "Career Development: An Outline of Issues for Men." *Personnel and Guidance Journal,* 1981, *60* (4), 231–237.

Skovholt, T. M., Schauble, D. G., and Davis, R. (eds.). *Counseling Men.* Pacific Grove, Calif.: Brooks/Cole, 1980.

Sloan, A. "The Hit Men." *Newsweek,* Feb. 26, 1996, pp. 44–48.

Smith, S. "Age and Sex Differences in Children's Opinion Concerning Sex Differences." *Journal of Genetic Psychology,* 1939, *54,* 17–25.

Sorensen, G., and Mortimer, J. T. "Implications of the Dual Roles of Adult Women for Their Health." In J. T. Mortimer and M. Borman (eds.), *Work Experience and Psychological Development Throughout the Life Span.* Boulder, Colo.: Westview Press, 1988.

Stark, A. "Women in a Postindustrial Society." Paper presented at the Sixteenth Congress of the International Association for Educational-Vocational Guidance, Stockholm, Aug. 7, 1995.

Steenbarger, B. N. "All the World Is Not a Stage: Emerging Contextualist Themes in Counseling and Development." *Journal of Counseling and Development,* 1991, *70* (2), 288–296.

Steenbarger, B. N. "A Multicontextual Model of Counseling: Bridging Brevity and Diversity." *Journal of Counseling and Development,* 1993, *72* (1), 8–15.

Sternberg, B. von. "U.S. Worried About Children Having Children." *Minneapolis Star Tribune,* Feb. 11, 1994, pp. 2A, 25A.

Stoltz-Loike, M. *Dual Career Couples: New Perspectives in Counseling.* Alexandria, Va.: American Counseling Association, 1992.

Subich, L. M. "How Personal Is Career Counseling?" *Career Development Quarterly,* 1993, *42* (2), 129–131.

Sue, D. W. "A Diversity Perspective on Contextualism." *Journal of Counseling and Development,* 1991, *70* (2), 300–301.

Sue, D. W. "Multicultural Organizational Development: Implications for the Counseling Profession." In J. G. Ponterotto and others (eds.), *Handbook of Multicultural Counseling.* (pp. 474–492) Thousand Oaks, Calif.: Sage, 1995.

Sue, D. W., Arredondo, P., and McDavis, R. J. "Multicultural Counseling Competencies and Standards: A Call to the Profession." *Journal of Counseling and Development,* 1992, *70* (4), 477–486.

Sue, D. W., Ivey, A. E., and Pedersen, P. B. *A Theory of Multicultural Counseling and Therapy.* Pacific Grove, Calif.: Brooks/Cole, 1996.

Sue, D. W., and Sue, D. *Counseling the Culturally Different: Theory and Practice.* New York: Wiley, 1990.

Super, D. E. "Vocational Adjustment: Implementing a Self-Concept." *Occupations,* 1951, *30,* 88–92.

Super, D. E. "A Life-Span, Life-Space Approach to Career Development." *Journal of Vocational Behavior,* 1980, *16* (3), 282–298.

Super, D. E. "Life Career Roles: Self-Realization in Work and Leisure." In D. T. Hall and Associates, *Career Development in Organizations.* San Francisco: Jossey-Bass, 1986.

Super, D. E. "The Two Faces of Counseling: Or Is It Three?" *The Career Development Quarterly,* Dec. 1993, 42 (3), 132–136.

Super, D. E., and Overstreet, P. L. *The Vocational Maturity of Ninth Grade Boys.* New York: Teachers College Press, 1960.

Super, D. E., and Sverko, B. (eds.). *Life Roles, Values, and Careers.* San Francisco: Jossey-Bass, 1995.

Swiss, D. J., and Walker, J. P. *Women and the Work-Family Dilemma.* New York: Wiley, 1993.

Theobald, R. *The Rapids of Change: Social Entrepreneurship in Turbulent Times.* Indianapolis, Ind.: Knowledge Systems, 1987.

Thomas, D. A., and Alderfer, C. P. "The Influence of Race on Career Dynamics: Theory and Research on Minority Career Experiences." In M. B. Arthur, D. T. Hall, and B. S. Lawrence (eds.), *Handbook of Career Theory.* (pp. 133–158) Cambridge: Cambridge University Press, 1989.

Tinsley, H.E.A., and Tinsley, D. J. "A Theory of the Attributes, Benefits, and Causes of Leisure Experience." *Leisure Science,* 1986, *8,* 1–45.

Trickett, E. J., Watts, R. J., and Birman, D. (eds.). *Human Diversity: Perspectives on People in Context.* San Francisco: Jossey-Bass, 1994.

"Two Studies of Married Dads Say Those in Two-Income Families Earn Less." *Minneapolis Star Tribune,* Oct. 14, 1994, p. 17A.

United Nations. "Convention to Eliminate All Forms of Discrimination Against Women (CEDAW)." In United Nations, *Human Rights: A Compilation of International Instruments.* New York: United Nations, 1983.

U.S. Department of Labor. "The American Work Force, 1992–2005." *Occupational Outlook Quarterly,* Fall 1993 (special issue).

Vaill, P. "Seven Process Frontiers for Organization Development." In W. Sikes, A. Drexler, and J. Gant (eds.), *The Emerging Practice of Organization Development.* (pp. 261–272) Alexandria, Va.: NTL Institute for Applied Behavioral Science, 1989.

Vondracek, F. W., Lerner, R. M., and Schulenberg, J. E. *Career Development: A Life-Span Developmental Approach.* Hillsdale, N.J.: Erlbaum, 1986.

Vondracek, F. W., and Schulenberg, J. E. "Counseling for Normative and Nonnormative Influences on Career Development." *Career Development Quarterly*, 1992, *40*, 291–301.

Vontress, C. E. "Traditional Healing in Africa: Implications for Cross-Cultural Counseling." *Journal of Counseling and Development*, 1991, *70* (1), 242–249.

Voydanoff, P. "Work and Family: A Review and Expanded Conceptualization." In E. B. Goldsmith (ed.), *Work and Family: Theory, Research, and Applications*. (pp. 1–22) Thousand Oaks, Calif.: Sage, 1989.

Walker, B. A. "The Value of Diversity in Career Self-Development." In D. T. Hall (ed.), *Career Is Dead—Long Live Career! A Relational Approach to Careers*. (pp. 265–277) San Francisco: Jossey-Bass, 1996.

Walker, B. A., and Hanson, W. C. "Valuing Differences at Digital Equipment Corporation." In S. Jackson and Associates (eds.), *Diversity in the Workplace: Human Resource Initiatives*. New York: Guilford Press, 1992.

Walker, J. *I'll Take Charge*. St. Paul: National 4-H Project, Center for Youth Development and Research, University of Minnesota, 1989.

Walker, L. S., Rozee-Koker, P., and Wallston, B. S. "Social Policy and the Dual-Career Family: Bringing the Social Context into Counseling." *Counseling Psychologist*, 1987, *15* (1), 97–121.

Watts, A. G. "Toward a Policy for Lifelong Career Development: A Trans-Atlantic Perspective." Keynote address, Fifth National Career Conference of the National Career Development Association, San Francisco, July 8, 1995.

Weitzman, L. B. *The Divorce Revolution: The Unexpected Social and Economic Consequences for Women and Children in America*. New York: Free Press, 1985.

White, J. L., and Parham, T. A. *The Psychology of Blacks: An African-American Perspective*. (2nd ed.) Upper Saddle River, N.J.: Prentice Hall, 1990.

Wigglesworth, D. C. "Meeting the Needs of the Multicultural Work Force." In J. M. Kummerow (ed.), *New Directions in Career Planning and the Workplace*. Palo Alto, Calif.: Consulting Psychologists Press, 1991.

Williams, C. L., and Berry, J. W. "Primary Prevention of Acculturative Stress Among Refugees: Application of Psychological Theory and Practice." *American Psychologist*, 1991, *46* (6), 632–641.

Williams, J. E., and Best, D. L. *Measuring Sex Stereotypes: A Thirty-Nation Study*. Thousand Oaks, Calif.: Sage, 1982.

"Without Money, She Finds She Has No Value." *Minneapolis Star Tribune*, Dec. 20, 1991, p. 27A.

Worthington, E. L. "Religious Faith Across the Lifespan: Implications for Counseling and Research." *Counseling Psychologist,* 1989, *17* (4), 555–612.

Yang, J. "Career Counseling of Chinese-American Women: Are They in Limbo?" *Career Development Quarterly,* 1991, *39* (4), 350–359.

Yankelovich, D. *New Rules: Searching for Self-Fulfillment in a World Turned Upside Down.* New York: Random House, 1981.

Yates, G. G. "Spirituality and the American Feminist Experience." *Signs,* 1983, *9,* 59–72.

Zedeck, S. (ed.). *Work, Families, and Organizations.* San Francisco: Jossey-Bass, 1992.

Name Index

Subject Index

A

"Absence, the Presence of," 180

Acculturation, minority group, 158–159, 266–267

Activities and applications, ILP, 265, 287–312; for career professionals, 308–312; change agent model use, 308–309; change inhibitors and facilitators identification, 185, 309–311; change response, 305; Circle of Life, 282–283, 312; connectedness and community tasks, 311–312; connecting family and work, 295–298; dreams and hopes, 304–305; encountering "the Other," 310; exploring spirituality, 301–305; finding our core, 301–302; finding work that needs doing, 291; gender-role transcenders, 293–294; global context, 291; holistic development, 292; interdisciplinary origins discussion, 290; leadership styles discussion, 308; life planning quilt, 289–290; life roles identification, 295–296; managing personal transitions, 305–308; multiple identities awareness, 299; mutual planning by partners, 297–298; new paradigm thinking, 288–289; partnership society visualization, 294–295; provider roles, 296–297; racial privilege awareness, 162–163; rebirth fantasy, 299–301; search for purpose, 302–303; self-sufficiency and connectedness, 292–293; a sense of time, 303–304;

taking risks, 306–308; valuing pluralism and inclusivity, 299–301; 310. *See also* Critical tasks, the six ILP; Interventions, ILP; *Chapter Ten Resource*

Adaptations to transition (Schlossberg model), 220–224, 225, 279–280, 303–304; case study, 224–229. *See also* Change; Transitions, personal

Adult development, and life stages, 22, 91–92

"Adversive racism," 182

Advocacy, of human rights, 68–71

Affirmative action, 160, 172

African Americans, 101, 167, 175, 182–183, 186; racial consciousness stages in, 46–47

Age factors, 69, 97, 105, 122–123

Ageism, 183

Agency and communion: gender-role dimensions of, 108–110; self-sufficiency and connectedness metaphor of, 110–112

Agency, a sense of, 15

Ambition and lifestyles, 198–200

American Association of University Women, 101

American Counseling Association (American Association for Counseling and Development), 74–75, 195

American Educational Research Association, 79

Androgyny, 103

Applications: ILP student, 273–274

Assessment instruments, 208, 209,

166; racist and sexist, 167,
173–174; role, 9, 31, 94–95; of
women, 31, 100–101
Stockbrokers, 197–198
Storytelling, use of, 79, 171, 203, 209;
career, 211, 212–213. *See also* Personal quilt, the author's
Stress, 20; acculturation, 76, 158–159;
coping resources, 142; in dual-earner couples, 138, 141–142,
149–150; male gender-role, 39–40,
42–43, 94–95. *See also* Change
Strong Interest Inventory, 212
Students, assisting. *See* Career counselors
Subjective and objective careers, 231
Subjectivity: of decision making,
234–235; and qualitative research,
27–28, 79–80, 269–270, 277
Success, vocational: and lifestyles,
197–200; men's, 39–40, 95; and
money, 196–198; two-earner family issues, 134–135, 227
Sweden, 274–275
Synchronism, marital-occupational,
126, 140–141, 227
System, family chores, 136, 141
System of Interactive Guidance and
Information (SIGI), 4–5
Systems approach to career counseling, 4–5, 22, 111, 112, 168, 259,
264; Change Agent as Process
Helper, 270–272; of VR/EGs,
166–167. *See also* Career guidance

T
"Tale of O" (video), 143
Task sharing, two-earner family, 127,
128, 136, 141, 256, 274–275
Taxation, 204
Technology, the constructive use of,
54–56
Temporary work, 10, 61, 230
Terminology: career professionals, 52,
180; of diversity, 156–160; gender
stereotypes, 31; ILP, 14–15; inclusive language, 180

Theaters, life, 6, 25; SOFI contexts,
86, 91–92, 264
Theology, 56–57
Theory. *See* Career development theory; Literature, career development
"Think globally, act locally," 16, 50,
254
Time: and downshifting, 199–200;
family, 97, 143–144, 145, 201, 206;
on the job, 198, 200; leisure, 26,
88–91, 141, 231; life and livelihood, 198–200, 264; and money,
204; personal, 198–199, 204, 206;
transition duration, 222, 228, 230,
231–232; workplace flexibility,
169–170
Time orientation, 165, 303
Traditions: career theory, 44, 45, 166;
changing societal, 278–279; and
detraditionalization, 59, 115, 128,
177–178; gender-role dimensions,
95, 108–110, 133, 175, 177–178,
281; morality and multicultural,
177–178, 278–279; of science, 195;
and VR/EGs, 166, 175, 177–178.
See also Gender-role system; Multiculturalism
Training, 183, 273–274
Trait and factor approach, 1, 3
Transactional career patterns, 8
Transcendence, gender-role, 280–281, 293–294
Transformations of society, 280–282.
See also Change; Society
Transition Coping Guide (TCG), 224,
265
Transitions, personal, 216–220,
257–258; adaptations to, 220–224,
225; and changing work patterns,
10–11, 276; chronic, 220–221; coping strategies, 228–229, 230; cross-cultural experience, 266–267; and
decision making, 232–236; disruptiveness factors, 22; endings and
beginnings (Bridges), 216–217,
231; job loss case study, 224–229;

This constitutes a continuation of the copyright page.

Chapter Six excerpts from "White Privilege and Male Privilege: A Personal Account of Coming to See Correspondences Through Work in Women's Studies," © 1988 Peggy McIntosh. Working Paper Series No. 189, Center for Research on Women, Wellesley College, Wellesley MA 02128-8259. This work may not be reproduced without permission of the author.

Chapter Nine excerpts from *Quilters* copyright © 1986, by Molly Newman and Barbara Damashek. Music and lyrics, copyright © 1986, by Barbara Damashek. Based on the book, *The Quilters: Women and Domestic Art.* Copyright © 1977, Patricia Cooper Baker and Norman Buferd.

CAUTION: The reprinting of *Quilters* included in this volume is reprinted by permission of the author and Dramatists Play Service, Inc. The stock and amateur performance rights in this play are controlled exclusively by Dramatists Play Service, Inc., 440 Park Avenue South, New York, N.Y. 10016. No stock or amateur production of the play may be given without obtaining in advance, the written permission of the Dramatists Play Service, Inc., and paying the requisite fee. Inquiries regarding all other rights should be addressed to Helen Merrill, Ltd., 435 West 23rd Street, Suite 1-A, New York, N.Y. 10011.